Game Programming with Silverlight™

Michael Snow

Course Technology PTR
A part of Cengage Learning

COURSE TECHNOLOGY
CENGAGE Learning™

Australia • Brazil • Japan • Korea • Mexico • Singapore • Spain • United Kingdom • United States

COURSE TECHNOLOGY
CENGAGE Learning™

Game Programming with Silverlight™
Michael Snow

Publisher and General Manager, Course Technology PTR: Stacy L. Hiquet

Associate Director of Marketing: Sarah Panella

Manager of Editorial Services: Heather Talbot

Marketing Manager: Jordan Casey

Senior Acquisitions Editor: Emi Smith

Project/Copy Editor: Kezia Endsley

Technical Editor: Tim Heuer

PTR Editorial Services Coordinator: Jen Blaney

Interior Layout Tech: Macmillan Publishing Solutions

Cover Designer: Mike Tanamachi

Proofreader: Kate Shoup

Indexer: Kelly Henthorne

Library of Congress Control Number: 2008940729

ISBN-13: 978-1-59863-906-3

ISBN-10: 1-59863-906-4

Course Technology, a part of Cengage Learning
20 Channel Center Street
Boston, MA 02210
USA

Cengage Learning is a leading provider of customized learning solutions with office locations around the globe, including Singapore, the United Kingdom, Australia, Mexico, Brazil, and Japan. Locate your local office at: **international.cengage.com/region**

Cengage Learning products are represented in Canada by Nelson Education, Ltd.

For your lifelong learning solutions, visit **courseptr.com**

Visit our corporate website at **cengage.com**

Printed in Canada
1 2 3 4 5 6 7 12 11 10 09

To my wife and children for all the joy they bring to my life.

Acknowledgments

I would like to thank my manager Vinaya Bhushana Gattam Reddy for his incredible leadership and mentorship at Microsoft. Also, I would like to thank Patrick Kutch for his inspiration and vision when I was new to software development.

Thanks to Tim Heuer and Kezia Endsley for taking the time to review this book. Also thanks to Patrick Duquette, Nikola Mihaylov, and John Weise for their input and comments.

For game art contributions I would like to give a special thanks to Raymond Jacobs (see http://www.edigames.com/morningswrath) and Ori Cohen (see http://www.garagegames.com/products/rtskit). Also, thanks to GarageGames.com for having an awesome portal where developers can obtain great artwork.

About the Author

Mike Snow is a Senior Lead Software Design Engineer in Test at Microsoft. He has over two decades of experience as a hobbyist game developer. He is the creator of one of the original multiplayer text-based LP MUDs (see http://en.wikipedia.org/wiki/LPMud) called *Tsunami Realms*. Currently he is a strong advocate for game programming with Silverlight and owns a game-centric "Silverlight Tips of the Day" blog that can be found at http://www.silverlight.net/blogs/msnow. When he is not focused on Silverlight, he enjoys the outdoors, especially participating in Adventure Racing. Mike Snow lives in Sammamish, Washington, with his wife and four kids.

Contents

Introduction

Why Silverlight?

The Internet is growing at an extremely fast rate. It's estimated that in 2008 around 23% of the world's population (about 1,565 million people) were using the Internet (see http://www.internetworldstats.com/emarketing.htm). This is up from just 0.4% (about 16 million people) back in 1995. If you think about it, that's an extraordinarily large potential customer base to target for your web-based applications. However, with growth comes evolution. The quality of games that was acceptable back in 1995 is no longer acceptable today. Just as Windows-based games have evolved so have the web-based games. Today, customers are coming to expect the same type of rich and powerful experience on the web that they receive through Windows-based applications.

The technology Microsoft provides to best achieve this goal is called Silverlight. Silverlight is a framework that developers can leverage to build these rich, web-based Internet applications. It is an especially ideal platform for rapid casual game development. Why, you ask? Take a look at some of the many features supported by Silverlight:

- A consistent experience through multiple browsers including, but not limited to, Microsoft IE, Mozilla Firefox, and Apple Safari. Your game will look and feel the same across these browsers without the need to re-engineer it for a specific platform.

- Cross-platform support running on Microsoft Windows, Unix/Linux, and Apple OSes.
- When users connect to your Silverlight application, they will always be automatically updated with the most recent versions. That is, there is no need for a patch or product version update solution for your Silverlight applications.
- 3D perspective transforms and hardware acceleration.
- Networking support, including HTTP over TCP, WCF web services, SOAP, REST, Binary XML, and ASP.NET AJAX services.
- High-definition video and audio streaming in 720p HDTV video modes.
- Multiple libraries of pre-made Silverlight controls.
- Free developer tools for designing, editing, building, debugging, running, and deploying your Silverlight application.
- A powerful XAML-based GUI.
- A .NET framework programming model using languages such as C# and Visual Basic.
- XML support through LINQ to XML or XmlReader.
- Animation through threading and timers.
- Vector graphics, images, text, and brushes.

The list goes on, but I think you get the idea! You have a powerful framework and toolset that can be used to rapidly build games without a single tooling cost to you.

Why Gaming?

Gaming is a big business that continues to grow quickly. In 2010, the industry is projected to reach $42B, up from $28.5B in 2005 (see http://www.dfcint.com). There are many options for generating revenue via a game, including one-time payments, subscriptions, and in-game and web-based advertising. Whatever method you choose, the web is a great medium to deliver your game to customers. Whether or not you are in it for the money, I believe you will find game development to be a very rewarding experience that you will learn a lot from. It can help you grow technically as a developer, a designer, and an artist and in the end you will have produced a fun product that has the potential to entertain many people.

What's New with Silverlight 3

The book was written and targeted for Silverlight version 3. This release encompasses an incredible set of new features and improvements that target RIA, and media and graphics scenarios. Here are some of the features that were introduced in Silverlight 3:

- Perspective 3D graphics
- H.264/AAC media playback
- Built-in data-binding validation
- Text rendering for animation
- Pixel shaders effects (blur, drop shadow, and custom)
- Local messaging
- Merged resource dictionaries
- Multi-select list boxes
- Raw audio/video support
- Save File dialog box
- Image refinements
- Animation easing
- XAML element data-binding
- `CaretBrush` on `TextBox`
- Transparent cached extensions
- GPU acceleration
- Application object extensibility
- Style updates (dynamic changes and `BasedOn`)

- Media logging
- Listening to handled routed events
- Compressed fonts from JS
- Local font support
- `SystemColors` for high-contrast mode
- Browser navigation support
- Out-of-browser applications
- Improved XAP compression
- Bitmap caching
- Bitmap APIs
- Binary XML
- Advanced accessibility features

The coming chapters cover and explain examples on how to leverage many of these new features.

About This Book

My goal with this book is to help you learn how to make successful games with Silverlight. To accomplish this, I have divided this book into 11 chapters, where each chapter builds upon the previous chapter by covering a wide variety of topics and techniques used to build a multiplayer online adventure game. The complete source for this game, including the world editor, client, and server application is available for you to download. It is my greatest hope that you will soon understand my overwhelming enthusiasm and excitement around Silverlight for game development!

Target Audience

This book is targeted at hobbyist and professional game programmers alike. At a minimum, readers should have an intermediate level of understanding of C# and the .NET framework. Although Silverlight supports other .NET languages, such as Visual Basic, IronPython, and IronRuby, C# is used exclusively throughout this book.

Downloading the Code

If you purchased this book, you can download the source code for the world editor, client, and server application at http://code.msdn.microsoft.com/Silverlight.

System Requirements

You need Microsoft Windows® XP, Windows® Vista, Win7, Windows® Server 2003 or 2008, and 512MB RAM to use the latest version of Silverlight.

Welcome to the book; let's get started!

CHAPTER 1

SILVERLIGHT 101

All About Silverlight

Silverlight is a powerful framework that developers can leverage to build rich, web-based Internet applications. Since its conception and the release of Silverlight 1.0 in 2006, Microsoft has taken Silverlight to phenomenally new heights and is fully committed to the success, support, and continued non-stop growth and evolution of Silverlight.

Silverlight is built upon a lightweight version of the .NET framework. By being lightweight, it provides the user with a fast download experience. By leveraging the .NET framework, Silverlight adopts features such as automatic memory management through garbage collection, JIT compilation, managed exception handling, security enforcement, and type safety verification.

Silverlight applications are built using a declarative markup language called Extensible Application Markup Language, or XAML, with code-behind files written in a .NET language such as C# or Visual Basic. Silverlight is designed to be loaded on single web page. It can be a full-frame application or just a portion of the page interacting with other content depending upon your preference. In addition, you can have multiple Silverlight controls on single web page. From a user/client perspective, Silverlight is a free browser plug-in that must be installed before the user can preview the application on the page. If the user does not have the client installed when connecting to a page, a link to the Silverlight installer is provided.

Silverlight's Tools

The Silverlight tools are add-ons to Visual Studio 2008 SP1 that provide users with the following support:

- The tools needed to build, debug, and run Silverlight applications, including the ability to remote-debug Silverlight applications on a Mac
- Service reference support
- Silverlight-specific WCF templates
- Visual Basic and C# project templates
- IntelliSense and code generators for XAML
- A design preview surface for your XAML
- Integration with Expression Blend 2 SP1

The DLR (dynamic language runtime), which gives you an alternate choice to using C# and Visual Basic by allowing you to build applications in languages such as IronPython, IronRuby, or managed Jscript, is available for download at http://www.codeplex.com/dlr.

The Silverlight tools for Visual Studio also come packaged with the Silverlight SDK, which provides the user with more than 50 high-quality controls. This is up from around 20 controls in Silverlight 2. These controls include objects such as buttons, images, list boxes, tree views, date pickers, and more. This chapter includes examples showing how to use these controls.

All About XAML

XAML, pronounced *zammel*, stands for Extensible Application Markup Language. It is a XML-based declarative markup language created by Microsoft and is used by both Silverlight and the Windows Presentation Foundation (WPF). You might also find it very similar to HTML. Because XAML is XML based, it must be well-formed, which means it must adhere to rules such as case sensitivity, closing tags, and whitespace.

In Silverlight, XAML is primarily used to declare and lay out all of the controls for your application. These controls include objects such as rectangles, text boxes, labels, media elements, and more. Each XAML file can be augmented by a code-behind file where all the programmatic logic for the control is added using a

.NET language such as C# or VB. Code-behind files have direct access to all the controls that are declared in their XAML files.

The following is an example of the XAML needed to declare a text box in the page.xaml file:

```
<Canvas>
      <TextBox>
      </TextBox>
</Canvas>
```

Although this is nothing too fancy, each control has properties that can be set to further customize the control. There are four primary syntaxes used to set the properties of a control that you should be aware of. These include the following:

- Attribute Syntax
- Property Element Syntax
- Content Element Syntax
- Collection Syntax

Attribute Syntax

The first method, which will be used extensively through this book, is called Attribute Syntax. Using Attribute Syntax, properties are set inline within the XAML of the control declaration. For example, to set the width, foreground, and background color properties of a text box, you could declare it like this:

```
<Canvas>
<TextBox Width="200" Background="Black" Foreground="White"/></Canvas>
```

You can also apply a unique identifier to a control via the `x:Name` property. The example here sets the `TextBox` identifier to `myTB`.

```
<Canvas>
<TextBox x:Name="myTB" Width="200" Background="Black" Foreground="White"/>
</Canvas>
```

Now that it is set, you can reference this control from your code-behind. For example, to change the height of the text box you could do this:

```
private void UpdateTextBoxHeight(double height)
{
    myTB.Height = height;
}
```

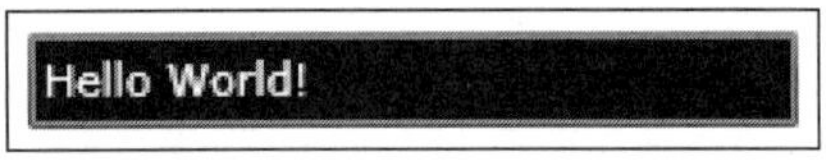

Figure 1.1
Basic Text Box

Figure 1.1 shows what this text box would look like if rendered with the text "Hello World" typed in it.

Property Element Syntax

Using Property Element Syntax, each property is declared as a child of the control rather than inline. The `TextBox` code shown in the previous section using Property Element Syntax would look like this:

```
<Canvas>

     <TextBox>
         <TextBox.Name>myTB</TextBox.Name>
         <TextBox.Width>200
         </TextBox.Width>
         <TextBox.Background>
                 <SolidColorBrush Color="Black"/>
         </TextBox.Background>
         <TextBox.Foreground>
                 <SolidColorBrush Color="White"/>
         </TextBox.Foreground>
     </TextBox>
</Canvas>
```

Content Element Syntax

A few controls also support what is called Content Element Syntax. These controls have a property that you can omit the name for by simply declaring the content within the object tags. For example, a `TextBlock` allows you to omit the `Text` property that is usually declared like this:

```
<TextBlock Text="Hello World"/>
```

Using Content Element Syntax, you can declare it like this:

```
<TextBlock>
    Hello World
</TextBlock>
```

Collection Syntax

Using Collection Syntax, you can essentially do a call to the `Add()` method to add one more element to a collection for a control. The following example creates a rectangle filled with a `LinearGradientBrush`. The `LinearGradientBrush` contains a collection of `GradientStop` objects. The following example adds a `GradientStop` twice to the collection:

```
<Canvas>
    <Rectangle Width="200" Height="200">
        <Rectangle.Fill>
            <LinearGradientBrush>
                <LinearGradientBrush.GradientStop>
                    <GradientStopCollection>
                        <GradientStop Offset="0.0" Color="Black" />
                        <GradientStop Offset="1.0" Color="White" />
                    </GradientStopCollection>
                </LinearGradientBrush.GradientStop>
            </LinearGradientBrush>
        </Rectangle.Fill>
    </Rectangle>
</Canvas>
```

While this code looks a little lengthy, the good news is the XAML parser implicitly knows the type of the collection, which allows you to omit the object element and the property element so that you can simply declare it like this:

```
<Rectangle Width="200" Height="200">
    <Rectangle.Fill>
    <LinearGradientBrush>
        <GradientStop Offset="0.0" Color="Black" />
        <GradientStop Offset="1.0" Color="White" />
    </LinearGradientBrush>
    </Rectangle.Fill>
</Rectangle>
```

The result of this code is shown in Figure 1.2.

Events

XAML also provides the ability to attach events to your controls. To do this, you simply follow the syntax `Event Name = Event Handler Function`. For example, if

Figure 1.2
Rectangle with `GradientStop` Collection

you want to monitor when the mouse enters and leaves a rectangle, you would do this:

```
<Rectangle MouseEnter="RC_MouseEnter" MouseLeave="RC_MouseLeave"></Rectangle>
```

Your code-behind would contain these two event handler functions:

```
private void RC_MouseEnter(object sender, MouseEventArgs e)
{
}

private void RC_MouseLeave(object sender, MouseEventArgs e)
{
}
```

The most common events that a Silverlight control will have include the following:

- `BindingValidationError`—Event fired when a data-validation error is reported by a binding source.
- `GotFocus`—Event fired when the control receives focus.
- `KeyDown`—Event fired when a key is pressed if the control has focus.
- `KeyUp`—Event fired when a key is released if the control has focus.
- `LayoutUpdated`—Event fired when the layout changes. For example, a browser is resized.

- `Loaded`—Event fired when the control has been created and added to the object tree.
- `LostFocus`—Event fired if the control loses focus.
- `LostMouseCapture`—Event fired if the control loses mouse capture.
- `MouseEnter`—Event fired if the mouse has entered the boundaries of the control.
- `MouseLeave`—Event fired if the mouse has left the boundaries of the controls.
- `MouseLeftButtonDown`—Event fired when the left mouse button is pressed over the control.
- `MouseLeftButtonUp`—Event fired when the left mouse button is released over the control.
- `MouseMove`—Event fired when the mouse is moved over the control.
- `SizeChanged`—Event fired when either the `ActualHeight` or `ActualWidth` properties of the object have changed.

Final Notes

Anything declared in XAML can also be programmatically created. To re-create the `TextBox` declared previously, you could use the following code:

```
TextBox tb = new TextBox();
tb.Background = new SolidColorBrush(Color.FromArgb(255, 0, 0, 0));
tb.Foreground = new SolidColorBrush(Color.FromArgb(255, 255, 255, 255));
tb.Width = 200;
LayoutRoot.Children.Add(tb);
```

As you can see, this is less straightforward when compared with declaring it in XAML. You must also remember to manually add the control to the Silverlight tree; otherwise, the control will not be visible.

An Overview of Silverlight Controls

Silverlight Tools for Visual Studio also comes packaged with numerous pre-built Silverlight XAML controls. Silverlight XAML controls make up UI elements such as buttons, check boxes, text boxes, rectangles, and so on. They allow developers

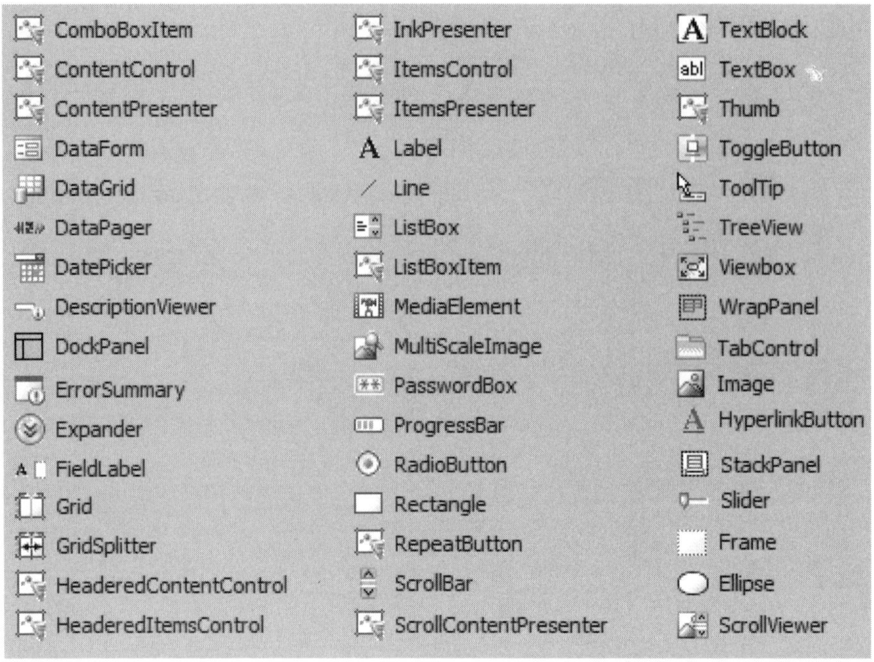

Figure 1.3
Silverlight XAML Controls

to quickly add specific functionality to their applications. The complete list of controls, found in your Toolbox pane, is shown in Figure 1.3. The Toolbox pane can be opened via View > Toolbox. To add a control, you simply double-click it or drag/drop to it to the appropriate place in your XAML source.

An collection of Silverlight 2 and Silverlight 3 controls, components, themes, and utilities are available through the Silverlight Toolkit. This toolkit can be downloaded free of charge from http://www.codeplex.com/Silverlight. There is also a dedicated forum for these controls at http://silverlight.net/forums/35.aspx. Once installed, the controls will automatically show up in your Toolbox.

For third-party controls that do not come with a setup application, you can follow these steps to manually add the controls to your Toolbox:

1. Right-click on the Toolbox pane and choose Add Tab from the context menu.
2. Give it a name, such as "Third-Party Controls."
3. Right-click on the newly created tab and select Choose Items from the context menu. This will open the Choose Toolbox Items dialog box, as seen in Figure 1.4.

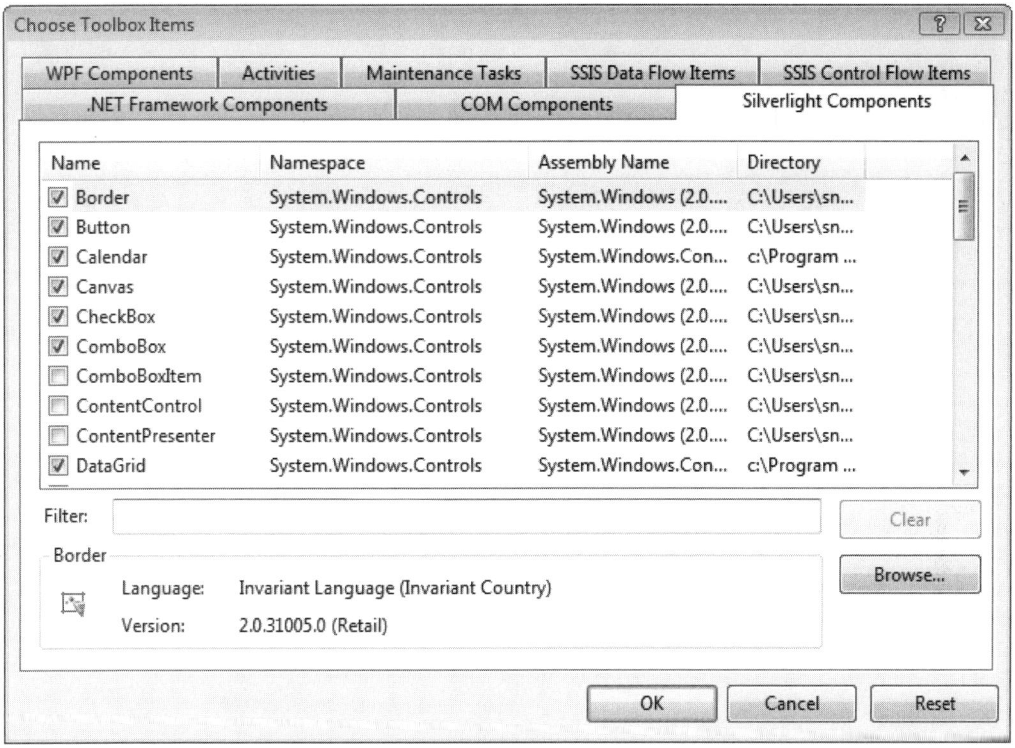

Figure 1.4
Choose Toolbox Items Dialog Box

4. Select the Silverlight Components tab.
5. Click the Browse button and browse to the location of the component that contains the third-party controls.
6. Double-click the component to add it and click the OK button when you are done.

At this point, you will have all the controls added to your new tab in the Toolbox, as seen in Figure 1.5.

The following sections describe a number of controls from the SDK.

AutoCompleteBox

This control combines a drop-down popup with a text box. As you type in the text box, items displayed in the drop-down popup are automatically filtered by the text you are typing.

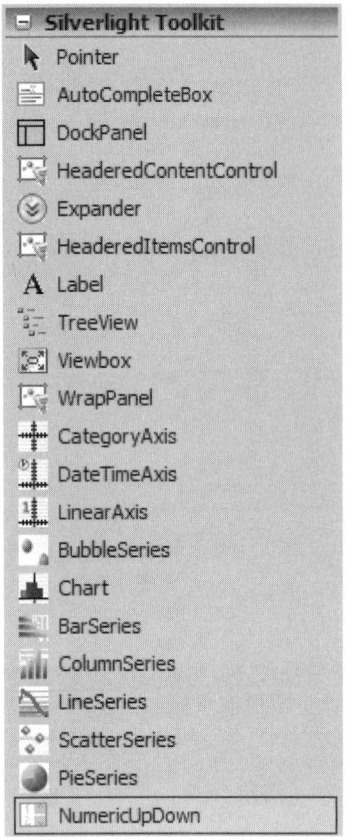

Figure 1.5
Silverlight Toolkit Controls

To declare it in XAML, do the following:

```
<input:AutoCompleteBox x:Name="acBox" Width="100"/>
```

To dynamically add items in C#, do the following:

```
acBox.ItemsSource = new string[]
     { "Hello", "Hi", "Howdy", "Greetings", "Goodbye" };
```

As you can see in Figure 1.6, typing the letter H will filter out all items that do not start with H.

DockPanel

The `DockPanel` control allows you to arrange other controls horizontally or vertically, relative to each other. The order in which you declare the panels will

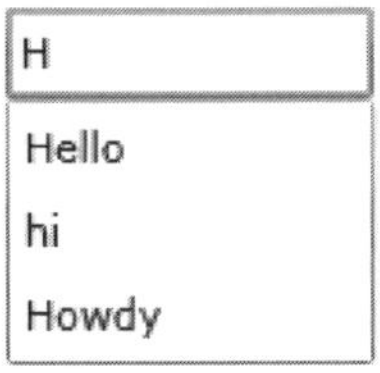

Figure 1.6
`AutoCompleteBox` Control

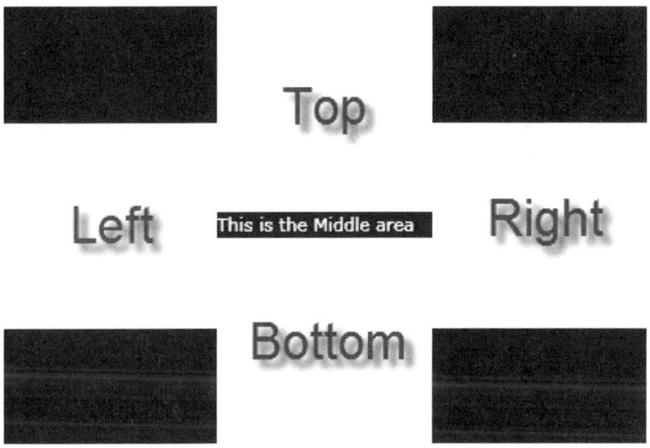

Figure 1.7
`DockPanel` Control

make a difference in how they are arranged. The following XAML example shows four images that are docked to the top, bottom, left, and right. The background of the `DockPanel` control is black so that you can see where the images are placed relative to each other.

```
<controls:DockPanel LastChildFill="True" Background="Black">
    <Image Source="left.png" controls:DockPanel.Dock="Left"/>
    <Image Source="right.png" controls:DockPanel.Dock="Right"/>
    <Image Source="top.png" controls:DockPanel.Dock="Top"/>
    <Image Source="bottom.png" controls:DockPanel.Dock="Bottom"/>
    <TextBlock Foreground="White">This is the Middle area</TextBlock>
</controls:DockPanel>
```

Figure 1.7 shows an example of four images docked to the left, right, top, and bottom with a non-docked `TextBlock` in the middle.

HeaderedContentControl

This is a base class for all controls that contain a single set of content and a header. To declare it in XAML, do the following:

```
<controls:HeaderedContentControl>
    <controls:HeaderedContentControl.Header>
        <TextBlock>This is the Header</TextBlock>
    </controls:HeaderedContentControl.Header>
    <controls:HeaderedContentControl.Content>
        <Image Source="Mage.png"></Image>
    </controls:HeaderedContentControl.Content>
</controls:HeaderedContentControl>
```

Figure 1.8 shows an example of how this control would look with a `TextBlock` as a header and an `Image` control as the content.

Expander

This is a control that has a header with collapsible content. In the example that follows, a `TextBlock` is declared to be the header and three images are placed in a `StackPanel` to be the content. For each image, the example specifies a margin of 10 in order to provide spacing between the images.

```
<controls:Expander BorderBrush="Black" Width="128">
    <controls:HeaderedContentControl.Header>
        <TextBlock>Map Tiles</TextBlock>
    </controls:HeaderedContentControl.Header>
    <controls:HeaderedContentControl.Content>
        <StackPanel>
            <Image Margin="10" Source="earth.png"/>
            <Image Margin="10" Source="brick.png"/>
            <Image Margin="10" Source="stone.png"/>
        </StackPanel>
    </controls:HeaderedContentControl.Content>
</controls:Expander>
```

Figure 1.8
HeaderedContentControl

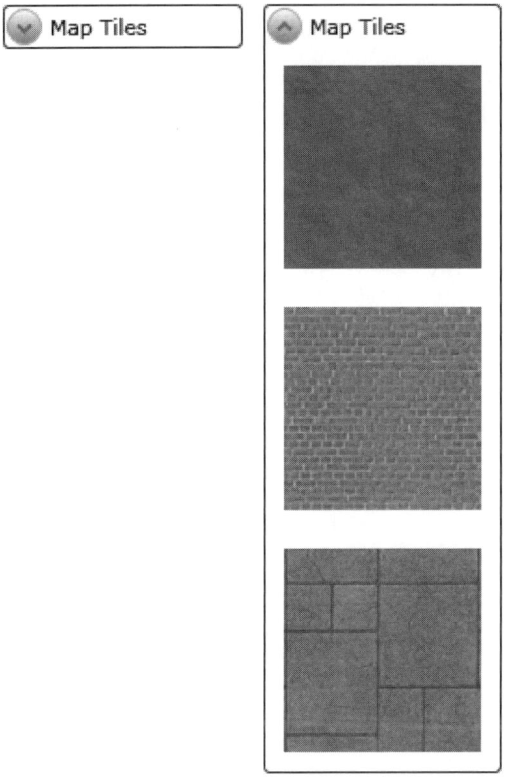

Figure 1.9
`Expander` Control

Figure 1.9 shows this expander before expansion (on the left) and after expansion (on the right).

HeaderedItemsControl

This control allows you to have multiple items under a single header. The example that follows shows how to bind the data you want to place in the content by setting the `ItemSource` for it in the C# code. To declare it in XAML, do the following:

```
<controls:HeaderedItemsControl x:Name="headeredCtrl">
    <controls:HeaderedItemsControl.Header>
        <TextBlock>This is the header</TextBlock>
    </controls:HeaderedItemsControl.Header>
    <controls:HeaderedItemsControl.ItemTemplate>
        <DataTemplate>
            <TextBlock Text="{Binding}"/>
```

```
        </DataTemplate>
    </controls:HeaderedItemsControl.ItemTemplate>
</controls:HeaderedItemsControl>
```

To dynamically set the source in C#, do the following:

```
headeredCtrl.ItemsSource = new string[] { "Hello", "there.", "How are you?" };
```

A preview of what you would see when this code is run is shown in Figure 1.10.

`Label`

This control represents the text label for a control. For example, you can set the font name and font size in the `Label` control and its content will inherit those values. To declare it in XAML:

```
<controls:Label FontFamily="Verdana" FontSize="20">
    <StackPanel>
        <TextBlock>Hello</TextBlock>
        <TextBlock>There</TextBlock>
    </StackPanel>
</controls:Label>
```

Figure 1.11 shows a screenshot of the result. Notice that both of the text blocks inherited the font name and size.

`TreeView`

This important control displays hierarchical data in a tree view that you can expand and collapse. At the root, you declare a `TreeView` control and all children

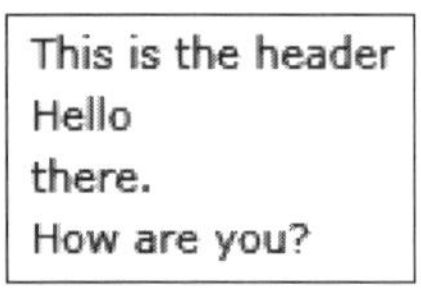

Figure 1.10
`HeaderedItemsControl`

Figure 1.11
`Label` Control

are declared as a `TreeViewItem`. You can have any level of children that you need. For example, to declare it in XAML, do the following:

```
<controls:TreeView>
    <controls:TreeViewItem Header="Cars" IsExpanded="True">
        <controls:TreeViewItem Header="Ford"/>
        <controls:TreeViewItem Header="Honda"/>
        <controls:TreeViewItem Header="Toyota"/>
    </controls:TreeViewItem>
    <controls:TreeViewItem Header="Sport Cars" IsExpanded="True">
        <controls:TreeViewItem Header="Porsche"/>
        <controls:TreeViewItem Header="Ferrari">
    </controls:TreeViewItem>
        <controls:TreeViewItem Header="Lamborghini" IsExpanded="True">

            <controls:TreeViewItem Header="Miura"/>
            <controls:TreeViewItem Header="Espada"/>
            <controls:TreeViewItem Header="Islero"/>
            <controls:TreeViewItem Header="Jarama"/>
            <controls:TreeViewItem Header="Urraco"/>
            <controls:TreeViewItem Header="Countach"/>
        </controls:TreeViewItem>
    </controls:TreeViewItem>
</controls:TreeView>
```

Figure 1.12 shows the tree view fully expanded.

Figure 1.12
`TreeView` Control

ViewBox

Content within a `ViewBox` control will stretch and scale to fit the available space. For example, the following XAML declares an image in a `ViewBox` three times, each time increasing the scale of the `ViewBox` by 100 pixels. The original image size is 96 × 96 pixels.

```
<controls:Viewbox Height="100" Width="100">
    <Image Source="Mage.png"/></controls:Viewbox>
<controls:Viewbox Canvas.Left="50" Height="200" Width="200">
    <Image Source="Mage.png"/></controls:Viewbox>
<controls:Viewbox Canvas.Left="150" Height="300" Width="300">
    <Image Source="Mage.png"/>
</controls:Viewbox>
```

As seen in Figure 1.13, the mage image is scaled to fill the `ViewBox` it is in.

WrapPanel

A `WrapPanel` control organizes controls from left to right, moving content to a new line when it reaches the right edge. The XAML example that follows declares a `WrapPanel` that is 500 pixels in width and then fills it with 13 images. Once an image reaches the right border, it is wrapped to a new line, as seen in Figure 1.14.

```
<controls:WrapPanel Width="500">
    <Image Stretch="None" Source="attacke0000.png"></Image>
    <Image Stretch="None" Source="attacke0001.png"></Image>
    <Image Stretch="None" Source="attacke0002.png"></Image>
    <Image Stretch="None" Source="attacke0003.png"></Image>
```

Figure 1.13
ViewBox Control

```
    <Image Stretch="None" Source="attacke0004.png"></Image>
    <Image Stretch="None" Source="attacke0005.png"></Image>
    <Image Stretch="None" Source="attacke0006.png"></Image>
    <Image Stretch="None" Source="attacke0007.png"></Image>
    <Image Stretch="None" Source="attacke0008.png"></Image>
    <Image Stretch="None" Source="attacke0009.png"></Image>
    <Image Stretch="None" Source="attacke0010.png"></Image>
    <Image Stretch="None" Source="attacke0011.png"></Image>
    <Image Stretch="None" Source="attacke0012.png"></Image>
</controls:WrapPanel>
```

NumericUpDown

This control combines a text box with a spinner control that allows you to increase or decrease the value in the text box as seen in Figure 1.15. Here's an example of how to create one in XAML:

```
<input:NumericUpDown Width="100" Minimum="0" Maximum="100" Value="33"
      Increment="1" IsEditable="True" DecimalPlaces="1">
</input:NumericUpDown>
```

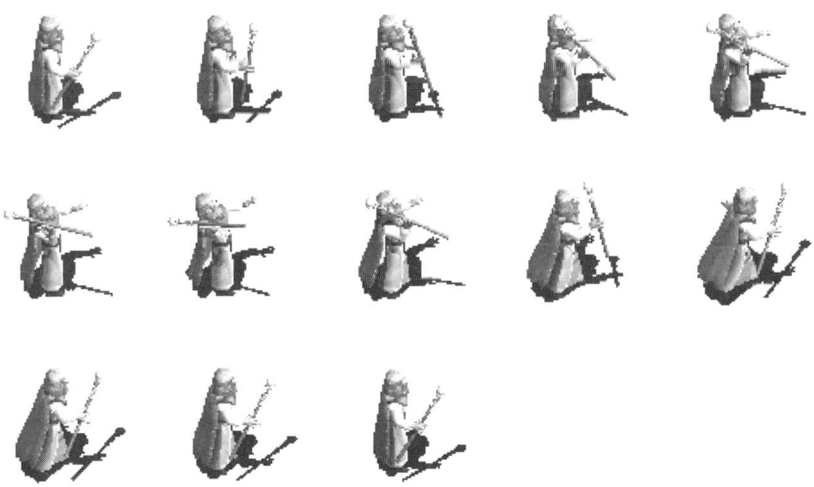

Figure 1.14
Wrap Panel

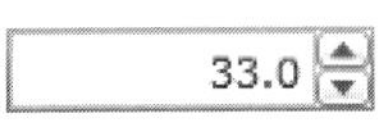

Figure 1.15
Numeric Up/Down Control

Chart

This control allows you to represent data in the form of a bar, column, pie, line, or point chart. Data in the graph is identified through DependentValueBinding and IndependentValueBinding. IndependentValueBinding represents the data you want to measure, whereas DependentValueBinding represents the quantity of each data item. For example, in Figure 1.16, you will see a chart of application bugs where the count is the DependentValueBinding and the bug status is the IndependentValueBinding.

The XAML needed to create this chart is as follows:

```
<chartingToolkit:Chart x:Name="myChart" Width="500" Height="300">
    <chartingToolkit:Chart.Series>
        <chartingToolkit:ColumnSeries Title="Bugs"
            ItemsSource="{Binding}"
            DependentValuePath="Value"
            IndependentValuePath="Key"
            IsSelectionEnabled="True"/>
    </chartingToolkit:Chart.Series>
</chartingToolkit:Chart>
```

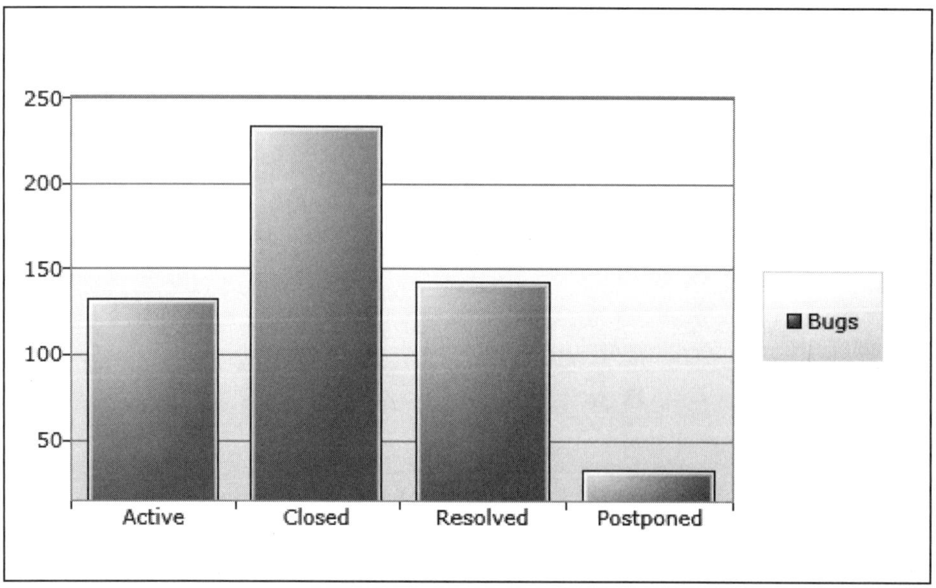

Figure 1.16
Column Chart

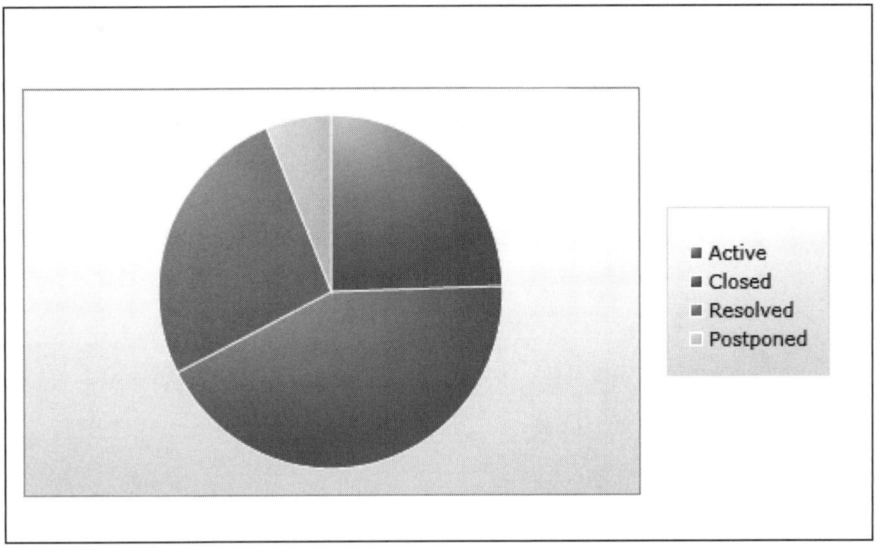

Figure 1.17
Pie Chart

In your code-behind, you could set the your data like this:

```
myChart.DataContext = new KeyValuePair<string, int>[]
{
    new KeyValuePair<string,int>("Active",133),
    new KeyValuePair<string,int>("Closed",233),
    new KeyValuePair<string,int>("Resolved",143),
    new KeyValuePair<string,int>("Postponed",33)
};
```

You can easily change the type of chart by setting the series to be an `AreaSeries`, `BarSeries`, `BubbleSeries`, `ColumnSeries`, `LineSeries`, `PieSeries`, or `ScatterSeries`. For example, changing the chart from a `ColumnSeries` to a `PieSeries` will result in a pie chart shown in Figure 1.17.

DatePicker

The `DatePicker` control allows you to set a date in a `TextBlock` by clicking on a button that brings up a calendar control from which you can select any date. The XAML needed to create the `DatePicker` is as follows:

```
<controls:DatePicker x:Name="myDatePicker"></controls:DatePicker>
```

Figure 1.18
`DatePicker`

Figure 1.18 shows the control in action.

You can monitor the `SelectedDataChange` event, which will fire when the data for this control has been set or changed.

For example:

```
myDatePicker.SelectedDateChanged +=
    new EventHandler<SelectionChangedEventArgs>
    (myDatePicker_SelectedDateChanged);
void myDatePicker_SelectedDateChanged(object sender, SelectionChangedEventArgs e)
{
    // Example: 12/01/2009 12:00:00 AM
    DateTime dateTime = (DateTime) myDatePicker.SelectedDate;
    // Example: 12/01/2009
    string date = myDatePicker.Text;
}
```

Using Themes

Themes are useful because they allow you to essentially skin your controls with a common look and feel. The Silverlight Toolkit comes with the following themes:

- Bubble Crème
- Bureau Black
- Bureau Blue

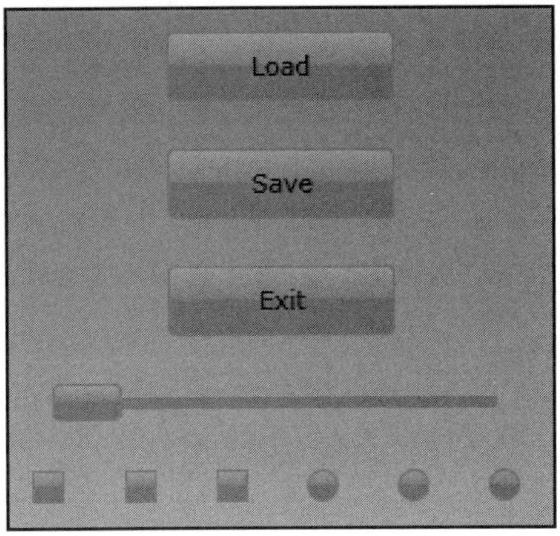

Figure 1.19
Themed Controls

- Expression Dark
- Expression Light
- Rainier Purple
- Rainier Orange
- Shiny Blue
- Shiny Red
- Twilight Blue
- Whistler Blue

To add a theme to your control, you simply drag/drop it from the Toolbox into your XAML code. Any controls contained within the theme will have the theme applied to it. The following XAML demonstrates applying the Expression Light Theme to a variety of controls. The result can be seen in Figure 1.19.

```
<expressionLight:ExpressionLightTheme Margin="20">
    <StackPanel>
        <Button Margin="10" Width="100" Height="30" Content="Load"/>
        <Button Margin="10" Width="100" Height="30" Content="Save"/>
        <Button Margin="10" Width="100" Height="30" Content="Exit"/>
        <Slider Margin="10" Width="200"></Slider>
        <StackPanel Orientation="Horizontal">
```

```
            <CheckBox Margin="10"></CheckBox>
            <CheckBox Margin="10"></CheckBox>
            <CheckBox Margin="10"></CheckBox>
            <RadioButton Margin="10"></RadioButton>
            <RadioButton Margin="10"></RadioButton>
            <RadioButton Margin="10"></RadioButton>
        </StackPanel>
    </StackPanel>
</expressionLight:ExpressionLightTheme>
```

Third-Party Controls

In addition to the controls that come packaged with the SDK and Silverlight Toolkit, you can also find a great number of third-party controls from a variety of companies. For example, ComponentArt is one such company whose controls I have used and really like. You can preview their Silverlight controls at http://www.componentart.com/products/silverlight. Figure 1.20 shows their `TreeView`, `Menu`, and `ContextMenu` controls.

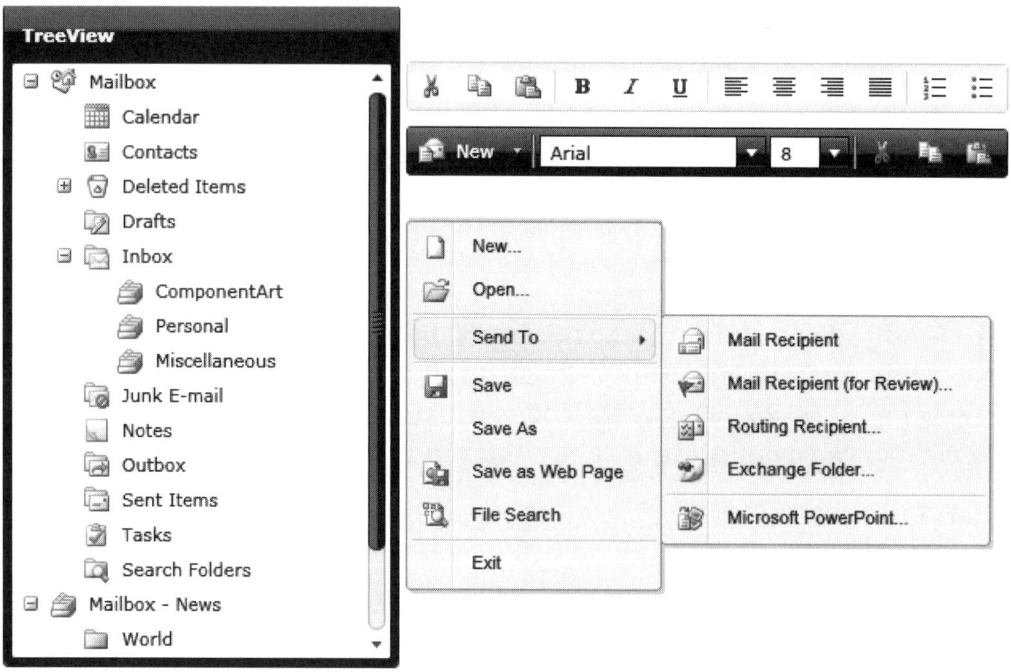

Figure 1.20
Some of ComponentArt's Controls

Summary

This chapter covered the basic concepts of Silverlight, including the tools and controls made available to you to build Silverlight applications. The next chapter covers the Silverlight project system in detail. It shows you everything needed to create, build, and debug Silverlight applications using Silverlight Tools.

CHAPTER 2

Getting Started

Before you dive into creating a Silverlight game, there are a few steps you will need to take to get ready. These steps, covered in this chapter, include the following:

- Gathering the tools you need
- Creating a Silverlight application project
- Exploring your project files
- Taking a peek at Visual Studio 2010
- Using common Silverlight utility functions

Gathering the Tools You Need

To begin, you will need to have the following tools installed in order to develop an application for Silverlight using Visual Studio 2008 SP1.

Visual Studio 2008 with Service Pack 1

This tool is primarily used for editing, building, debugging, running, and deploying your Silverlight applications. You can download a free copy of the Visual Web Developer Express version of Visual Studio 2008 SP1 at http://www.microsoft.com/express/download. Make certain to have the Web Authoring feature for VS installed, since this is a required feature for website development.

Silverlight Tools for Visual Studio 2008 Service Pack 1

The Silverlight Tools installer comes packaged with the Silverlight developer runtime, Silverlight SDK, and the add-on needed to create Silverlight applications in Visual Studio. The most recent version of Silverlight Tools can be found on the http://silverlight.net/GetStarted page. If you have an older version of Silverlight, the installer will automatically update your version.

Expression Blend 2 SP1

Although optional, you might also want to consider installing Expression Blend 2 SP1. This tool is primarily used by designers for creating the graphical interface of a Silverlight application. It comes with a powerful interactive WYSIWYG (what you see is what you get) design surface. For more info on Blend and to try out a demo, visit http://www.microsoft.com/expression/products/Overview.aspx?key=blend. Although Expression Blend isn't covered in detail in this book, it is a great tool to add to your arsenal for designer-related work.

Creating a Silverlight Application Project

The first step to creating a new Silverlight application is to create a Silverlight application project using Visual Studio 2008. To accomplish this, follow these steps:

1. Launch Visual Studio 2008.
2. From the File menu, choose New Project. This will bring up the New Project dialog box, as shown in Figure 2.1.
3. In the Project Types window, expand the Visual C# node and select Silverlight. C# is used exclusively in this book, but as an alternative you can also use Visual Basic.
4. In the Templates window, select Silverlight application.
5. Specify a name you want to give your application, such as "RPG."
6. Specify the path where you want to store the project files, such as c:\projects.
7. Verify that you have .NET Framework 3.5 selected in the top-right corner.
8. Click on the OK button when you're ready.

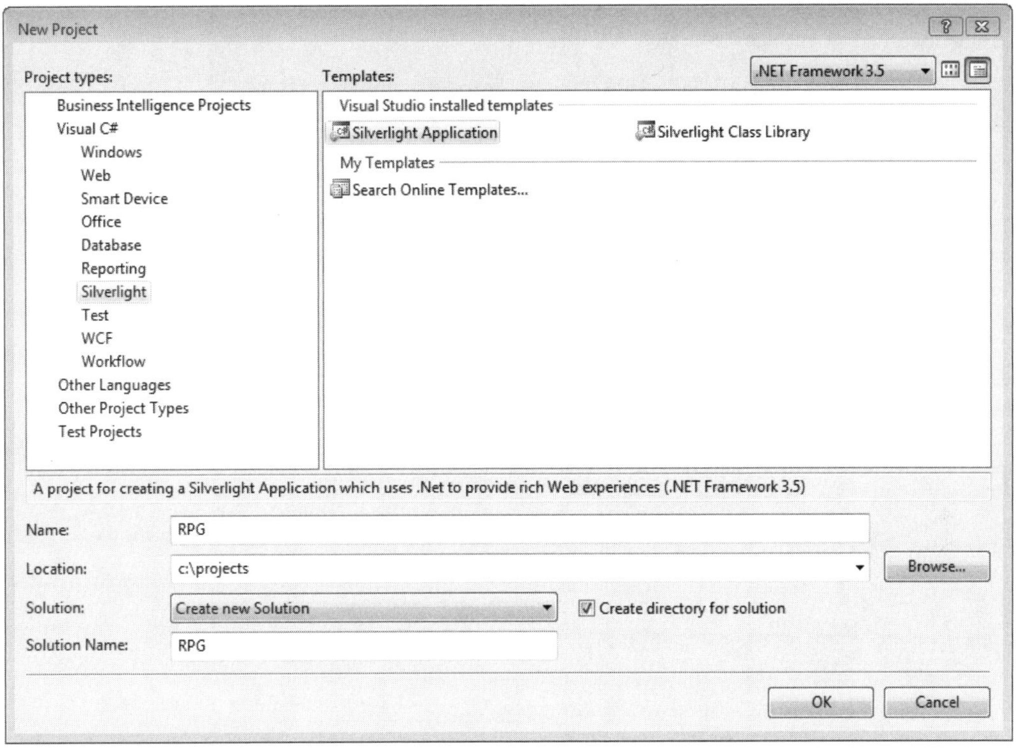

Figure 2.1
Visual Studio 2008 New Project Dialog Box

Once you click on the OK button, you will be shown the New Silverlight Application dialog box, as shown in Figure 2.2. This dialog box is used to associate or link a Silverlight application with a website.

The New Silverlight Application dialog box gives you two options:

- Host the Silverlight Application in a New Website. This option, checked by default, will generate a new website and will perform all the necessary configuration steps needed for the website to automatically work with your new Silverlight application.
- Test Page Generation. Unchecking option #1 will cause a test page that hosts your Silverlight application to be dynamically created at runtime. Because there is no website associated with the project, this is the right option to choose if you plan to deploy your Silverlight application to an existing website at a later time.

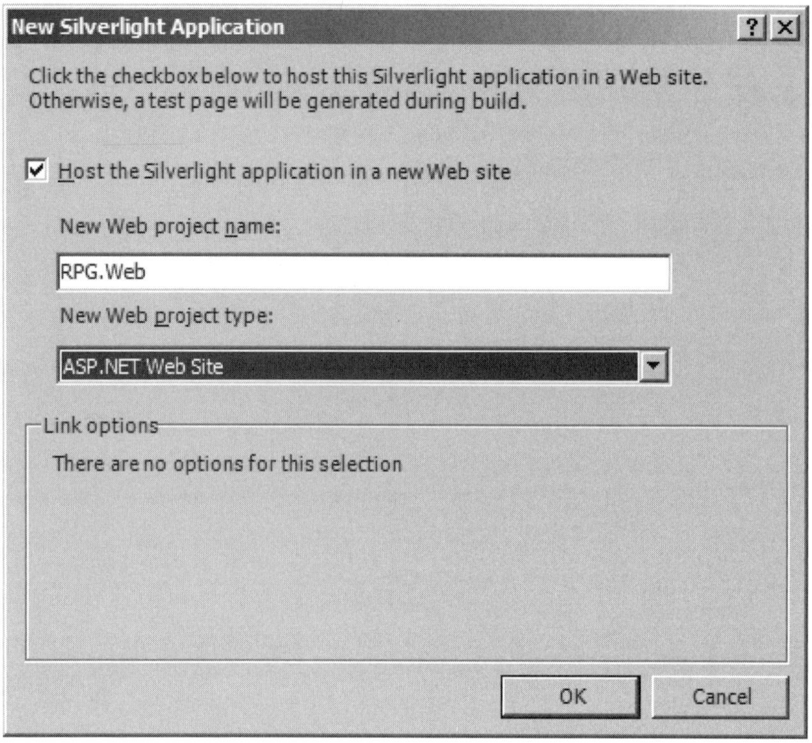

Figure 2.2
New Silverlight Application Dialog Box

The Link Options section has options listed only when you are adding a new Silverlight application project to an existing website. The options, which are self-explanatory, include the following:

- Add a test page that references this application
- Make it the start page
- Enable Silverlight debugging (disables JavaScript debugging)

Choose the default option and click the OK button to proceed. At this stage, as shown in Figure 2.3, you will now have an empty Silverlight application project.

Exploring the Silverlight Application Project

Now that you have created a Silverlight application project, this section steps you through the different parts of Visual Studio that make up your Silverlight application project. By default, you can see in Figure 2.3 that there are four windows.

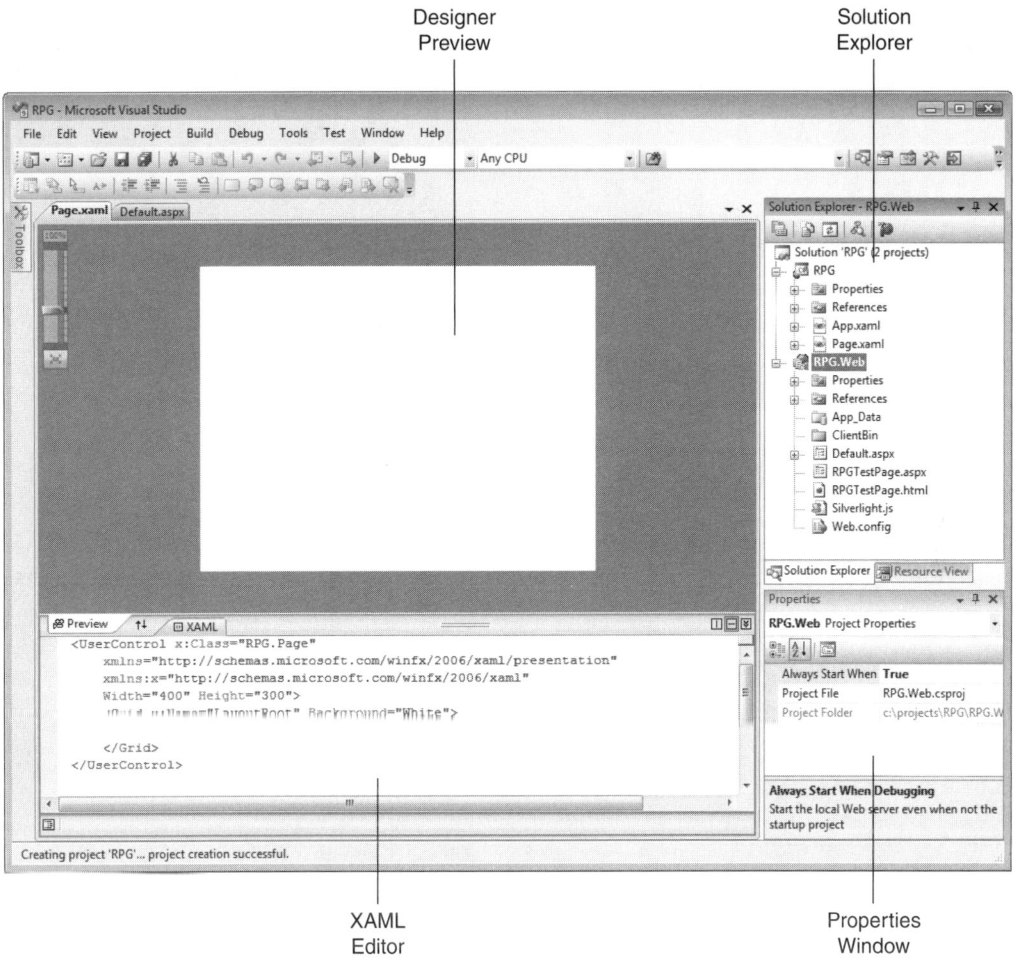

Figure 2.3
Empty Silverlight Application Project

The Designer Preview

This window, shown in Figure 2.4, gives you a non-interactive preview of the your XAML, showing you what it would look like if it was rendered in your browser. There is a zoom bar on the left side of the window that allows you to zoom in and out of the control. This preview window is only available in Silverlight 3 beta releases and earlier. This is due to incompatibilities with the final version of Silverlight 3. However, if you want to work with a designer window, I recommend you check out Visual Studio 2010. Not only is the designer present in Visual Studio 2010, but it is also fully interactive window. See the section "Taking a Peek at Visual Studio 2010" later in this chapter for more details.

Figure 2.4
Designer Preview Window

Figure 2.5
XAML Source Code Editor

The XAML Code Editor

This window, shown in Figure 2.5, is your XAML source code editor. Using the first two buttons in the upper-right corner, you can rearrange the layout of the designer and code editor to be a vertical or horizontal split. The third button allows you to collapse the source code editor pane.

Solution Explorer

As shown in Figure 2.6, the Solution Explorer lists all the files that are associated with your solution. In Visual Studio, a *solution* is a collection of code files and other resources that are used to build your application. All the information that

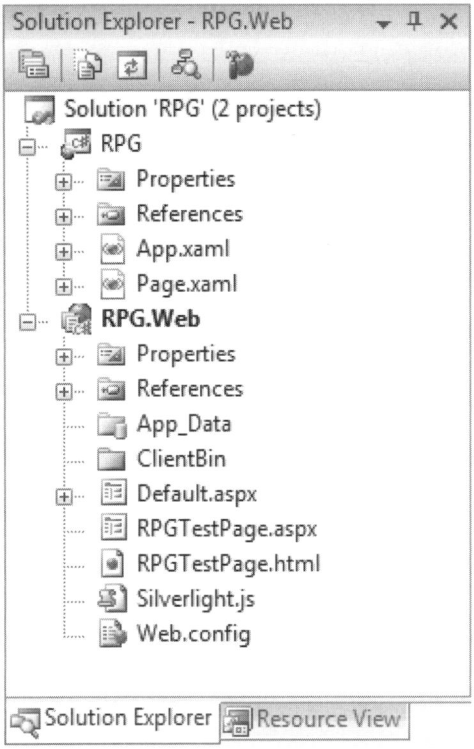

Figure 2.6
Solution Explorer

makes up a solution is stored as an SLN file on your computer. Each solution can contain multiple projects, which are stored as CSPROJ files on your computer. In your case, you currently have two projects in the solution—the Silverlight application project and the website project. The Solution Explorer is used to manage and browse all the files contained within the solution file. This chapter explores the contents of the projects in a later section.

Properties Window

The Properties window, shown in Figure 2.7, can be opened by pressing F4 on the keyboard or by choosing Properties from the context menu of the Solution Explorer. The Properties window can be used to view and edit properties and events of selected objects. Above the grid in Figure 2.7 is the object list, which allows you to choose which object you want to preview. Property editing for XAML objects is not enabled in Visual Studio 2008 but it is enabled for Visual Studio 2010.

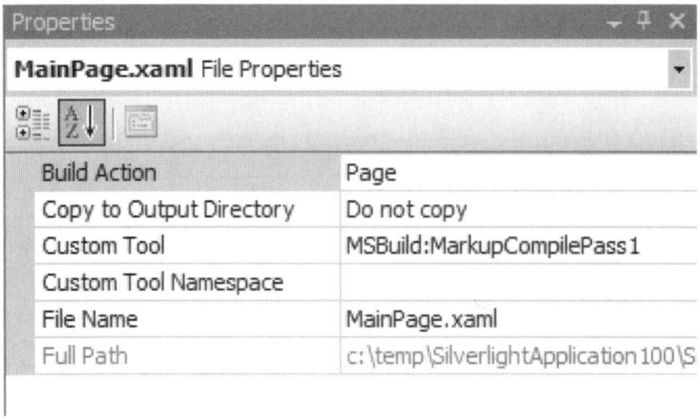

Figure 2.7
Properties Window

Exploring Your Project Files

This section walks you through the individual files that make up your default website and Silverlight application projects. It explains the purpose of each file generated and explains how, specifically, the file is used.

Website Project

Now that you have created a new solution, take a look in your Solution Explorer and you will see there are two separate projects added to the solution. The first one is your Silverlight application. If you named your solution RPG, this project would also be called RPG. The second project is the website that hosts your Silverlight application. It will have a .web extension, such as rpg.web. On the website, you will notice there are three types of web pages that you can choose from:

- **RPGTestPage.aspx**—An ASPX page pre-configured to load and display your Silverlight component
- **RPGTestPage.html**—A HTML page pre-configured to load and display your Silverlight component
- **Default.aspx**—An empty web page with a code-behind file

You can choose which file to use by default by right-clicking on the file and selecting Set As Start Page. This action will cause this page to be loaded and run during execution. If you open the testpage.aspx file, you will see the following markup code:

```
<%@ Page Language="C#" AutoEventWireup="true" %>
<%@ Register Assembly="System.Web.Silverlight"
    Namespace="System.Web.UI.SilverlightControls" TagPrefix="asp" %>
<!DOCTYPE html PUBLIC "-//W3C//DTD XHTML 1.0 Transitional//EN"
   "http://www.w3.org/TR/xhtml1/DTD/xhtml1-transitional.dtd">
<html xmlns="http://www.w3.org/1999/xhtml" style="height:100%;">
<head runat="server">
     <title>RPG</title>
</head>
<body style="height:100%;margin:0;">
     <form id="form1" runat="server" style="height:100%;">
          <asp:ScriptManager ID="ScriptManager1" runat="server">
          </asp:ScriptManager>
          <div style="height:100%;">
          <asp:Silverlight ID="Xaml1" runat="server"
               Source="~/ClientBin/RPG.xap" MinimumVersion="2.0.31005.0"
               Width="100%" Height="100%" />
          </div>
     </form>
</body>
</html>
```

There are two distinct declarations that are needed in order for the Silverlight control to be hosted on the web page. The first requirement is that you must register the assembly `System.Web.Silverlight`, as shown here:

```
<%@ Register Assembly="System.Web.Silverlight"
    Namespace="System.Web.UI.SilverlightControls" TagPrefix="asp" %>
```

The second requirement is that you must declare the Silverlight control itself, as follows:

```
<asp:Silverlight ID="Xaml1" runat="server" Source="~/ClientBin/RPG.xap"
     MinimumVersion="2.0.31005.0" Width="100%" Height="100%" />
```

The ID is needed if you want to reference this Silverlight control. The source points to a file with an .xap extension. This file contains all your project output files. It is essentially a zip file that has been renamed with the extension .xap. If you were to unzip this file, you would see a file called rpg.dll, which contains your

Silverlight component as well as an application manifest file that references the rpg.dll.

In addition to the website files there is also a file called Silverlight.js. This file contains a number of helper functions for your web page. These functions include a utility that checks to see if Silverlight is installed and a function to create and load the Silverlight control. For the most part, you can just leave this file alone.

Silverlight Application Project

In your Silverlight application project, you will notice that the following two files with their corresponding code-behind files were automatically generated and added to your project. Each file serves a distinct purpose:

- **App.xaml**—This file is primarily used for global declaration and application-specific events. It is most commonly used to declare resources such as styles and brushes that are referenced across the application. The default app.xaml file contains the following:

```
<Application xmlns="http://schemas.microsoft.com/winfx/2006/xaml/
  presentation"xmlns:x="http://schemas.microsoft.com/winfx/
  2006/xaml" x:Class="RPG.App">
      <Application.Resources>
      </Application.Resources>
</Application>
```

- **App.xaml.cs**—This is the app.xaml's code-behind file. You will notice there are three events added by default:

  `Application_Startup()`—Place any code you want to execute before the application starts here.
  `Application_Exit`—Place any code you want to execute when the application is exiting here.
  `Application_UnhandledException`—Place any code you need here to process unhandled exceptions.

- **Mainpage.xaml**—This is the main file you will be working with when creating your game. With the exception of custom controls, all of your UI, sound objects, and so on can be declared in the page.xaml file. All named objects declared in page.xaml are automatically known in the code-behind file page.xaml.cs. As an alternative approach, anything that you declare in page.xaml can also be programmatically created in the code-behind file. The default page.xaml file contains the following:

```
<UserControl x:Class="RPG.Page"
xmlns="http://schemas.microsoft.com/winfx/2006/xaml/presentation"
xmlns:x="http://schemas.microsoft.com/winfx/2006/xaml"
Width="400" Height="300">
<Grid x:Name="LayoutRoot" Background="White">
</Grid>
</UserControl>
```

As you can see from the code, a single `UserControl` is declared with its namespaces and dimensions are defined. By default, a single empty `Grid` control is declared as its only child. If you were to run the application now, you would see an empty white page, since the `Grid` contains no children and has no rows or columns associated with it.

- **Page.xaml.cs**—By default this file contains the `Page` class declaration with its constructor. This class inherits from a `UserControl`, which is the base class for any Silverlight-based application. A single call to `InitializeComponent()` is made from within the constructor in order to load the component.

```
using System;
using System.Collections.Generic;
using System.Linq;
using System.Net;
using System.Windows;
using System.Windows.Controls;
using System.Windows.Documents;
using System.Windows.Input;
using System.Windows.Media;
using System.Windows.Media.Animation;
using System.Windows.Shapes;

namespace RPG
{
        public partial class Page : UserControl
        {
            public Page()
            {
                InitializeComponent();
            }
        }
}
```

Taking a Peek at Visual Studio 2010

In Visual Studio 2010, the Silverlight tools, runtime, and SDK come packaged with the product. Because of this, you no longer need to go through a separate installation process to install these products. The primary new features for Visual Studio 2010 covered here include the following:

- Silverlight framework multi-targeting
- Interactive XAML designer
- Interactive Properties window

To see the differences, start by creating a new project in Visual Studio 2010. As you can see in Figure 2.8, the New Project dialog box looks much different than it did in Visual Studio 2008.

As with Visual Studio 2008, you can target the .NET framework, except now version 4.0 is available. Choose 4.0 and select the Silverlight Application template,

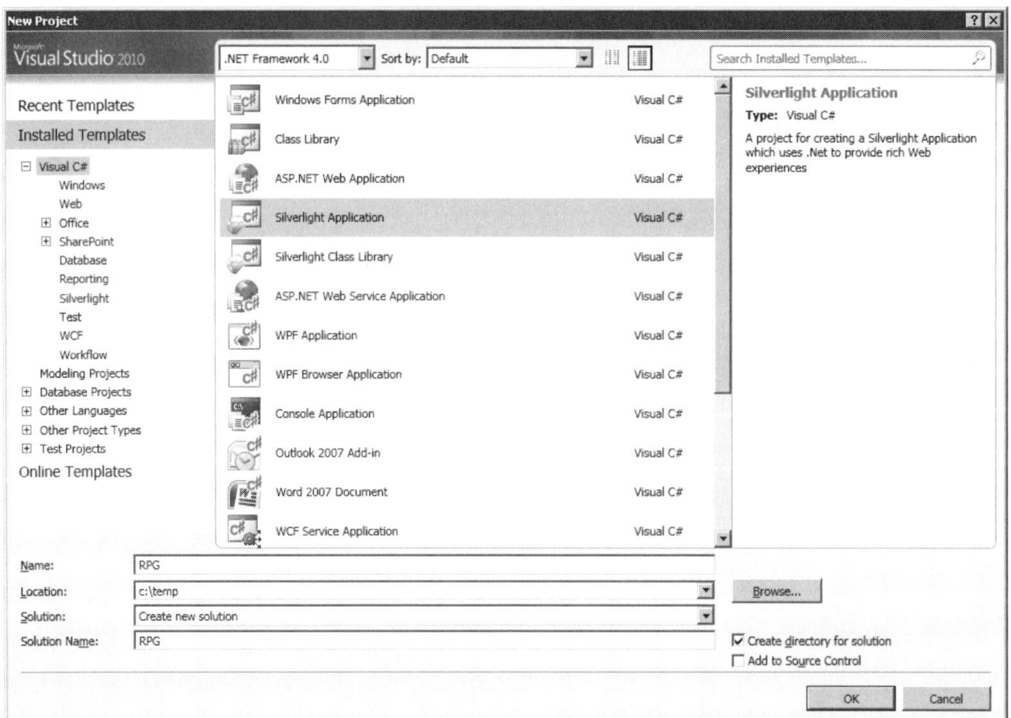

Figure 2.8
New Project Dialog Box

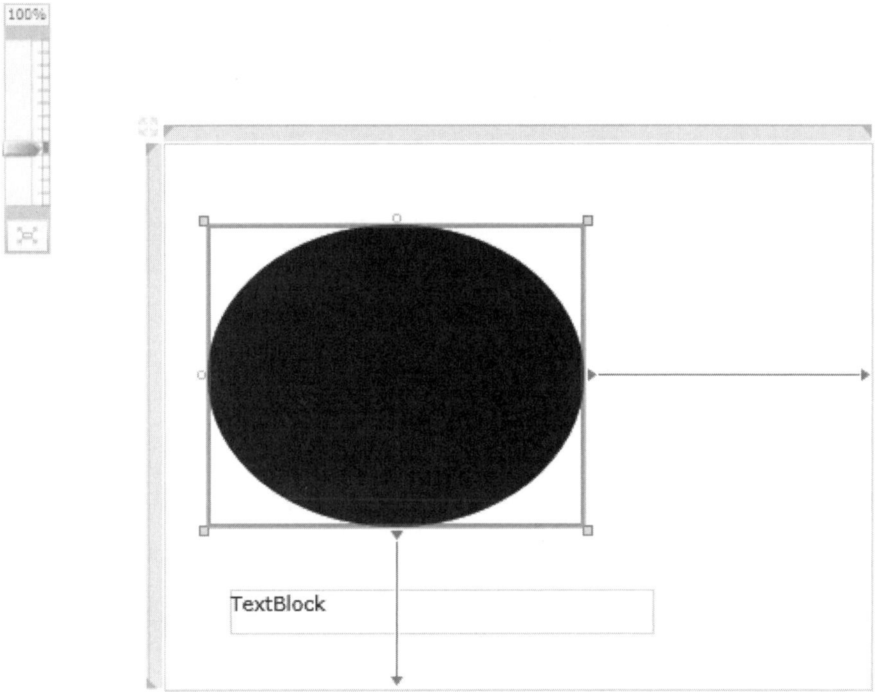

Figure 2.9
Interactive Designer

clicking OK once you have set your project name and location. This will bring up the same New Project dialog box as seen in Figure 2.8. The primary change in this dialog box is the option to choose which version of Silverlight you want to target. Choose Silverlight 3 and click OK when you are ready.

The XAML designer has gone from being preview-only to being fully interactive. You can directly drag/drop controls from the Toolbox to the designer surface. From there, you can select controls, and then resize and re-position the controls anywhere on the surface. Figure 2.9 shows the designer surface with an ellipse selected.

You can also dynamically add rows and columns to a `Grid` control by clicking anywhere along the border of the designer. In Figure 2.10, you can see this being done. Notice it shows you the number of pixels between each row and column along the border.

The next new feature is the interactive Properties window. You can now select individual XAML controls and their properties and events will be displayed in the

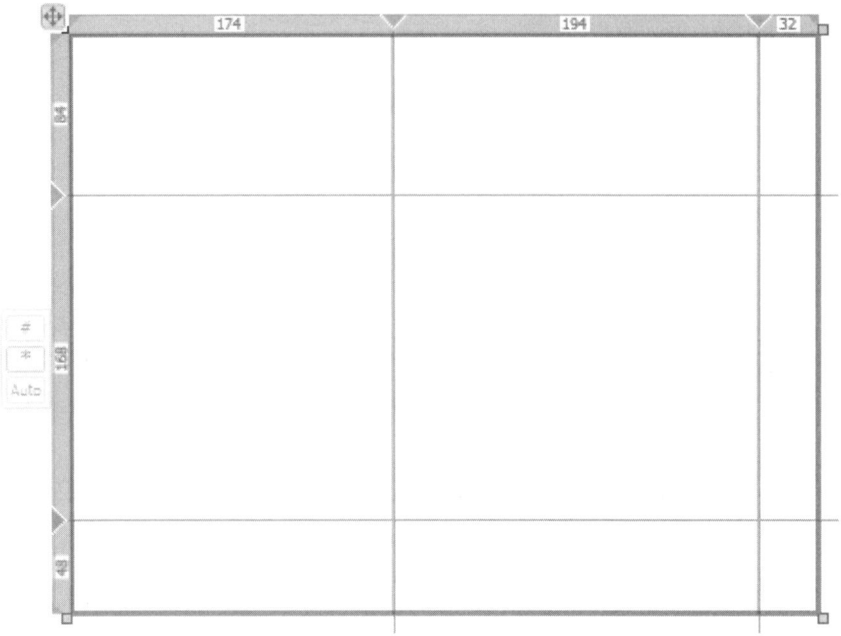

Figure 2.10
Grid Editing

Properties window. This window is fully interactive; it allows you to edit and apply changes to the control's properties and events. Figure 2.11 shows this window.

Using Common Silverlight Utility Functions

Now that you have a Silverlight project up and running, this chapter concludes by showing you how to create a static `Utility` class that can be called from anywhere in your project. To start, add a new class to the Silverlight application project you created earlier. Follow these steps to do so:

1. Right-click on your Silverlight application project in the Solution Explorer.
2. From the context menu, select Add > New Item. This will bring up the Add New Item dialog box, as seen in Figure 2.12.
3. Under Templates, select Class, as shown in Figure 2.12. Rename it utils.cs.
4. Click the Add button when you're done.

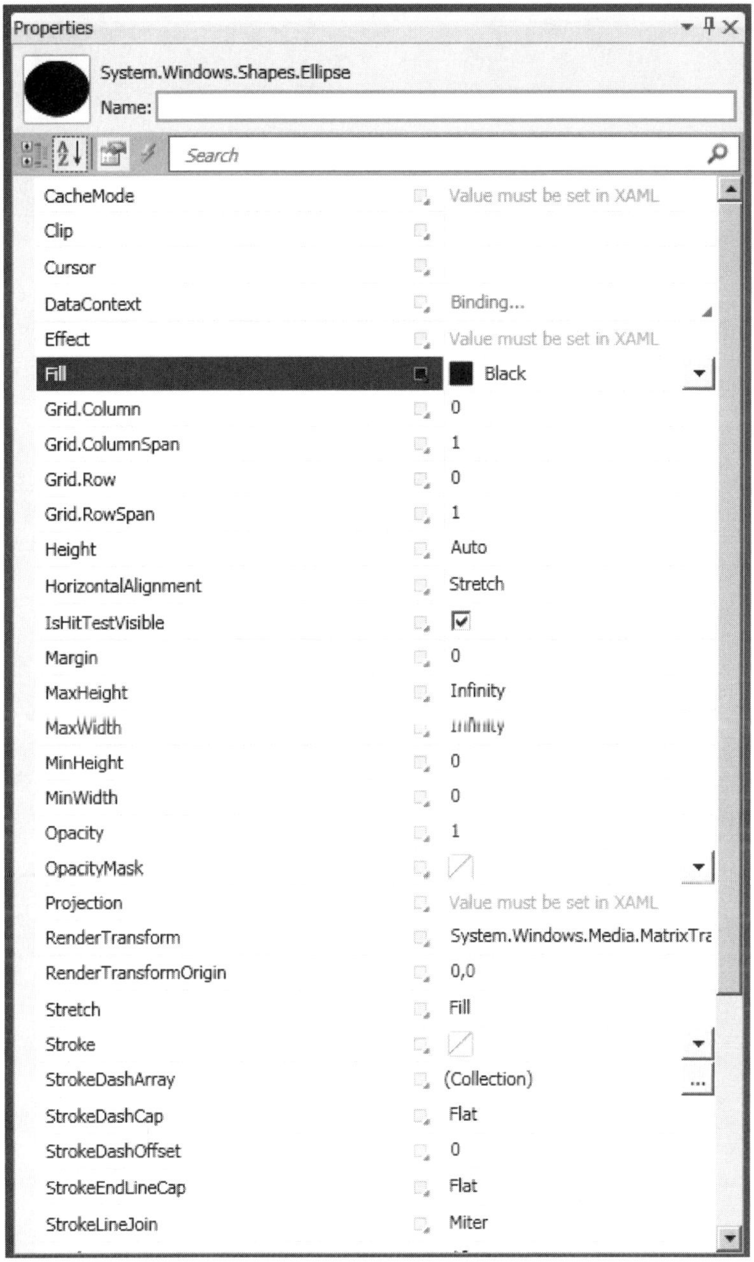

Figure 2.11
Interactive Properties Window

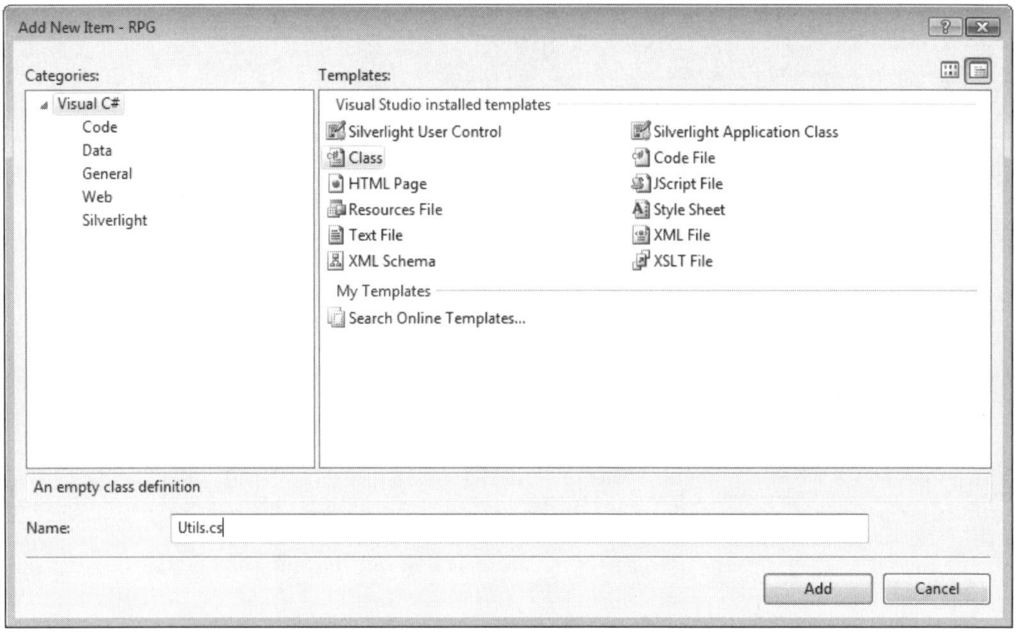

Figure 2.12
Adding a New Class

At this point, you will have an empty `Utils` class. Add to the `Utils` class a static constructor that you will use to initialize any class objects:

```
public class Utils
{
    static Utils()
    {
    }
}
```

The first utility you can add is a random number generator. This example uses a single function called `RndGen()` that will return an integer given a minimum and maximum integer value. In the constructor of the `Utils` class, you can instantiate the random object.

```
static Random _random;
static Utils()
{
        _random = new Random();
}
```

```
public static int RndGen(int min, int max)
{
        return _random.Next(min, max);
}
```

Here's an example using this method that returns a random number between 0 and 100:

```
int rndNumber = Utils.RndGen(0,100);
```

Summary

This chapter covered the tools needed to create, build, and run Silverlight applications. Also, it discussed how to create Silverlight application projects from scratch, including how each file generated by default is used. Finally, the chapter dove into showing you what's new for Visual Studio 2010 and how to create a simple utility class. The next chapter helps you familiarize yourself further with Silverlight by going over a series of tutorials. These tutorials discuss tips and techniques for accomplishing a wide variety of tasks using Silverlight.

CHAPTER 3

What's New with Silverlight 3

Silverlight 3 comes packed with a large set of new features that make developing applications, including games, a much more powerful experience. This chapter reviews each of the following new features, which are most applicable to game development:

- Perspective transforms
- Pixel effects
- Navigation template
- `SaveFileDialog`
- `CaretBrush` on `TextBox`
- Bypassing the image cache
- Image opened event
- Multi-selection list box
- Pixel APIs
- System colors
- Text rendering for animation

- GPU/hardware acceleration
- Media support for H.264/AAC media playback
- Local connection
- Animation easing
- Out-of-browser applications
- Data validation
- Network change detection
- Binary XML
- Merged resource dictionaries

Not included here but also new to Silverlight 3 are

- Raw audio/video support
- Transparent cached extensions
- Application object extensibility
- Style updates (dynamic changes and `BasedOn`)
- Media logging
- Listening to handled routed events
- Compressed fonts from JS
- Local font support

Perspective Transforms

Perspective transforms allow you to apply non-affine transformations to objects. Although this does not yet support true 3D, it does allow you simulate certain 3D scenarios. For example, you can rotate, scale, and translate objects live against a 3×3 matrix, giving them the proper perspective depth.

This feature will allow you to greatly enhance your UI. No longer does your UI have to be flat and 2D. Now you can add compelling effects to your site to entice your customers. Hit testing works against the final rendered rotational boundaries of the object.

To accomplish this, each `UIElement` now has a property called `Projection`. In Silverlight, a `UIElement` is the base class for almost all visible objects or controls. To the `Projection` property, you can apply a `PlaneProjection` that will indicate how to rotate, scale, and translate the object.

To illustrate this, the following example applies a `PlaneProjection` to an image. Note that you can do the same thing for any `UIElement`. The following code declares an image of a rock `gollum`. A 60-degree rotation is applied in each direction, as you can see in Figure 3.1. This is done by setting the properties `RotationX`, `RotationY`, and `RotationZ` to the given degrees.

```
<Image Source="gollum.png">
    <Image.Projection>
        <PlaneProjection RotationX="60"></PlaneProjection>
    </Image.Projection>
</Image>
<Image Source="gollum.png">
    <Image.Projection>
        <PlaneProjection RotationY="60"></PlaneProjection>
    </Image.Projection>
</Image>
<Image Source="gollum.png">
    <Image.Projection>
        <PlaneProjection RotationZ="60"></PlaneProjection>
    </Image.Projection>
</Image>
```

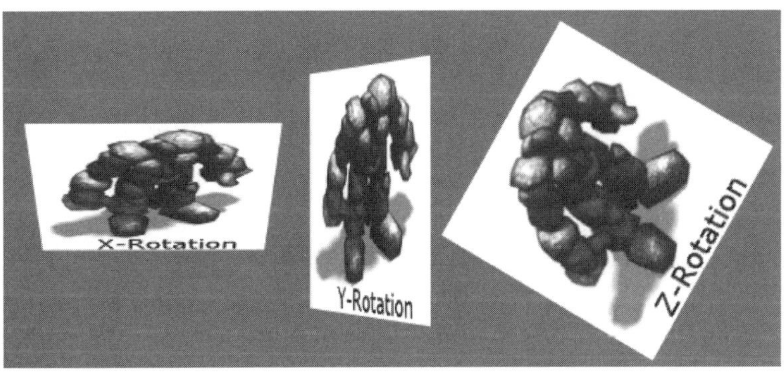

Figure 3.1
Perspective Transforms

You can also specify the center of rotation via the properties CenterOfRotationX, CenterOfRotationY, and CenterOfRotationZ. By default, the center is in the middle, which is defined as 0.5 for X and Y and 0.0 for Z. Values go from 0.0 to 1.0.

In order to set translate transforms for an object, you will need to set the properties LocalOffsetX, LocalOffsetY, and LocalOffsetZ. These values allow you to position the object along a vector after the rotation has occurred. By default, all these properties are set to 0.0. GlobalOffsetX, GlobalOffsetY, and GlobalOffsetZ offer the same functionality except that they translate along the screen coordinates instead of a vector.

Pixel Effects

Pixel shaders allow you to programmatically color and manipulate pixels for a wide range of effects. Using the High Level Shader Language (HLSL), you can now create and use pixel shaders and apply them to your UI elements. For now, you can use only the Pixel Shader 2.0 specification. By default, Silverlight 3 comes with two shaders: drop shadow and blur.

The following code shows you how to apply the built-in blur shader. Blur is affected by its Radius property. The larger the radius, the blurrier the content gets, as you can see in the result shown in Figure 3.2.

```
<StackPanel Orientation="Horizontal">
    <Image Width="200" Source="dragon.png" Margin="3">
        <Image.Effect>
            <BlurEffect Radius="0"></BlurEffect>
        </Image.Effect>
    </Image>
    <Image Width="200" Source="dragon.png" Margin="3">
        <Image.Effect>
            <BlurEffect Radius="5"></BlurEffect>
        </Image.Effect>
    </Image>
    <Image Width="200" Source="dragon.png" Margin="3">
        <Image.Effect>
            <BlurEffect Radius="10"></BlurEffect>
        </Image.Effect>
    </Image>
</StackPanel>
```

Figure 3.2
Blur Shader

The built-in drop shadow shader allows you to produce a shadow in the background of your object. You can apply any combination of the following properties to your drop shadow:

- `BlurRadius`—The amount of blur applied to the shadow. By default, it is 5.
- `Color`—The color of the shadow. By default, it is black.
- `Direction`—Sets the direction the shadow falls in degrees. By default, it is 315.
- `Opacity`—Indicates the opacity of the shadow. By default, it is 1 for no opacity.
- `ShadowDepth`—The offset of the shadow to the object. By default, it is 5.

The following code sets both the `Color` and the `Direction`, resulting in the effect shown in Figure 3.3.

```
<Image Source="mushroom.png" Margin="3">
   <Image.Effect>
     <DropShadowEffect Color="Red" Direction="-103"></DropShadowEffect>
   </Image.Effect>
</Image>
```

Figure 3.3
Drop Shadow Shader

Only one shader can be applied to an element at a time. However, you can work around this by nesting controls, applying a separate shader to each. For example, if you want both a blur and a drop-shadow effect, you could do something like this:

```
<Canvas>
    <Canvas.Effect>
        <DropShadowEffect></DropShadowEffect>
    </Canvas.Effect>
    <Image Source="mushroom.png" Margin="3">
        <Image.Effect>
            <BlurEffect></BlurEffect>
        </Image.Effect>
    </Image>
</Canvas>
```

With this code, you get both shaders applied to the image, resulting in the effect shown in Figure 3.4.

In addition to using the built-in shaders, you can write your own HLSL shader and apply it to your controls. Tutorials on how to build shader files and a library of additional shader effects can be found at http://wpffx.codeplex.com.

To demonstrate how to load and apply a custom pixel shader file, I have created a sample class called `EdgeEffect`. This class loads a binary file called EdgeEffect.ps, creating a `PixelShader` from the content of the file.

```
using System.Windows.Media.Effects;

public class EdgeEffect : ShaderEffect
{
   public EdgeEffect()
    {
        PixelShader = _shader;
```

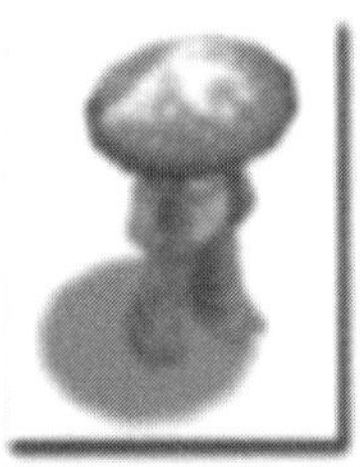

Figure 3.4
Applying Multiple Shaders

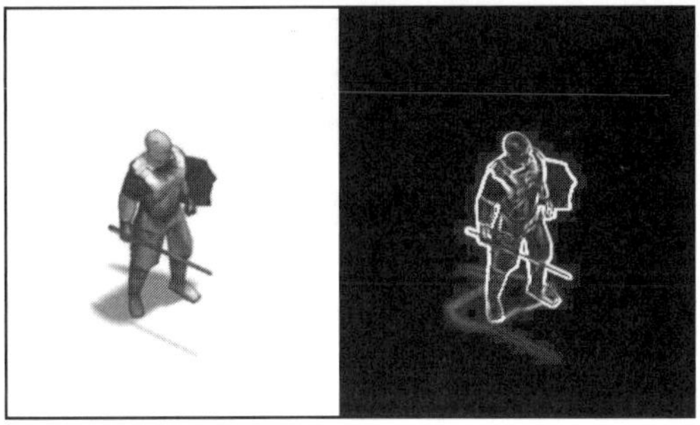

Figure 3.5
Custom Edge Effect

```
        this.DdxUvDdyUvRegisterIndex = 4;
    }
    private static PixelShader _shader =
      new PixelShader() { UriSource = new Uri("EdgeEffect.ps", UriKind.Relative) };
}
```

The following `Image` control shows how to apply this effect to a control:

```
<Image x:Name="MyImage" Stretch="None" Source="man.png"/>
```

Applying the effect to the image is as easy as this:

```
public void ApplyPixelShader()
{
    efx = new EdgeEffect();
    MyImage.Effect = efx;
}
```

Figure 3.5 shows the before and after result of applying this `EdgeEffect` shader.

When adding shader files to your Visual Studio projects, make certain to set your shader files to `Build Acton=Content` so that they will get copied into your XAP file.

Navigation Template

Silverlight 3 Tools introduced a new template called the Navigation template. This template demonstrates how to use the Back and Forward buttons of your browser to navigate through your application. When a user clicked the Back button in Silverlight 2, the browser would leave the Silverlight application and return to the previously viewed website. Now you can control the events associated with these buttons by giving your application a navigation history.

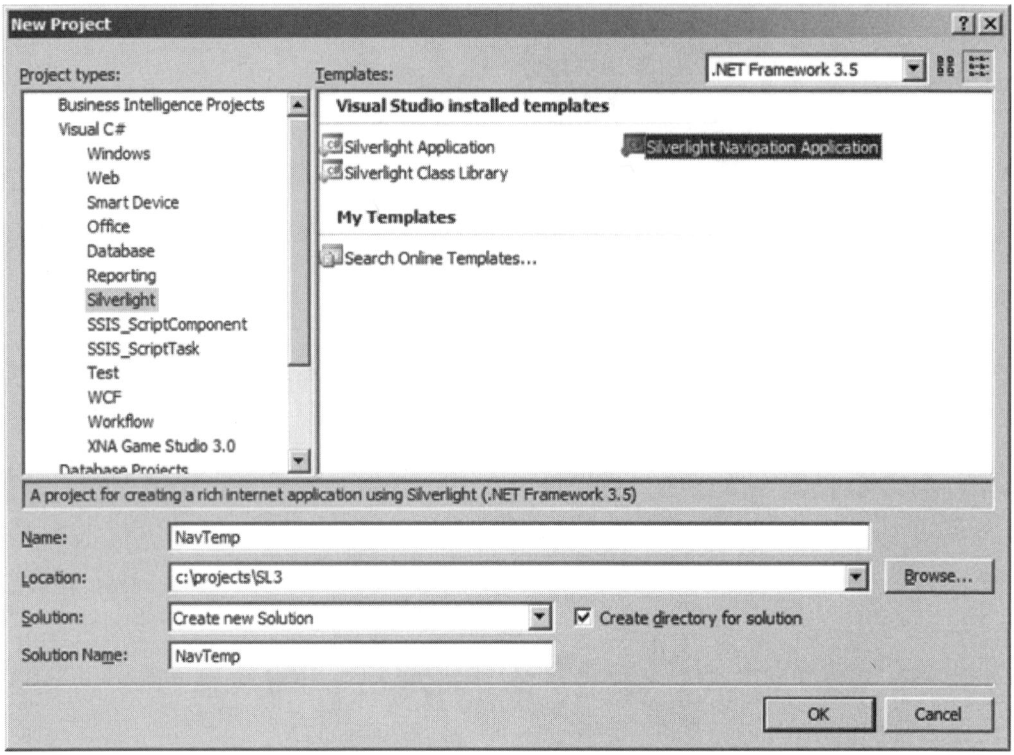

Figure 3.6
New Project Dialog Box

To use this template, open Visual Studio and select File > New Project. This will bring up the New Project dialog box, as shown in Figure 3.6.

Select the Silverlight Navigation Application template and click OK to create the application. When you run the application, you will see a base template that you can use to build your application around. See Figure 3.7.

Clicking the About button in the upper-left corner will navigate the frame to a new control. Notice in Figure 3.8 the Back button is now active in your browser. If you click this button, it will return you to the home page of your Silverlight application.

To add the same functionality to an existing site, you need to follow these steps:

1. Add a reference to System.Windows.Controls.Navigation.dll.
2. In your control, add the following reference:

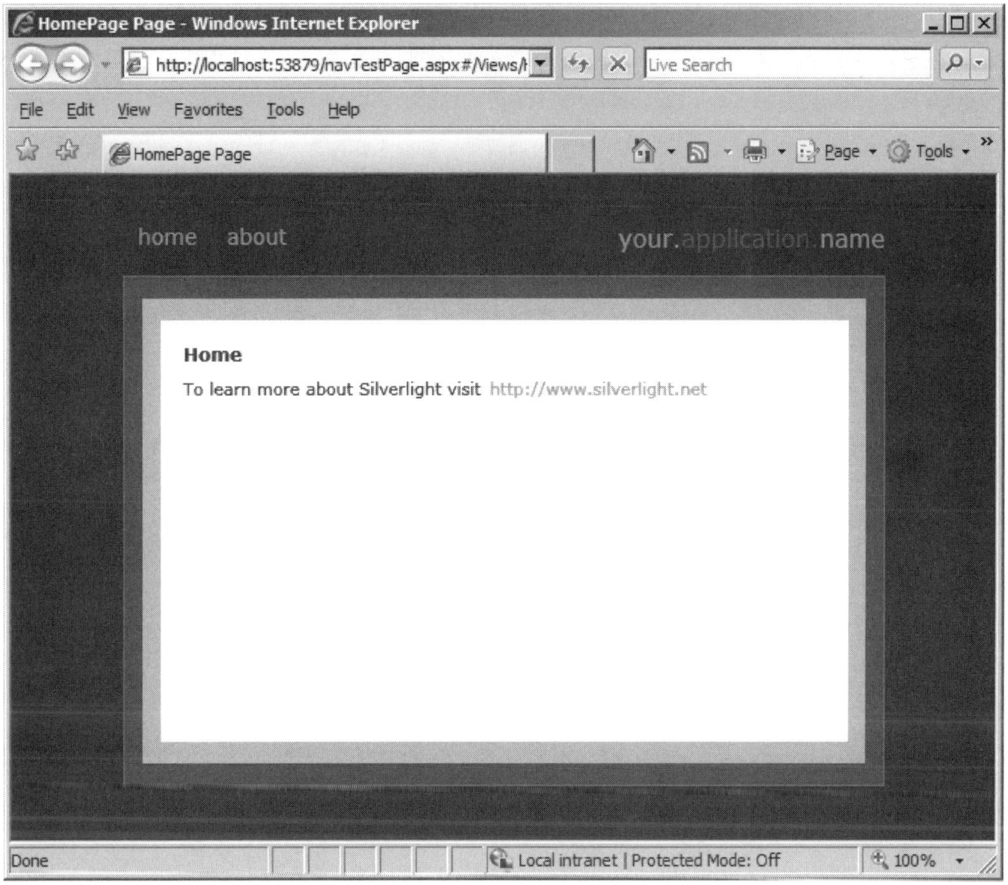

Figure 3.7
Navigation Template

```
xmlns:navigation=
   "clr-namespace:System.Windows.Controls;
   assembly=System.Windows.Controls.Navigation
```

3. Add a Navigation frame to your application, pointing it to your main page:

```
<navigation:Frame x:Name="Frame" Source="/Views/HomePage.xaml"
                    HorizontalContentAlignment="Stretch"
                    VerticalContentAlignment="Stretch"
                    Padding="15,10,15,10"
                  Background="White"/>
```

4. Make a call to `this.Frame.Navigate(URI)` to add the navigational history to your browser.

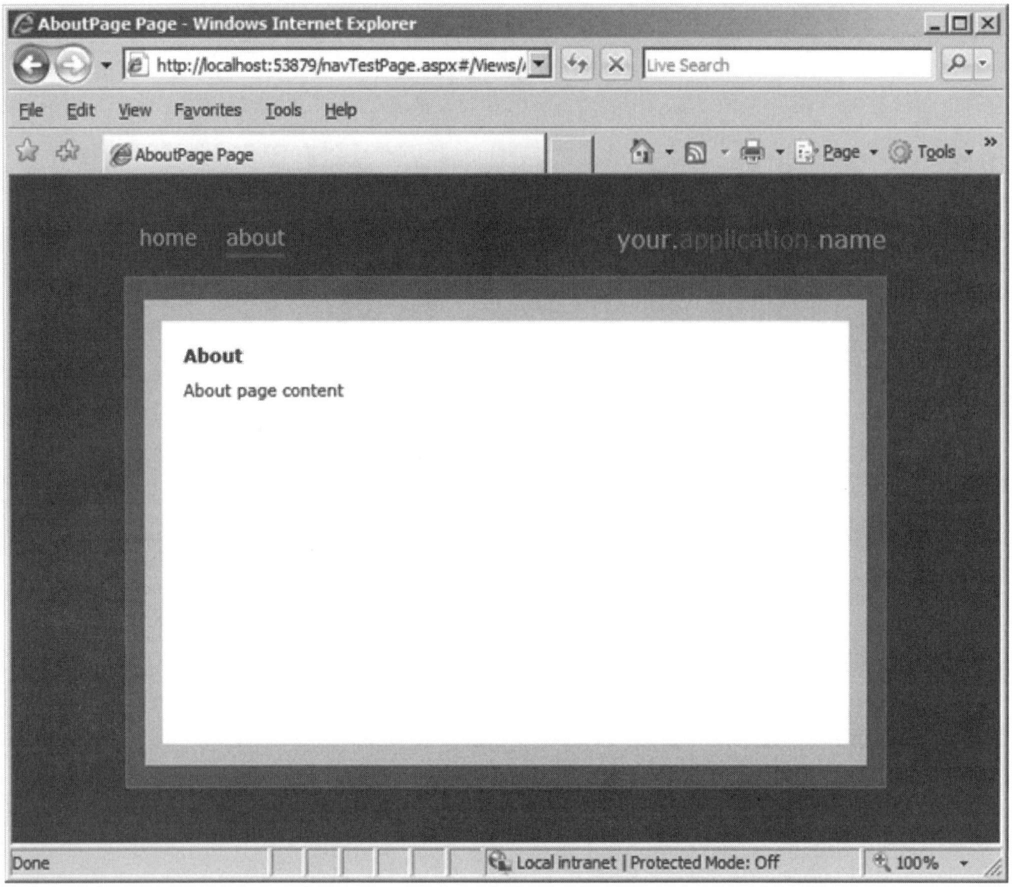

Figure 3.8
Back Button Enabled

SaveFileDialog

With Silverlight 2, you had the option to open files via the `OpenFileDialog` but, due to security concerns, no option to save files. This was a real barrier for developers who needed to save content locally to their clients' machines. Fortunately, Silverlight 3 made way for the `SaveFileDialog` function. This function opens a dialog box, thus allowing users to browse and specify the location where they want to save.

The following code shows you how to invoke the `SaveFileDialog`. Notice that the dialog box does not give you the name of the file but rather a stream pointer that you can use to save data to.

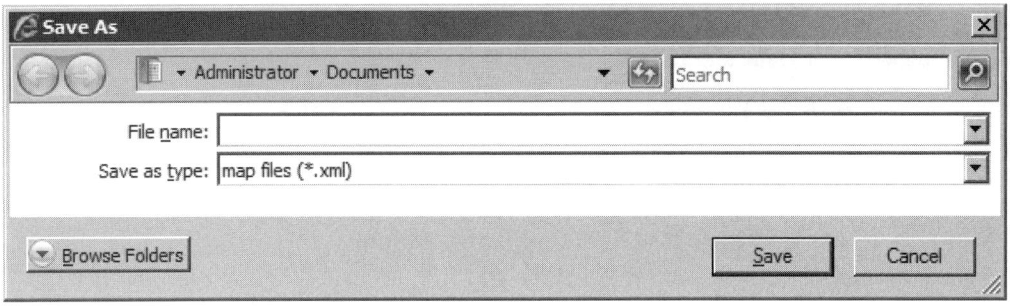

Figure 3.9
Save As Dialog Box

```
SaveFileDialog sfd = new SaveFileDialog();
sfd.Filter = "map files (*.xml)|*.xml|All files (*.*)|*.*";
sfd.ShowDialog();
System.IO.Stream stream = sfd.OpenFile();
```

Use the `Filter` property to specify the extension of the file you want to save. The result of running this code would be the dialog box shown in Figure 3.9. `SaveFileDialog` must be called from a user-initiated action, like a button click.

CaretBrush

You can now apply a style to the caret that appears in the `TextBox` and `PasswordBox` controls. Since this caret is black by default, this can be problematic if you want to use dark, custom colors for your background. For example, if the background of the text box is black, you won't be able to see the caret since by default it is also black.

Caret is a property of `TextBox` that can be set to a brush. This example sets the caret to be a white brush:

```
<TextBox Width="400" Height="60" FontSize="40"
         Foreground="White" Background="Black">
    <TextBox.CaretBrush>
        <SolidColorBrush Color="White"></SolidColorBrush>
    </TextBox.CaretBrush>
</TextBox>
```

Because the caret can be any brush, you can apply a number of great effects to it. For example, you can make it a `LinearGradientBrush`. The following XAML turns the caret into a gradient that goes from white to black. Notice that the example scales the X direction three times to make the cursor wider and more visible.

Figure 3.10
Custom `CaretBrush`

```
<TextBox Width="100" Height="60" FontSize="40"
         Foreground="White" Background="Black">
    <TextBox.RenderTransform>
        <ScaleTransform ScaleX="3" ScaleY="1"/>
    </TextBox.RenderTransform>

    <TextBox.CaretBrush>
        <LinearGradientBrush MappingMode="RelativeToBoundingBox"
                             StartPoint="0,0" EndPoint="0,1">
            <LinearGradientBrush.GradientStops>
                <GradientStop Color="White" Offset="0" />
                <GradientStop Color="Black" Offset="1" />
            </LinearGradientBrush.GradientStops>
        </LinearGradientBrush>

    </TextBox.CaretBrush>
</TextBox>
```

Figure 3.10 shows a screenshot of the solid white and gradient cursor examples.

Bypassing the Image Cache

By default, Silverlight leverages an image cache for images using the URI of the image as the key. The image is not reloaded as long as the URI stays the same. However, there are times when you will want the image to be reloaded. To accommodate this, `BitmapImage` objects can set their `CreationOptions` to `BitmapCreateOptions.IgnoreImageCache`. The following code shows you how:

```
Image img = new Image();
Uri uri = new Uri("MyImage.png", UriKind.Relative);
BitmapImage bi = new System.Windows.Media.Imaging.BitmapImage(uri);
bi.CreateOptions = BitmapCreateOptions.IgnoreImageCache;
img.Source = bi;
```

The default remains `BitmapCreateOptions.None`, so you will need to set it if you want it to bypass the image cache.

ImageOpened Event

In Silverlight 2, it was difficult to determine when an image was completely loaded. Knowing this is important for many reasons, including getting the image's true dimensions. The primary problem was that the DownloadProgress event was fired at 100% before the image was completely decoded. So checking the ActualWidth and ActualHeight properties of the image would intermittently fail. This is now fixed in Silverlight 3 with the introduction of a new event called ImageOpened. The following code shows you how it works:

```
private void LoadImage(string fileName)
{
    Image img = new Image();
    Uri uri = new Uri(fileName, UriKind.Relative);
    img.Source = new System.Windows.Media.Imaging.BitmapImage(uri);
    img.ImageOpened += new EventHandler<RoutedEventArgs>(Image_ImageOpened);
}

void Image_ImageOpened(object sender, RoutedEventArgs e)
{
    Image img = (Image)sender;
    BitmapImage bi = (BitmapImage)img.Source;
    double width = bi.PixelWidth;
    double height = bi.PixelHeight;
}
```

Multi-Selection List Box

Multi-selection is now supported in list boxes. There are three modes you can set to a list box:

- Single—Only one item can be selected at a time.
- Multiple—Multiple items can be selected without having to hold down a modifier key.
- Extended—Multiple items can be selected with the Ctrl modifier key.

To enable this functionality on a list box, you simply have to set the SelectionMode property of the ListBox object like this:

```
<ListBox SelectionMode="Extended">
    <ListBoxItem Content="Item #1" IsSelected="True" />
```

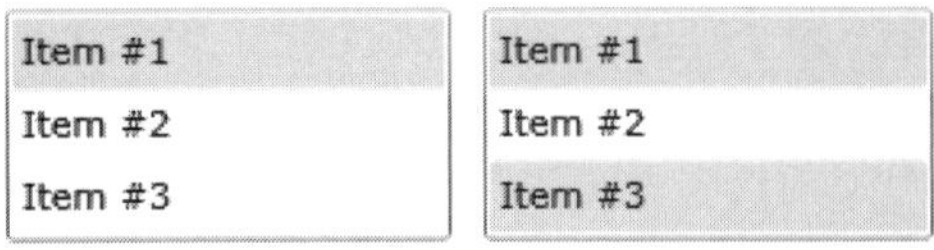

Figure 3.11
Multiple Selection

```
    <ListBoxItem Content="Item #2" />
    <ListBoxItem Content="Item #3" />
</ListBox>
```

To specify which list-box item is selected by default, set the property `IsSelected = true`. If `SelectMode` is either `Extended` or `Multiple`, you can set multiple list-box items to `IsSelected = true`.

```
<ListBox SelectionMode="Extended">
    <ListBoxItem Content="Item #1" IsSelected="True"/>
    <ListBoxItem Content="Item #2" IsSelected="False"/>
    <ListBoxItem Content="Item #3" IsSelected="True"/>
</ListBox>
```

Figure 3.11 shows the result of these two list boxes.

Pixel APIs

A new object called `WriteableBitmap` is available that allows you to directly manipulate pixels on an image. To create a `WriteableBitmap` you will need to specify the pixel width, height, and format. All pixels are initialized to black or 0. To create a 128 × 128 image, you would declare it as such:

```
WriteableBitmap wb = new WriteableBitmap(128,128,PixelFormats.Bgr32);
```

Alternatively, you can create a `WriteableBitmap` by setting it to a `BitmapSource` directly:

```
WriteableBitmap wb = new WriteableBitmap(bitmapSource);
```

If you have an existing image, you can copy its contents directly onto the `WriteableBitmap` via the `Render` function. This function takes two parameters—the image you want to copy and any transform you wish to apply to the image.

```
wb.Render(MyImage, new ScaleTransform());
```

Figure 3.12
WriteableBitmap

From here, you can use the WriteableBitmap as a brush if you want to have it rendered in your application. The following example declares a rectangle.

```
<Rectangle x:Name="MyRect" Height="128" Width="128" />
```

You can then create an ImageBrush object and set its source to be the WriteableBitmap. Finally, you fill the rectangle with the brush you just created:

```
ImageBrush brush = new ImageBrush();
brush.ImageSource = wb;
MyRect.Fill = brush;
```

When you run this code, you will get a rectangle filled with your image, as seen in Figure 3.12.

Individual pixels can be set by indexing into the WriteableBitmap. You will need to Lock() the object before making changes. After you are done, you will want to call Invalidate() to request a redraw of the entire bitmap followed by Unlock() to release it.

For example:

```
WriteableBitmap wb = new WriteableBitmap(128,128,PixelFormats.Bgr32);
wb.Render(MyImage, new ScaleTransform());
ImageBrush brush = new ImageBrush();
brush.ImageSource = wb;
MyRect.Fill = brush;
wb.Lock();
wb[0] = 0; // Set the pixels color by the index
wb.Invalidate();
wb.Unlock();
```

System Colors

In Silverlight 2, you could determine if the system is running in high-contrast mode. Silverlight 3 enables you to determine information about system color settings. This will allow you to set a contrast that matches your user's settings. The color settings include the following:

- `ActiveBorderColor`
- `ActiveCaptionColor`
- `AppWorkspaceColor`
- `DesktopColor`
- `ControlColor`
- `ControlLightLightColor`
- `ControlDarkColor`
- `ControlTextColor`
- `ActiveCaptionTextColor`
- `GrayTextColor`
- `HighlightColor`
- `HighlightTextColor`
- `InactiveBorderColor`
- `InactiveCaptionColor`
- `InactiveCaptionTextColor`
- `InfoColor`
- `InfoTextColor`
- `MenuColor`
- `MenuTextColor`
- `ScrollBarColor`

- ControlDarkDarkColor
- ControlLightColor
- WindowColor
- WindowFrameColor
- WindowTextColor

To access this data, Silverlight introduced a new class called `SystemColors`, which is available through the `System.Windows.SystemColors` namespace.

For example, if you have a rectangle like this:

```
<Rectangle x:Name="MyRect" Width="100" Height="100"/>
```

You can set its fill color to be the system `ActiveCaption` color:

```
MyRect.Fill=newSolidColorBrush(System.Windows.SystemColors.ActiveCaptionColor);
```

Text Rendering for Animation

`RenderOptions` (part of the `System.Windows.Media` namespace) has a new property called `TextRenderingMode`. By setting `RenderingOptions.TextRenderingMode` to `TextRenderingMode.RenderForAnimation`, you can now to turn off text-rendering optimizations. This enhances performance when users zoom in or scroll text. Figure 3.13 shows some intensive text rendering, including animated rotating and zooming. With this setting enabled, the application runs more smoothly and more efficiently.

The following code shows an example of how to set this for a `TextBox` control:

```
RenderOptions.SetTextRenderingMode(MyTextbox,
            TextRenderingMode.RenderForAnimation);
```

GPU/Hardware Acceleration

Silverlight 3 supports harnessing the client's graphics processor unit (GPU) for rendering graphics. The GPU is a processor attached to your graphics card that is generally used for calculating floating-point operations. In addition, it contains a number of graphics primitives that will save you a lot of CPU time.

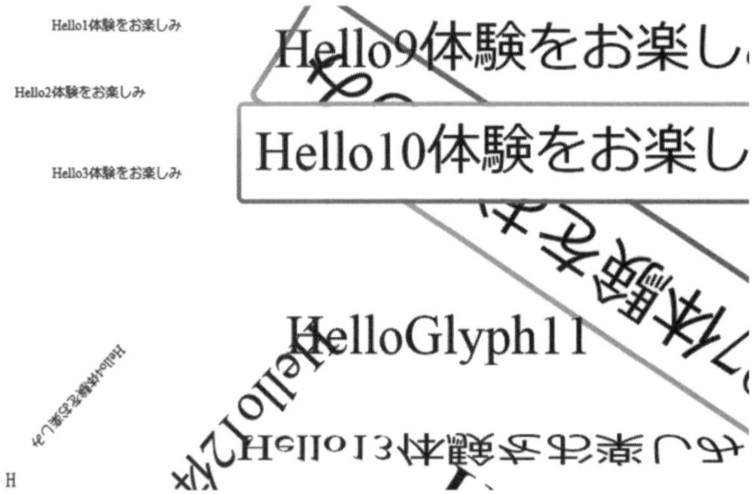

Figure 3.13
Text Rendering for Animation

Hardware acceleration is probably one of the most important features to the game developer. It adds supports stretching, blending, and blitting directly on the graphics card. Stretching pixels is very match-intensive, so by leveraging the GPU, performance is greatly improved.

By default, this option is disabled, and to use it you must enable it both at the Silverlight plug-in level as well as the individual control level. To enable it on your Silverlight plug-in, simply add the parameter `EnableGPUAcceleration` to your HTML, as seen here in bold:

```
<object data="data:application/x-silverlight-2," type="application/
             x-silverlight-2"><param name="EnableGPUAcceleration"
             value="true" />
</object>
```

For ASPX, `EnableGPUAcceleration` is added as an attribute, as seen here in bold:

```
<asp:Silverlight ID="Silverlight1" EnableGPUAcceleration="true"
  runat="server" Source="~/ClientBin/MyApp.xap"
  MinimumVersion="3.0.40307.0"/>
```

At the control level, you can enable hardware acceleration for a given control by setting `CacheMode="Bitmap"`. For example, to enable it for an image, you do this:

```
<Image CacheMode="BitmapCache" Source="MyImage.png"/>
```

Currently, `BitmapCache` is the only option. It causes visual elements (and all their children) to be cached as bitmaps after they have already been rendered. Once these items are cached, your application can bypass the expensive rendering phase for the cached elements and just display them.

If you want to test what is being cached in your application, add the attribute `EnableCacheVisualization` to your Silverlight plug-in. For example:

```
<asp:Silverlight EnableCacheVisualization="true"
   ID="Silverlight1" EnableGPUAcceleration="true"
   runat="server" Source="~/ClientBin/MyAPp.xap"
   MinimumVersion="3.0.40307.0"/>
```

Uncached objects will appear tinted, whereas cached objects will not be tinted. For Macs, this feature is supported only in full screen.

Ideally, this feature should be used only when the following operations are being performed:

- Transformations (translating, rotating, stretching, and so on)
- Clipping
- Blending

Media Support for H.264/AAC Media Playback

Silverlight 3 now supports native H.264 Advanced Audio Coding (AAC), IIS 7 smooth streaming, and full high-definition 720+ playback. This allows for full-screen, stutter-free video directly to the desktop.

With IIS Media Services, users will experience smoother video streaming since it will detect and switch in real-time the quality of your video quality depending upon your current bandwidth and CPU status.

Although Silverlight 2 supported VC-1/WMA media formats, Silverlight 3 offers support for MPEG-4 based H.264 AAC Audio, which means higher-quality content can be delivered.

Since Silverlight 3 supports GPU acceleration, video can now leverage the GPU for hardware acceleration. This allows for true high-definition video at 720p+.

Local Connection

With this new feature, you can now have two separate Silverlight applications communicate with each other on the client side without the need for round-tripping to the server. This circumvents the need to leverage the HTML DOM bridge or scriptable objects. Implementing this feature is fairly straight forward. The following code shows you how to listen for messages:

```
LocalMessageReceiver receiver = new LocalMessageReceiver("R2D2");
receiver.MessageReceived += new
     EventHandler<MessageReceivedEventArgs>(receiver_MessageReceived);
receiver.Listen();

void receiver_MessageReceived(object sender, MessageReceivedEventArgs e)
{
    string message = e.Message;
}
```

You need to reference the namespace `System.Windows.Messaging` to make these calls. The constructor for `LocalMessageReceiver` takes any unique identifier you want to use for sending and receiving. When a message is received, the event `MessageReceived()` is called.

This next block of code shows you how to send messages:

```
LocalMessageSender sender = new LocalMessageSender("R2D2");
sender.SendCompleted +=
        new EventHandler<SendCompletedEventArgs>(sender_SendCompleted);
sender.SendAsync("Hello World!");

void sender_SendCompleted(object sender, SendCompletedEventArgs e)
{
    // message sent
}
```

Notice that you must use the same unique identifier in both the send and receive code.

Animation Easing

Animation easing allows you to apply built-in animation functions that are used when animating your Silverlight controls. The result is a variety of animation effects that make your controls move in a more realistic way. In many cases, by using animation easing, you can avoid having to go through all the hard work to figure out how to apply physics to your world objects. For example, you can add springiness to your controls, set how many times you want it to bounce when it hits a destination point, and so on. The functions that you can set (all of these are found in the `System.Windows.Media.Animation` namespace) include the following:

- `BackEase`—Moves the object backward by an amount specified through its amplitude before moving forward.
- `BounceEase`—Creates an effect like a bouncing ball.
- `CircleEase`—Accelerates the animation based upon a circular function.
- `CubicEase`—Accelerates the animation based upon a cubic function.
- `ElasticEase`—Uses springiness and oscillation to animate.
- `ExponentialEase`—Accelerates the animation based upon an exponent value.
- `PowerEase`—Accelerates the animation based on a power of time.
- `QuadraticEase`—Accelerates the animation based on the square of time.
- `QuarticEase`—Accelerates the animation based on the cube of time.
- `QuinticEase`—Accelerates the animation based on the time to the power of 5.
- `SineEase`—Accelerates the animation along a sine wave.

Each of these can have an `EasingMode` set to one of the following options:

- `EaseOut`—Ease takes place at the beginning of the animation.
- `EaseIn`—Ease takes place at the end of the animation.
- `EaseInOut`—`EaseIn` takes place for half the animation, followed by `EaseOut`.

A good way to visualize the acceleration for these is to take a look a Figure 3.14. This figure is a screenshot of the `EasingFunction` tool window found in `ExpressionBlend`. This tool window gives you an acceleration visualization cue for each of the available functions.

To set an easing function for a control (such as an `Image` control), you will need to first associate the control with a `Storyboard`. A `Storyboard` is essentially a timer

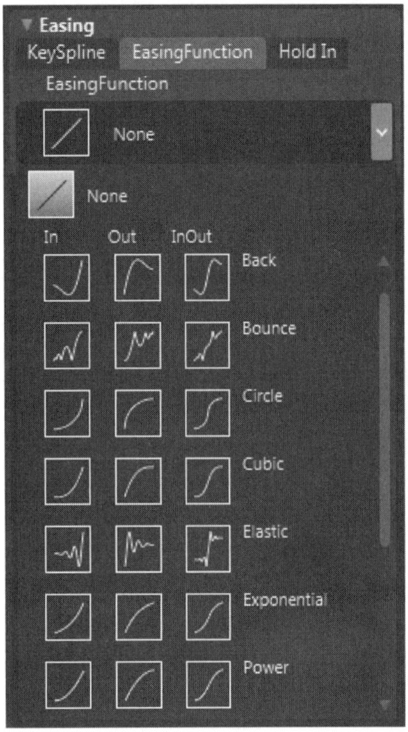

Figure 3.14
EasingFunction

that drives the animation for the object over a specified timeline. Storyboard objects are covered in detail in Chapter 7, "Animation." The easing function gets applied directly to the animation object associated with the Storyboard.

The following XAML shows an Image control that points to an image of a soccer ball. The Storyboard contains an animation of type DoubleAnimation. This animation targets the Image object and its Top property (or the Y coordinate) for animation. In the animation, the Top property is set to go from 0 to 1000 over a period of five seconds. Applied to the animation's EasingFunction is a BounceEase (in bold), which is configured to make the image control bounce two times once it reaches its destination.

```
<Canvas x:Name="LayoutRoot" Background="White">
    <Canvas.Resources>
        <Storyboard x:Name="BallSB">
            <DoubleAnimation x:Name="BallDA" Completed="DoubleAnimation_
                                                                Completed"
```

```
            From="0" To="1000" Duration="0:0:05"
Storyboard.TargetName="TargetBall"
Storyboard.TargetProperty="(Canvas.Top)">
                <DoubleAnimation.EasingFunction>
                    <BounceEase x:Name="Easing" Bounces="2"
EasingMode="EaseOut" Bounciness="2"/>
                </DoubleAnimation.EasingFunction>
            </DoubleAnimation>
        </Storyboard>
    </Canvas.Resources>
    <Image x:Name="TargetBall" Source="soccerball.png"
     ImageOpened="Image_ImageOpened"/>
</Canvas>
```

To start the animation, you simply have to call `BallSB.Start()`. The result will be a ball that that drops down from Y=0 to Y=1000, gradually speeding up over five seconds and finally bouncing twice once it reaches the bottom.

Out-of-Browser Applications

This feature allows you to create Silverlight applications that run in their own window outside of your browser. Your application can have its own shortcut with an icon in the Start menu and/or the desktop.

To enable this functionality in your Silverlight application, you simply add the following XML to your AppManifest.xml. This XML contains the name, title, and description of your application.

```
<Deployment.ApplicationIdentity>
    <ApplicationIdentity
        ShortName="My Application"
        Title="My Cool Out of Browser Application">
        <ApplicationIdentity.Blurb>OOB Demonstration
        </ApplicationIdentity.Blurb>
    </ApplicationIdentity>
</Deployment.ApplicationIdentity>
```

The AppManifest.xml file is located in your Silverlight applications Properties folder. Once you have added this XML, you run your Silverlight like normal in the browser. Right-click on the application in the browser and you will notice the option to install the application is now enabled, as seen in Figure 3.15.

Figure 3.15
Out of Browser

Figure 3.16
Install Application

Figure 3.17
Out-of-Browser Shortcut Icon

Selecting Install My Application onto This Computer will bring up the dialog box shown in Figure 3.16. In this dialog box, you can confirm the locations (Start menu and/or desktop) where you want to install the shortcuts that will launch your application out of browser.

Clicking OK in this dialog box will cause the shortcut icon seen in Figure 3.17 to be generated.

Figure 3.18
Out of Browser Application

After the shortcut is generated, the application will automatically launch out of browser, as can be seen in Figure 3.18.

To remove the application, you right-click on the out-of-browser application and choose Remove This Application from the context menu, as seen in Figure 3.19.

You can customize the icon for the shortcut by setting `ApplicationIdentity.Icons` in the AppManifest.xml. The following example shows how to do this:

```
<Deployment.ApplicationIdentity>
  <ApplicationIdentity
      ShortName="My Application"
      Title="My Cool Out of Browser Application">
    <ApplicationIdentity.Blurb>OOB demonstration</ApplicationIdentity.Blurb>
    <ApplicationIdentity.Icons>
      <Icon Size="16x16">16.png</Icon>
      <Icon Size="32x32">32.png</Icon>
      <Icon Size="64x64">64.png</Icon>
      <Icon Size="128x128">128.png</Icon>
    </ApplicationIdentity.Icons>
```

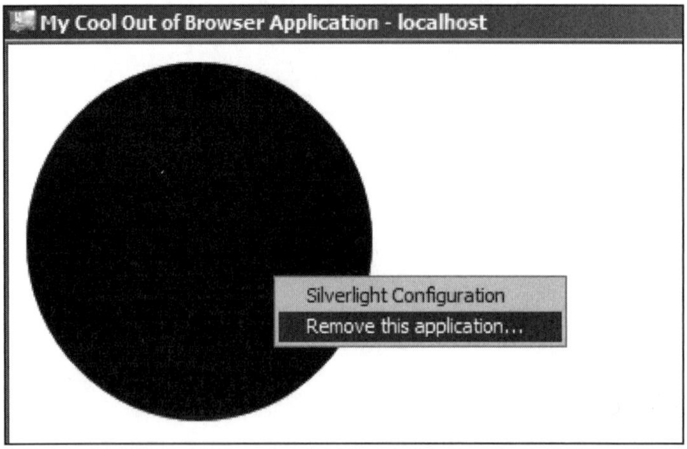

Figure 3.19
Remove Application

```
  </ApplicationIdentity>
</Deployment.ApplicationIdentity>
```

The individual images will need to be added to your Silverlight application. In the Properties window for each image, make certain to set the `Build Action = Content` and `Copy To Output Directory = Copy if newer`.

Data Validation

Using data validation, you can separate your validation logic from your UI elements. This is a common best practice that is easy to implement in Silverlight. To demonstrate how this works, the following example uses a text box that accepts a number within the range of 1-10. The validation logic is contained in a class called `UIDataValidation`. In Figure 3.20, you can see the before and after that occurs when typing a number that is not within the range of 1-10. An error message pops up and the text block is highlighted with a red border if the data inputted is not valid.

To see how this works, start by looking at the following XAML:

```
<UserControl x:Class="SilverlightApplication101.MainPage"
    xmlns="http://schemas.microsoft.com/winfx/2006/xaml/presentation"
    xmlns:x="http://schemas.microsoft.com/winfx/2006/xaml"
    xmlns:local="clr-namespace:SilverlightApplication101"
    Width="400" Height="300">
```

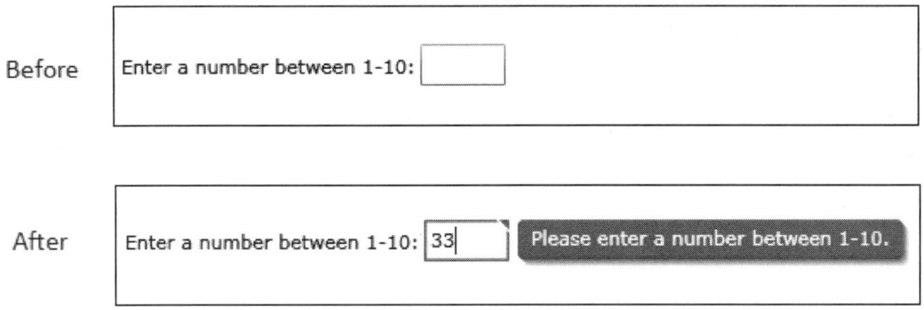

Figure 3.20
Data Validation

```
    <Canvas x:Name="LayoutRoot" Background="White">
        <Canvas.DataContext>
            <local:UIDataValidation />
        </Canvas.DataContext>
        <TextBlock Margin="5" x:Name="InputValue">Enter a number between 1-10:
        </TextBlock>
        <TextBox Canvas.Left="180" Width="50"
                    Text="{Binding Number, Mode=TwoWay,
                    ValidatesOnExceptions=True}"/>
    </Canvas>
</UserControl>
```

The `UIDataValidation` class that does the verification is declared under the `Canvas.DataContext` section shown in bold. With this declaration, the `Canvas` object and all its children will be able to reference properties in the `UIDataValidation` class that they wish to be called for UI verification. For example, the `TextBox` binds to the property `Number`. In this property, you should check to see if the value inputted is within the range of 1-10. If it's not, throw an exception. Since the text block sets `ValidatesOnException` to `true`, the binding engine will create a validation error if the exception gets thrown.

The following code is the class for `UIDataValidation`. You take the string that is inputted in the text box and convert it to an integer. To reiterate the point, any exception thrown by this property gets caught by the binding engine and is turned into a validation error. You throw an exception if the number inputted is not within the range of 1-10 or if you are able to convert the inputted string to an integer. For example, this could happen if the user types a non-numeric character. If you do throw an exception, you include a message in the thrown exception that gets displayed to the users, as seen in the after section of Figure 3.20.

```
public class UIDataValidation
{
    private string number;

    public string Number
    {
        get { return number; }
        set
        {
            try
            {
                int inputValue = (int) Convert.ToInt32(value);
                if(inputValue < 1 || inputValue > 10)
                    throw new Exception("Please enter a number between 1-10.");
            }
            catch
            {
                throw new Exception("Please enter a number between 1-10.");
            }
        }
    }
}
```

The previous example performed data verification on the `Text` property of a text box. The following example shows you how to bind data verification to the `SelectedItem` property of the `ListBox` control. In this example, you must check to see if a person's age is 18 years or more. If not, you throw an exception telling the users they must be at least 18 years of age to play this game. Figure 3.21 shows this process in action.

The following XAML creates the `TextBlock` that poses the age question and a `ComboBox` that allows the users to specify what age range they are in.

```
<TextBlock Canvas.Top="40">How old are you?</TextBlock>
<ComboBox Canvas.Top="60" Width="200"
  SelectedItem="{Binding AgeRange, Mode=TwoWay, ValidatesOnExceptions=True}">
```

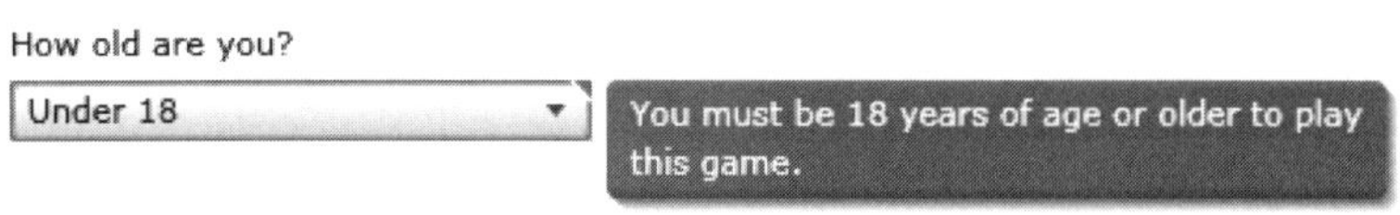

Figure 3.21
`ComboBox` Verification

```
    <sys:String>Under 18</sys:String>
    <sys:String>18 or older</sys:String>
</ComboBox>
```

The ComboBox binds to the property AgeRange in the UIDataValidation class. The following code is the property for AgeRange:

```
public string AgeRange
{
    get { return ageRange; }
    set
    {
        if (!string.IsNullOrEmpty(value) &&
            value.Equals("Under 18", StringComparison.OrdinalIgnoreCase))
        {
           throw new Exception("You must be 18 years of age
                                  or older to play this game.");
        }
        ageRange = value;
    }
}
```

There may be times when you will want to sweep through all your UI elements to see if any of them contain a validation error–for example, when a user clicks a button to submit a form. You can do this by calling Validation.GetErrors() and passing as the parameter the UI element you wish to verify. The following code shows you how to iterate through all your UI elements in your Silverlight tree and perform the data-validation check on each element. Any element that has an error is added to a list that you can then process:

```
List<ValidationError> errorList = new List<ValidationError>();

foreach ( UIElement element in this.LayoutRoot.Children )
{
    if ( (element as FrameworkElement) != null )
    {
        foreach ( ValidationError error in Validation.GetErrors( element ) )
        {
            errorList.Add( error );
        }
    }
}
```

Network Change Detection

For the first time, in Silverlight 3, you can detect if your Internet connection has changed or if it is available. To see if your Internet connection is available, you simply have to call `GetIsNetworkAvailable()`, which is part of the `System.Net.NetworkInformation` namespace. The following code demonstrates its use:

```
using System.Net.NetworkInformation;
public MainPage()
{
    InitializeComponent();

    if (NetworkInterface.GetIsNetworkAvailable())
    {
        StartMultiplayerGame();
    }
    else
    {
        ReportNetworkError();
    }
}
```

To monitor for the event that detects any change in the network availability, you can use the following code:

```
NetworkChange.NetworkAddressChanged += new
NetworkAddressChangedEventHandler(NetworkChange_NetworkAddressChanged);

void NetworkChange_NetworkAddressChanged(object sender, EventArgs e)
{
}
```

Binary XML

In addition to traditional text-based XML, Silverlight now supports XML in binary format. The advantage of using binary-based XML files is the files are smaller (compressed), which will result in better performance and greater speed when communicating with web services.

Merged Resource Dictionary

Merged resource dictionaries allow you to essentially manage resource dictionary files in separate files that you can then point to and reference from your XAML. For example, say you have two separate resource files, each containing their own set of style declarations. The following XAML shows you how to merge and reference the two resource files using a resource dictionary.

```
<Canvas x:Name="LayoutRoot" Background="White">
    <Canvas.Resources>
        <ResourceDictionary>
            <ResourceDictionary.MergedDictionaries>
                <ResourceDictionary Source="Resource1.xaml"/>
                <ResourceDictionary Source="Resource2.xaml"/>
            </ResourceDictionary.MergedDictionaries>
        </ResourceDictionary>
    </Canvas.Resources>
</Canvas>
```

The following is the content for each of the two resource files.

Resource 1:

```
<ResourceDictionary
    xmlns="http://schemas.microsoft.com/winfx/2006/xaml/presentation"
    xmlns:x="http://schemas.microsoft.com/winfx/2006/xaml"
    xmlns:sys-"clr-namespace:System;assembly=mscorlib">
    <sys:String x:Name="WelcomeMsg">Welcome to Tsunami Realms!</sys:String>
</ResourceDictionary>
```

Resource 2:

```
<ResourceDictionary
    xmlns="http://schemas.microsoft.com/winfx/2006/xaml/presentation"
    xmlns:x="http://schemas.microsoft.com/winfx/2006/xaml" >
    <SolidColorBrush x:Key="FontColor" Color="Pink" />
</ResourceDictionary>
```

The following XAML shows you how to reference the styles as a static resource from the different resource files:

```
<Canvas x:Name="LayoutRoot" Background="White">
    <Canvas.Resources>
```

Figure 3.22
Merged Dictionary Resources

```
        <ResourceDictionary>
            <ResourceDictionary.MergedDictionaries>
                <ResourceDictionary Source="Resource1.xaml"/>
                <ResourceDictionary Source="Resource2.xaml"/>
            </ResourceDictionary.MergedDictionaries>
        </ResourceDictionary>
    </Canvas.Resources>

    <TextBlock FontSize="25" Text="{StaticResource WelcomeMsg}"
               Foreground="{StaticResource FontColor}">
    </TextBlock>
</Canvas>
```

The result can be seen in Figure 3.22.

Summary

This chapter covered many of the new features found in Silverlight 3. Most of these new features are extremely useful for game development. Overall, these new and powerful features should give you a solid glimpse of what is possible with Silverlight. The next chapter discusses how to leverage these and other Silverlight features for game-development purposes.

CHAPTER 4

Silverlight Game Tips and Tricks

Whenever you adopt a new technology, you might find you spend a lot of time searching the Internet to find out how to accomplish certain tasks with this technology. Not only do you want to find how to do it but also find the best, most efficient way to do it. You may find there is often a big learning curve and you would like to just skip ahead to the snippets of code you need to get your job done. This chapter covers a number of such scenarios in order to show you how to do certain game-development tasks in Silverlight. My hope is that these tips and tricks will save you a lot of time and research.

This chapter covers the following topics:

- Creating the main game loop
- Putting your game in full-screen mode
- Accessing the HTML DOM from your game
- Centering your game window in the browser
- Setting browser cookies from your game
- Communicating with JavaScript
- Capturing browser resizes
- Communicating between the `Application` and `MainPage` classes

- Enabling and disabling your game controls
- Making a browser window pop up
- Dynamically loading and displaying your game
- Making your Silverlight control transparent
- Scaling your game controls in your browser
- Image loading
- Obtaining image dimensions
- Monitoring for mouse and keyboard events
- Cropping objects in your game
- Loading a Silverlight control within another Silverlight control
- Adding tooltips to buttons and objects
- Leveraging isolated storage for your game purposes
- Working with image source filenames
- Working with strokes and shapes
- Loading images from streams
- Loading and managing images in your game
- Setting the default browser from within VS
- Detecting mouse double clicks in your game

Creating the Main Game Loop

The main game loop is the non-stop beating heart of your game. It is essentially an infinite loop that is used for a variety of game-related task processing. For example, processing network communications, performing animation, and checking on player input and status are all examples of work items that can be done in the main game loop.

There are a variety of ways to create a main game loop in Silverlight, including using a `Storyboard` animation control or a `DispatcherTimer`. The technique I prefer is to use the `CompositionTarget.Rendering` event. This event is called once per frame just before the objects in the Silverlight composition tree are rendered. This ensures your rendering is in sync with your set frame rate.

Creating this event is as simple as the following:

```
public partial class Page : UserControl
{
    public Page()
    {
        InitializeComponent();
        CompositionTarget.Rendering += new EventHandler(MainGameLoop);
    }

    void MainGameLoop(object sender, EventArgs e)
    {
        // Put your game loop logic here (animation, etc.).
    }
}
```

Putting Your Game in Full-Screen Mode

Putting your game into full-screen mode will essentially cause your browser to disappear, with your game taking up the entire desktop space. It does not, however, change your desktop resolution. You will need to perform any necessary scaling to your game if you want your game to take up the entire space. Also, only one Silverlight application can be in full-screen mode at a time.

To go into full-screen mode, all you have to do is set `IsFullScreen` to `true`. This property can be found in the `Application.Current.Host.Content` namespace. This property can be set only in response to a user-input event handler such as a button click or else it will be ignored. That is, your game cannot automatically be launched into full-screen mode without permission from the user. This restriction is put in place for security purposes. Without it, users could spoof the appearance of the operating system or other such applications. The following code is an example of how you could toggle full-screen mode from a button click event:

```
private void Button_Click_Toggle_FullScreen(object sender, RoutedEventArgs e)
{
    if(true == Application.Current.Host.Content.IsFullScreen)
        Application.Current.Host.Content.IsFullScreen = false;
```

```
    else
        Application.Current.Host.Content.IsFullScreen = true;
}
```

When the application goes into full-screen mode, the user will see the message displayed in Figure 4.1, which will fade away after four seconds.

In order prevent password spoofing, keyboard inputs are restricted to the following keys while in full-screen mode:

- Spacebar
- Arrow keys
- Tab
- Home
- Enter
- End
- Page Up/Page Down

So, for example, users cannot type into a text box in full-screen mode. If you plan to design a full-screen application, you will have to keep this restriction in mind.

Accessing the HTML DOM from Your Game

The HTML Document Object Model (DOM) is accessible through the `HtmlPage.Document` object. In order for this object to be recognized, you will need to add a `using` statement to reference the namespace `System.Windows.Browser`. Through the DOM, you can make a number of changes to the web page that hosts your Silverlight control. In the code example that follows, `GetElementByID()` is called in the DOM to get access to the DIV that is wrapping the Silverlight control. Once you have the DIV object, you must call `SetStyleAttribute()` to toggle the color of the DIV to green or blue.

Figure 4.1
Full-Screen Mode Notification

```
private void Button_Click_Toggle_Page_Color(object sender, RoutedEventArgs e)
{
    HtmlDocument doc = HtmlPage.Document;
    HtmlElement div = doc.GetElementById("myDIV");
    string color = div.GetStyleAttribute("background");
    if(color == "green")
        div.SetStyleAttribute("background", "blue");
    else
        div.SetStyleAttribute("background", "green");
}
```

If you open the file default.aspx, you can see the DIV that has the ID `myDIV`.

```
<div id="myDIV" style="background:blue;width:1024px;height:768px">
   <asp:Silverlight ID="Xaml1" runat="server" Source="~/ClientBin/Chapter4.xap"
       MinimumVersion="2.0.31005.0" Width="800px" Height="600px" />
</div>
```

Notice that the size of the DIV is set to 1024×768 and the Silverlight control is 800×600. This way, the Silverlight control does not completely overlap and hide the DIV. Also, your application can enable or disable access to the DOM via the property `HtmlAccess`. The default is `true` if in same-domain applications but is `false` for cross-domain applications. At the plug-in level, you can set this to `Enabled`, `Disabled`, or `SameDomain`.

Centering Your Game Window in the Browser

There are times when you may want to keep your Silverlight application centered directly in the middle of the web browser. By default, the application is positioned in the upper-left corner. In order to accomplish this adjustment, you have to set the style of the DIV that encompasses your Silverlight control to `margin:auto`. You also need to change the width and height from 100% to a pixel dimension.

```
<div style="margin:auto;width:400px;height:300px">
   <asp:Silverlight ID="Xaml1" runat="server"
   Source="~/ClientBin/Chapter4.xap" MinimumVersion="2.0.31005.0"
   Width="100%" Height="100%" />
</div>
```

Now, as shown in Figure 4.2, the application is centered in the browser.

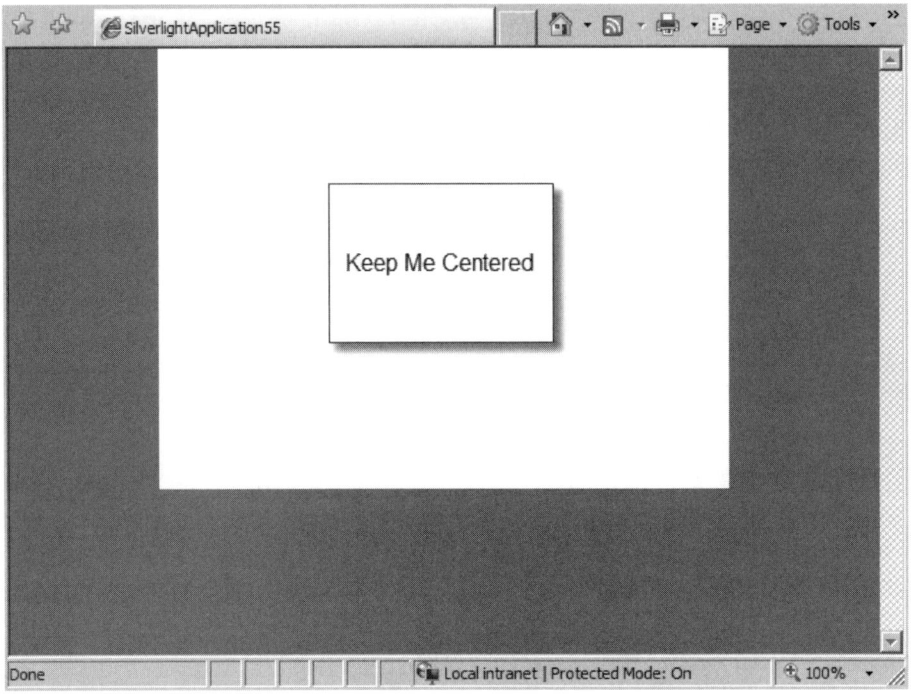

Figure 4.2
Centered Silverlight Control

Setting Browser Cookies from Your Game

Cookies are useful because they allow the server to store settings on the client that can be reloaded the next time the client accesses the page. Cookies are stored as strings of text. To set browser cookies, you return again to the `HtmlPage.Document` object. In order to set a cookie, you call `SetProperty()` with a string in the following format: `"`*`Key`*`=`*`Value`*`;expires=`*`ExpireDate`*`"`, where `Key` is any name you want to identity the key with and `value` is the value you want to identify with that key. *`Expires`* is the date this cookie is set to expire. For example:

```
private void SetCookie(string key, string value, double daysToExpire)
{
   DateTime expireDate = DateTime.Now + TimeSpan.FromDays(daysToExpire);
   string newCookie = key + "=" + value + ";expires=" + expireDate.ToString("R");
   HtmlPage.Document.SetProperty("cookie", newCookie);
}
```

Getting a cookie is a little different and unfortunately a bit more difficult. You will need to iterate through all cookies that are currently set until you find the one that matches the key you are searching for. In the following example, you return the value for a given key. If the key was not found, you return `null`.

```
private string GetCookie(string key)
{
    string[] cookies = HtmlPage.Document.Cookies.Split(';');
    foreach (string cookie in cookies)
    {
        string[] keyValue = cookie.Split('=');
        if (keyValue.Length == 2)
        {
            if (keyValue[0].ToString() == key)
                return keyValue[1];
        }
    }
    return null;
}
```

The following test method shows how to call the `set` and `get` cookie methods with the key being `"UserName"`, the value being `"Mike Snow"`, and the expiration date being seven days.

```
private void TestCookie()
{
    SetCookie("UserName", "Mike Snow", 7);
    string userName = GetCookie("UserName");
}
```

Communicating with JavaScript

Communication between JavaScript and Silverlight is fairly straightforward. In order to call Silverlight from JavaScript, you need to do the following:

- In the constructor of your Silverlight app, make a call to `RegisterScriptableObject()`. This call essentially registers a managed object for scriptable access by JavaScript code. The first parameter is any key name you want to give. This key is referenced in your JavaScript code when making the call to Silverlight.
- To call a function in JavaScript, you simply need to invoke it through the `Htmlpage.Window.Invoke()` method, where the first parameter is the method to call and the remaining parameters are the parameters that get passed to the JavaScript method.

- Add a function you want called in your Silverlight code. You must prefix it with the `[ScriptableMember]` attribute. From JavaScript, you can now call directly into your Silverlight function. This can be done through the document object. From the example that follows: `document.getElementById("silverlight Control"). Content.Page.UpdateText("Hello from JavaScript!");` where `silverlightControl` is the ID of my Silverlight control.

For example, in Silverlight, add the following code:

```
HtmlPage.RegisterScriptableObject("Page", this);
HtmlPage.Window.Invoke("TalkToJavaScript", "Hello from Silverlight");

[ScriptableMember]
public void UpdateText(string result)
{
    JSTextBoxMessage.Text = result;
}
```

The `JSTextBoxMessage` is a text-box control that you set with the message you receive from JavaScript. In the default.aspx file, add the function `TalkToJava Script()` that is called from your Silverlight code:

```
<script type="text/javascript">
    function TalkToJavaScript(data)
    {
        alert("Message received from Silverlight: " + data);
        var control = document.getElementById("silverlightControl");
        control.Content.Page.UpdateText("Hello from Javascript!");
    }
</script>
```

Capturing Browser Resizes

It is important to know when your browser is resized so you can properly position and resize your game surface and the controls it contains as needed. In order to accomplish this, you will need to subscribe to the event `App.Current. Host.Content.Resized`. For example:

```
App.Current.Host.Content.Resized += new EventHandler(Content_Resized);
```

This event will fire whenever the users resize their browser windows. When fired, you can capture the size of your browser by checking for the values `ActualWidth` and `ActualHeight`, as seen in the following code:

```
void Content_Resized(object sender, EventArgs e)
{
    double height = App.Current.Host.Content.ActualHeight;
    double width = App.Current.Host.Content.ActualWidth;
}
```

Communicating Between the Application and MainPage Classes

The Application class (app.xaml and app.xaml.cs) is primarily used for global events and declarations such as styles.

The primary events this class handles by default include the following:

- Application_Startup()—Called when the application starts.
- Application_Exit()—Called when the application is exiting.
- Application_UnhandledException()—Called when an unhandled exception has occurred.

The MainPage class (MainPage.xaml and MainPage.xaml.cs) is where you will typically put the core game logic and UI declarations. Now, what if you want to communicate with your game logic in your MainPage class when an event such as Application_Exit() is fired in the Application class?

In Application_Startup(), your Application class creates an instance of your MainPage class and stores it as a UIElement under the property RootVisual:

```
private void Application_Startup(object sender, StartupEventArgs e)
{
    this.RootVisual = new MainPage();
}
```

To illustrate the call, add a public getter function in page.xaml.cs:

```
private bool _done = false;

public bool Done
{
    get { return _done; }
    set { _done = value; }
}
```

In order to call any public members in the page class, you have to typecast `RootVisual` to be a `MainPage` since by default it is a `UIElement`. In app.xaml.cs, you can make a call to set `done = true` in the `MainPage` class when the application has exited:

```
private void Application_Exit(object sender, EventArgs e)
{
    ((MainPage)this.RootVisual).Done = true;
}
```

Enabling and Disabling Your Game Controls

Silverlight controls can be enabled and disabled via the property `IsEnabled`. This property is supported with all XAML controls found in the toolbox except those controls that are non-interactive (such as ellipses, images, lines, and so on). By default, all controls are enabled, so you need to set this property only if you want to set it to `false` in order to disable the control. In addition to the property `IsEnabled`, an event called `IsEnableChanged` is now available.

When `IsEnabled` is set to `false`, the control is grayed out and will not respond to user interaction. The following example shows two buttons—the first is one enabled and the second is one disabled. Figure 4.3 shows the enabled and disabled buttons.

```
<Button Width="120" Content="Enabled Button" ></Button>
<Button IsEnabled="False" Width="120" Content="Disabled Button" ></Button>
```

Making a Browser Window Pop Up

Say a user clicks on a button and you want to pop up a separate browser window and point the user to a specific web page. How do you do this in Silverlight? Silverlight supports a method called `HtmlPage.PopupWindow()`. For security reasons, this method can be used only in response to a user input such as a button click.

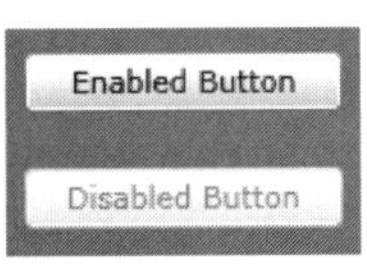

Figure 4.3
Enabled and Disabled Controls

To use this method, you need to add a reference to `System.Windows.Browser`. The call to `HtmlPage.PopupWindow()` takes three parameters:

- `Uri`—The location to browse to (such as http:///www.silverlight.net).
- `String`—The name you want to call the target window.
- `HtmlPopupWindowOptions`—A variety of options such as window positioning, sizing, whether the toolbar and menu bar are visible, and so on.

The following code demonstrates how to pop up a window in response to a button click from the user:

```
private void Button_Click_Popup_Browser(object sender, RoutedEventArgs e)
{
    HtmlPopupWindowOptions options = new HtmlPopupWindowOptions();
    options.Left = 0;
    options.Top = 0;
    options.Width = 800;
    options.Height = 600;
    if (true == HtmlPage.IsPopupWindowAllowed)
    HtmlPage.PopupWindow(new Uri("http://www.silverlight.net"), "new", options);
}
```

Dynamically Loading and Displaying Your Game

By default, Silverlight controls are statically declared in your web page file. The Silverlight control is essentially an ASP component that points to an XAP file. This XAP file is a zip file that contains the files and components needed to run your application. The Silverlight control declaration for this chapter is declared in the default.aspx file and looks like this:

```
<asp:Silverlight ID="Xaml1" runat="server" Source="~/ClientBin/Chapter4.xap"
    MinimumVersion="2.0.30523" Width="100%" Height="100%" />
```

So what if you want to your website to be able to change which Silverlight application is being loaded and displayed? This is useful, for example, if you want to switch which application a panel in your website is displaying. You can do this by dynamically creating a Silverlight component and adding it directly to your web page.

The following example shows two buttons on a web page. When clicked, each of these buttons will load a separate Silverlight application. Here, and in the code-behind file default.aspx.cs, you will see the two button event functions, one that loads the first application and one that loads the second application. In these functions, a new Silverlight object found in the namespace `System.Web.UI.SilverlightControls` is created. Once created, its source is set to point to the location of the Silverlight application's XAP file that you want to load. Optionally, you can also set `ID`, `width`, `height`, and `Windowless=true` parameters for the window. Once the window is created, you add it to the web page.

```
protected void OnShowFirstApp(object sender, EventArgs e)
{
    Silverlight sl = new Silverlight();
    sl.Source = "ClientBin/SilverlightApplication1.xap";
    sl.ID = "SilverlightApp1";
    sl.Width = new Unit(800);
    sl.Height = new Unit(600);
    sl.Windowless = true;
    SilverlightApp.Controls.Clear();
    SilverlightApp.Controls.Add(sl);
}

protected void OnShowSecondApp(object sender, EventArgs e)
{
    Silverlight sl = new Silverlight();
    sl.Source = "ClientBin/SilverlightApplication2.xap";
    sl.ID = "SilverlightApp2";
    sl.Width = new Unit(800);
    sl.Height = new Unit(600);
    sl.Windowless = true;
    SilverlightApp.Controls.Clear();
    SilverlightApp.Controls.Add(sl);
}
```

Making Your Silverlight Control Transparent

By default, the background of your Silverlight control is not transparent. Normally, it takes up the entire web page since the Silverlight control on the website is set to a width and height of 100%. However, if you want the Silverlight control to take up only a part of the web page, you may want to consider making it transparent so that it blends in with the background of your web page. In order to accomplish this, you will need to set two properties on your Silverlight control. The first is called `PluginBackground` and you will need to set this to `Transparent`. The second is `Windowless` and you will need to set this to `true`. Also, make certain the parent control of your Silverlight application does not have a background color. Keep in mind that setting a Silverlight control to be transparent can have a negative effect on performance. Set it to transparent only if you really need to.

For an ASPX page, you can set the transparency like this:

```
<asp:Silverlight PluginBackground="Transparent" Windowless="true"
   ID="Xaml1" runat="server" Source="~/ClientBin/SilverlightApplication40.xap"
   MinimumVersion="2.0.31222.0" Width="300px" Height="200px" />
```

For an HTML page, you will need to add these properties as `params` like this:

```
<object data="data:application/x-silverlight," type="application/
                                                x-silverlight-2" >
   <param name="source" value="ClientBin/SilverlightApplication40.xap"/>
   <param name="onerror" value="onSilverlightError" />
   <param name="pluginbackground" value="Transparent" />
   <param name="windowless" value="true" />
</object>
```

To demo this example, I have created a Silverlight application with a `TextBlock`, `Slider`, and `Ellipse`. I set the web page background color to gray. In Figure 4.4, where the top image is the transparent Silverlight control, you can see that the gray background renders through each control in the Silverlight application. The Silverlight application on the bottom of Figure 4.4 is not transparent and the background has defaulted to white.

Scaling Your Game Controls in Your Browser

The Silverlight control contains a property called `ScaleMode` that allows you to specify how the controls within your Silverlight application are scaled when your Silverlight control gets resized in the browser.

For example, if the width or height of your Silverlight control is set to be a percentage of your browser web page, when the browser page is resized, your Silverlight control will also get resized.

The three options available for the `ScaleMode` property are as follows:

- `None`—No scaling is performed.
- `Stretch`—Stretching is performed to fill the browser host area horizontally and vertically.
- `Zoom`—Scaling is performed to proportionally fill the browser.

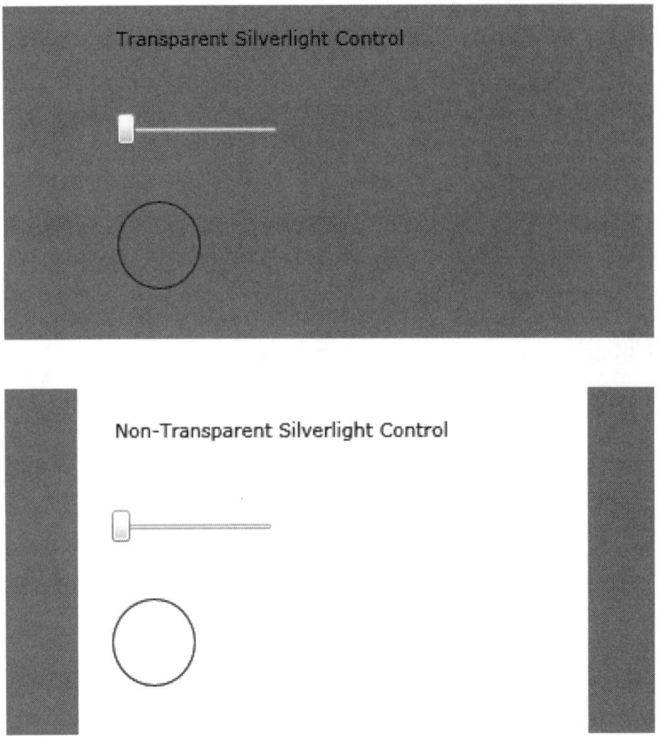

Figure 4.4
Transparent and Non-Transparent Silverlight Controls

The following is an example of how to set the `ScaleMode` property to `Stretch` in your Silverlight control:

```
<asp:Silverlight ID="Xaml1" ScaleMode="Stretch" runat="server"
    Source="~/ClientBin/SilverlightApplication52.xap"
    MinimumVersion="2.0.31222.0" Width="100%" Height="100%" />
```

Figures 4.5 and 4.6 show an example of a Silverlight app with a few random controls. In Figure 4.6, the browser has been resized and the controls have been stretched to match.

Image Loading

There are three steps needed to load an image in Silverlight:

1. Create a new `Image` control.
2. Create what's called a uniform resource identifier (URI). The URI is essentially a string that points to a resource. The resource can be locally

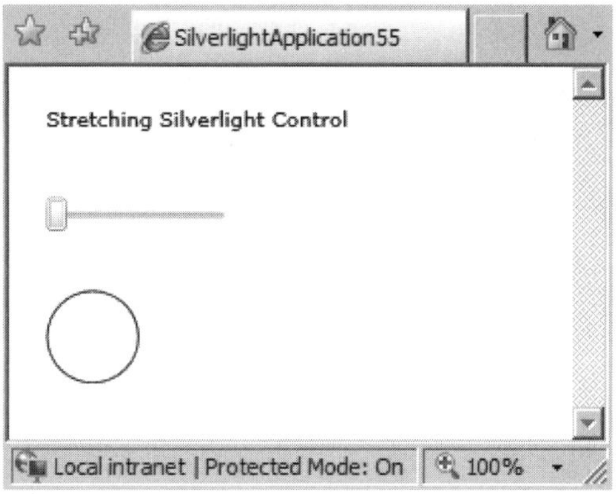

Figure 4.5
Before a Browser Resize

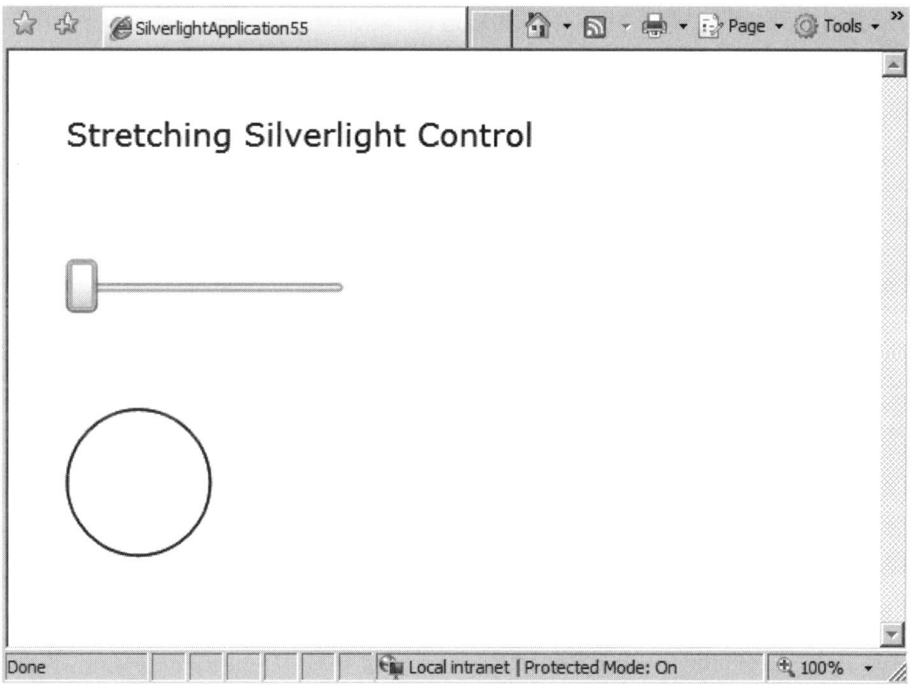

Figure 4.6
After a Browser Resize

in the project or out on the Internet. Images that are loaded locally must be first added to your Visual Studio project.

3. Create an `ImageSource` from the URI and set your image `Source` property to point to the `ImageSource`.

The following example has a static function called `LoadImage()` in the `Utils` class. This static function loads an image given a string that points to the resource file for your image in the project:

```
public static Image LoadImage(string imgResource)
{
   Image img = new Image();
   Uri uri = new Uri(imgResource, UriKind.Relative);
   ImageSource imgSource = new
      System.Windows.Media.Imaging.BitmapImage(uri);
      img.Source = imgSource;
      return img;
}
```

Here's an example of how to call this function:

```
Image img = Utils.LoadImage("adventure.png");
```

Obtaining Image Dimensions

Since Silverlight is based upon an asynchronous model, getting an image's width and height immediately after loading the image is not possible. However, you can monitor the download progress for the image and obtain the image dimensions once the download progress has reached 100%.

The following code shows a sample that demonstrates how to do this. But first, a few important notes:

- The example uses a `BitmapImage` instead of an `ImageSource` to load the image since `BitmapImage` has the event needed to monitor the download progress. `BitmapImage` requires the namespace `System.Windows.Media.Imaging`.
- `ActualWidth` and `ActualHeight` are calculated values. The calculation happens after a layout pass. Therefore, the image must be in the Silverlight tree in order for its size to be accounted for. To accomplish this, you can add the call `MapCanvas.Children.Add(grass);` this will add the image to the canvas.
- The image you are adding to your canvas must be first added to your Silverlight application project in Visual Studio. Make certain your path to this image is correct.

- The call to `Dispatcher.BeginInvoke(delegate() { ... } );` is required before you obtain the `Width/Height` or they might be intermittently zero.

```
public partial class Page : UserControl
{
    Image grassImg;

    public Page()
    {
        InitializeComponent();

        grassImg = LoadImage("grass.png");
        MapCanvas.Children.Add(grassImg);
    }
    private Image LoadImage(string path)
    {
        Image img = new Image();
        Uri uri = new Uri(path, UriKind.Relative);
        BitmapImage bitmapImage = new BitmapImage();
        bitmapImage.UriSource = uri;
        bitmapImage.DownloadProgress += new
          EventHandler<DownloadProgressEventArgs>
          (bitmapImage_DownloadProgress);

        img.Source = bitmapImage;
        return img;
    }

    void bitmapImage_DownloadProgress(object sender,
                    DownloadProgressEventArgs e)
    {
        if (e.Progress == 100)
        {
            Dispatcher.BeginInvoke(delegate()
            {
                double height = grassImg.ActualHeight;
                double width = grassImg.ActualWidth;
            });
        }
    }
}
```

Monitoring for Mouse and Keyboard Events

Silverlight has great support for keyboard and mouse event monitoring. You can listen for these events at the application level or even at the individual control level. For example, to listen for `KeyUp()` and `KeyDown()` events at the application level, you simply need to make the following calls:

```
this.KeyUp += new KeyEventHandler(Page_KeyUp);
this.KeyDown += new KeyEventHandler(Page_KeyDown);
```

Within the callback functions, you can determine which key was pressed by checking the `e.Key` value:

```
void Page_KeyDown(object sender, KeyEventArgs e)
{
    switch (e.Key)
    {
        case Key.Escape:
            break;
        case Key.Up:
            break;
        case Key.Down:
            break;
        case Key.Left:
            break;
        case Key.Right:
            break;
    }
}
```

The following mouse events are available:

- `MouseEnter`
- `MouseLeave`
- `MouseLeftButtonDown`
- `MouseLeftButtonUp`
- `MouseMove`

Listening to a mouse event is similar to how you listen to a keyboard event:

```
this.MouseLeftButtonDown += new MouseButtonEventHandler(Page_MouseLeftButtonDown);
this.MouseLeftButtonUp += new MouseButtonEventHandler(Page_MouseLeftButtonUp);
```

Cropping Objects in Your Game

If you want to display only part of an object, you can do so using the `Clip` property. The clip that you define is the area of the object that you want to be rendered. For example, let's say you have a rectangle defined like this:

```
<Rectangle Fill="White" Height="100" Width="200" StrokeThickness="3"
                                                 Stroke="Black">
</Rectangle>
```

Figure 4.7 shows a rendering of this unclipped rectangle.

If you only want to show part of the rectangle, you can apply a clip region to it like this:

```
<Rectangle Fill="White" Height="100" Width="200" StrokeThickness="3"
                                                 Stroke="Black">
   <Rectangle.Clip>
      <EllipseGeometry Center="0,0" RadiusX="80" RadiusY="80" />
   </Rectangle.Clip>
</Rectangle>
```

Figure 4.8 shows a rendering of the clipped rectangle.

Loading a Silverlight Control Within Another Silverlight Control

Let's say your site is written entirely in Silverlight but you want to be able to load and run a different Silverlight application within your main Silverlight application/site.

Figure 4.7
Unclipped Rectangle

Figure 4.8
Clipped Rectangle

The way you can do this is to add a second, hidden Silverlight control to your web page. You then set the `Source` for this second Silverlight control to be empty (`""`) until you want the Silverlight control to load and display. You must also put the control in a hidden DIV. You can load and unload this control as well and you can dynamically set it to point to different XAPs in order to load different applications on your site.

From your website, verify that you have two Silverlight controls declared. The first control is your main control:

```
<div style="height: 100%; z-index: 1; position: absolute;">
   <asp:Silverlight ID="Xaml1" runat="server" Source="~/ClientBin/SLDev.xap"
       MinimumVersion="2.0.30523" Width="100%" Height="100%" />
</div>
```

The second control is the one you will load and display within the main control:

```
<div id="myDIV" style="z-index: 2; display: none; position: absolute;
         padding-left: 0px; padding-top: 200px;">
     <asp:Silverlight ID="Silverlight1" runat="server" Source=""
         MinimumVersion="2.0.30523" Width="800px" Height="600px" />
</div>
```

Things to notice:

- The style z-index order is higher for the second Silverlight control than for the first so that the second one appears on top.
- The style `display` is set to `none` for the DIV of the second Silverlight control so that it is not displayed and does not interfere with mouse/keyboard input for the first Silverlight control.
- The style `position` is set to `absolute` so that the controls can float on top of each other. You will want to adjust `padding-left` and `padding-right` to properly position the control where you want it on your site.
- `Source =""` is set for the second Silverlight control to keep it from loading an application until you are ready.

To your website (that is, the default.aspx file), add two JavaScript functions that your Silverlight application can call to load and hide the second Silverlight control.

A few notes:

- The `LoadSilverlightControl()` function takes a parameter that contains the full path to the XAP you want to load–for example, `ClientBin\TankWar.xap`.

- For the Silverlight control, you call `setAttribute()` to change the source of the Silverlight control.
- For the DIV, you set the `style.display` setting to `block` so that it will display or to `none` to hide it.

```
<script type="text/javascript">
    function LoadSilverlightControl(ctrl)
    {
           var control = document.getElementById("Silverlight1");
           var div = document.getElementById("myDIV");
           div.style.display = "block";
           control.setAttribute("Source", ctrl);
    }
    function HideSilverlightControl()
    {
            var control = document.getElementById("Silverlight1");
            var div = document.getElementById("myDIV");
            div.style.display = "none";
            control.setAttribute("Source", "");
    }
</script>
```

The call from Silverlight to JavaScript to make the control load and run is as follows:

```
HtmlPage.Window.Invoke("LoadSilverlightControl", "ClientBin/TankWar.xap");
```

To hide it, use this call:

```
HtmlPage.Window.Invoke("HideSilverlightControl");
```

Adding Tooltips to Buttons and Objects

If you have a framework element in your game such as an image, button, text block, and so on, you can add a tooltip to it. Tooltips are usually small, boxed text blocks that pop up when users hover over the control. The purpose of the tooltip is to tell the user what the control does.

For example, as shown in Figure 4.9, say you have a toolbar of flags that represents the language a user can select. If users do not recognize a flag, they could hover over it, and the tooltip would indicate which language the flag represents. See Figure 4.10.

Figure 4.9
Silverlight Toolbar

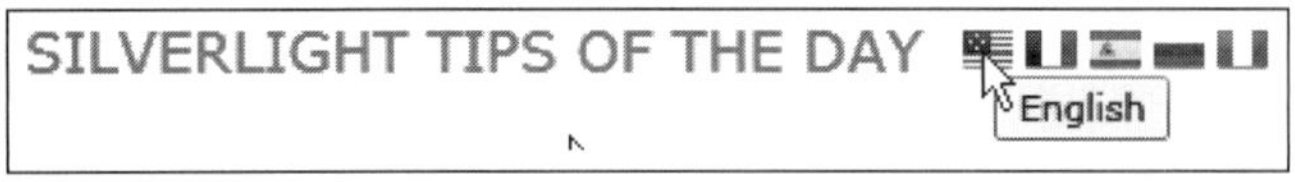

Figure 4.10
Silverlight Toolbar with Tooltip

Figure 4.11
Silverlight Toolbar with an Image as a Tooltip

To add a tooltip to a framework element, all you have to do is declare the property `ToolTipService.ToolTip`. For example:

```
<Image Source="images/france.png" ToolTipService.ToolTip="French">
```

A tooltip does not have to be only text; in fact, a tooltip can be any control you declare. For example, to make a tooltip an image, you would declare it as follows:

```
<Image Source="images/france.png" Width="16" Height="16">
    <ToolTipService.ToolTip>
<Image Source="images/france.png"></Image>
    </ToolTipService.ToolTip>
</Image>
```

The result when hovering over the French flag would be the French flag in a larger size, as seen in Figure 4.11.

Leveraging Isolated Storage for Game Purposes

Silverlight uses isolated storage as a virtual file system to store data in a hidden folder on your machine. It breaks the data into two separate sections—section 1 contains administrative information such as disk quota and section 2 contains the actual data. Each Silverlight application is allocated its own portion of the storage with the current quota set to be 1MB per application.

Advantages of isolated storage are as follows:

- Isolated storage is a great alternative to using cookies (as discussed in http://silverlight.net/blogs/msnow/archive/2008/07/15/tip-of-the-day-18-how-to-set-browser-cookies.aspx), especially when you are working with large sets of data. Examples of uses include adding undo functionality to your app, storing shopping-cart items, saving window settings, and storing any other settings so that your application can call them the next time it loads.

- Isolated storage stores information by the OS user, thus allowing server applications to dedicate unique settings per individual user.

Possible pitfalls of isolated storage include the following:

- Administrators can set a disk quota per user and assembly, which means there is no guarantee that space will be available. For this reason, it is important to add exception handling to your code.
- Even though isolated storage is placed in a hidden folder, it is possible, with a bit of effort, to find the folder. Therefore, the data stored is not completely secure, as users can change or remove files. It should be noted, though, that you can use the cryptography classes to encrypt data stored in isolated storage, thus preventing users from changing it.
- Machines can be locked down by administrative security policies, thereby preventing applications from writing to the `IsolatedStorage`. More specifically, code must have the `IsolatedStorageFilePermission` to work with isolated storage.

The following code is a quick look at how you can save and load data from `IsolatedStorage`. Note that you need to add a `using` statement to reference the namespace `System.IO.IsolatedStorage` as well as `System.IO`.

```
private void SaveData(string data, string fileName)
{
    using (IsolatedStorageFile isf =
          IsolatedStorageFile.GetUserStoreForApplication())
    {
        using (IsolatedStorageFileStream isfs =
              new IsolatedStorageFileStream(fileName, FileMode.Create, isf))
        {
            using (StreamWriter sw = new StreamWriter(isfs))
            {
                sw.Write(data);
                sw.Close();
            }
```

```
            }
        }
    }

    private string LoadData(string fileName)
    {
        string data = String.Empty;
        using (IsolatedStorageFile isf =
                IsolatedStorageFile.GetUserStoreForApplication())
        {
            using (IsolatedStorageFileStream isfs =
                    new IsolatedStorageFileStream(fileName, FileMode.Open, isf))
            {
                using (StreamReader sr = new StreamReader(isfs))
                {
                    string lineOfData = String.Empty;
                    while ((lineOfData = sr.ReadLine()) != null)
                      data += lineOfData;
                }
            }
        }
        return data;
    }
```

And finally, here's an example of how you could call these functions:

```
SaveData("Hello There", "MyData.txt");
string test = LoadData("MyData.txt");
```

Working with Image Source Filenames

There are times in your game development that you will want to know from where you loaded a specific image. The source filename can be retrieved through the `Uri` property of the image's `Source` property. You must first typecast the `Source` property to be a `BitmapImage` in order to get access to the `Uri`.

The following example shows a static function that is part of the `Utils` class called `GetImageSourceFile()`. This function takes as a parameter the target image and returns a string that points to the image's source file.

```
public static string GetImageSourceFile(Image img)
{
    BitmapImage bi = (BitmapImage) img.Source;
```

```
    Uri uri = bi.UriSource;
    return uri.OriginalString
}
```

Working with Strokes and Shapes

When dealing with shapes such as rectangles and ellipses, two properties that are commonly used to define the border are `Stroke` and `StrokeThickness`. `Stroke` specifies the color of the shape's border and `StrokeThickness` specifies the thickness of the border. The following code shows how this is done, with the result shown in Figure 4.12. The thickness of the stroke is 10 and the stroke is black in color.

```
<Ellipse Margin="10" Width="200" Height="200" Stroke="Black"
                                              StrokeThickness="10">
</Ellipse>
```

Two other properties that are not so commonly known are `StrokeDashArray` and `StrokeCap`. `StrokeDashArray` is used to draw the border as a series of dashes. You can set the length of each dash and the distance between each dash with this property. In addition, you can specify an array of these values, where the first value is the length and the second value is the distance. The pair value in the array is applied and then repeated once the array you specified runs out.

The following code draws a dash of length 1 with a distance of 5 between each dash. The thickness of the stroke determines the number of dashes that will appear. To best illustrate it, the thickness is set to 2. The result can be seen in Figure 4.13.

```
<Ellipse Margin="10" Width="200" Height="200" Stroke="Black"
    StrokeDashArray="1,5" StrokeThickness="2">
</Ellipse>
```

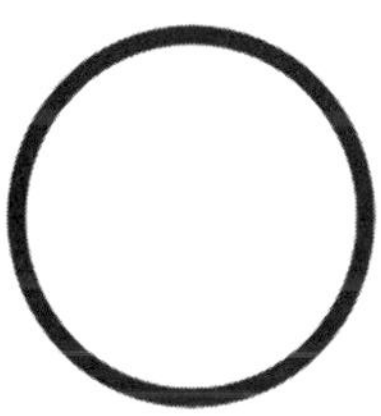

Figure 4.12
Ellipse with Border

Figure 4.13
Ellipse with **StrokeDashArray**

Figure 4.14
Ellipse with Another **StrokeDashArray**

This next example shows you how to create an array of values by setting two pair values. Note that you can have as many pair values as you want. The first pair has a stroke length of 1 followed by a gap of 5. The next pair has a stroke length of 10 followed by a gap of 2, as shown in Figure 4.14.

```
<Ellipse Margin="10" Width="200" Height="200" Stroke="Black"
    StrokeDashArray="1,5,10,2" StrokeThickness="2">
</Ellipse>
```

The `StrokeDapCap` property is used to specify how each of the individual dots is drawn. This value can be set to `Flat`, `Round`, `Square`, or `Triangle`. Figure 4.15 shows the result of each, zoomed in so you can see the details.

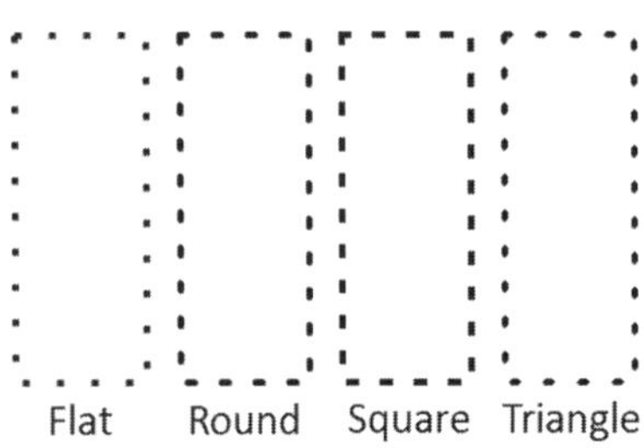

Figure 4.15
The **StrokeDapCap** Property

Loading Images from Streams

There are often times when you will want your users to open files such as images from the client machine. For example, in the Map Editor, you might want to add functionality that allows users to load their own custom images that can apply to the maps.

This can be accomplished by using the stream returned from the `OpenFileDialog`. Due to security reasons, files cannot be directly loaded unless using this dialog box where the client gets to pick which file to open. Also, `OpenFileDialog` can be called only in response to user input such as a button click.

To demonstrate this process, the example here creates a button to open the file and an `Image` object that will contain the image loaded from the stream. The XAML for this code is as follows:

```
<Canvas  x:Name="LayoutRoot" Background="White">
    <StackPanel  Orientation="Vertical">
        <Image x:Name="MyImage" Width="400" Height="300"/>
        <Button Width="100" HorizontalAlignment="Left"
              Content="Load Image" Click="Button_Click_Load_Image"/>
    </StackPanel>
</Canvas>
```

Finally, the event for the button click is as follows. This event prompts the user for files with the extension .png. Calling `File.OpenRead()` returns the stream needed to load the image. Calling `BitmapImage.SetSource()` with the stream will generate the `BitmapImage`. The result of this code after opening and loading an image can be seen in Figure 4.16.

```
private void Button_Click_Load_Image(object sender, RoutedEventArgs e)
{
    OpenFileDialog ofd = new OpenFileDialog();
    ofd.Filter = "PNG Files (*.png;*.png)|*.png;*.png | All Files (*.*)|*.*";
    ofd.FilterIndex = 1; if (true == ofd.ShowDialog())
    {
        System.IO.Stream stream = ofd.File.OpenRead();
        BitmapImage bi = new BitmapImage();
        bi.SetSource(stream);
        MyImage.Source = bi;
        stream.Close();
    }
}
```

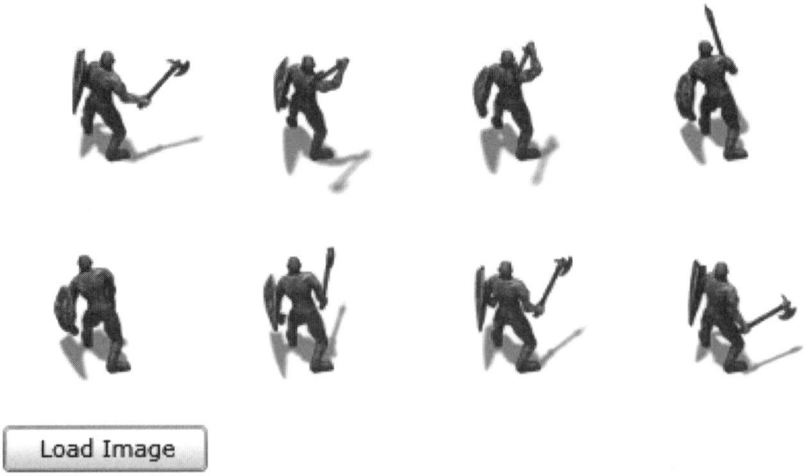

Figure 4.16
Loading an Image from a Stream

Loading and Managing Images in Your Game

If your game is large, you may want to consider loading images from an external server rather than having them all packaged into a single large XAP. Having a large XAP file can result in slow startup times for your game since the entire XAP must be downloaded before the game can commence. The following code demonstrates how to load an image from an external server resource. The `Uri` points to an external image. Since loading is done asynchronously, the program listens for the event `ImageOpened` to be fired before proceeding with the image. This event fires once the image is loaded and ready to render.

```
public partial class MainPage : UserControl
{
    private Image _gameImage = new Image();

    public MainPage()
    {
        InitializeComponent();
        this.Loaded += new RoutedEventHandler(MainPage_Loaded);
    }

    void MainPage_Loaded(object sender, RoutedEventArgs e)
    {
        BitmapImage bi = new BitmapImage();
        bi.UriSource =
        new Uri("http://www.silverlightdev.net/images/blogImages/Sample.png");
```

```
        _gameImage.Source = bi;
        _gameImage.ImageOpened +=
                    new EventHandler<RoutedEventArgs>(MyImage_ImageOpened);
    }

    void MyImage_ImageOpened(object sender, RoutedEventArgs e)
    {
        // Image load complete. Add it as needed
    }
}
```

Setting the Default Browser from Within VS

It is a good idea to try out your game in a variety of browsers before releasing it. In Visual Studio, you can change which browser (Internet Explorer, Firefox, and so on) you want to target when you launch and debug your game. To do this, right-click on your web page file in the Solution Explorer and choose Browse With. This will open the Browse Width dialog box, as seen in Figure 4.17. From there, you can simply select the browser you want to use and click the Set as Default button. In addition to targeting the browser of your choice, this dialog box also allows you to specify what resolution you want the browser to be when launched.

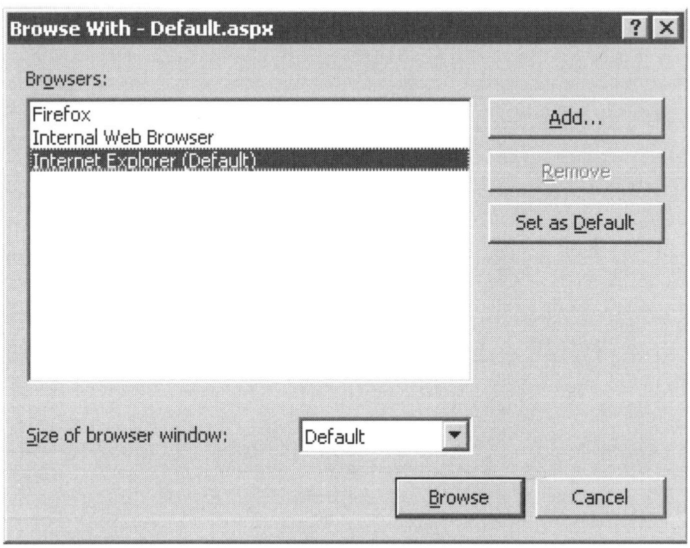

Figure 4.17
Target Browser

Detecting Mouse Double Clicks

Detecting left mouse clicks on objects is as easy as listening for the MouseLeftButtonDown event. But what if you want to detect a double click? This can be done by checking the elapsed delta in milliseconds between two left clicks. The following example uses 200 milliseconds as the maximum amount of time that is allowed to pass for the clicks to be considered a double click. The program also needs to make certain that the mouse wasn't moved during the clicks.

To accomplish this process, start by creating a DispatcherTimer that has an interval of 200 milliseconds. The DispatcherTimer is part of the System.Windows.Threading namespace. Once the timer event has fired, the timer is stopped, as can be seen in the following code. If the timer is stopped, too much time has gone by for it to be considered a double click.

```
public partial class MainPage : UserControl
{
    private Image _gameImage = new Image();
    private DispatcherTimer _doubleClickTimer = new DispatcherTimer();

    public MainPage()
    {
        InitializeComponent();

        _doubleClickTimer.Interval = new TimeSpan(0, 0, 0, 0, 200);
        _doubleClickTimer.Tick += new EventHandler(DoubleClick_Timer);
    }

    void DoubleClick_Timer(object sender, EventArgs e)
    {
        _doubleClickTimer.Stop();
    }
}
```

The following shows the code for the mouse-click event. If a single click has already happened and the timer is still enabled, you now have a double click to process.

```
void MainPage_MouseLeftButtonDown(object sender, MouseButtonEventArgs e)
{
    if (_doubleClickTimer.IsEnabled)
    {
        // Process double click at the determined location
```

```
        double posX = (double)e.GetPosition(LayoutRoot).X;
        double posY = (double)e.GetPosition(LayoutRoot).Y;
    }
    else
    {
        // Start a double click
        _doubleClickTimer.Start();
    }
}
```

Summary

This chapter covered a wide variety of techniques that you can use when building games with Silverlight. Hopefully, from these techniques, you have been able to gain a good understanding of how things work in Silverlight. The next chapter covers the useful tools you can leverage when building games and also covers art resources that are available to you.

CHAPTER 5

Creating the World

Now that you are familiar with the basics on how things are done in Silverlight, this chapter will get started with the actual steps needed to make a game. This chapter will be describing the type of game made here, the resources for artwork, and the model conversion and the Silverlight-based Map Editor that are used to create world maps to load into your game. A *map* is essentially a level, a zone, or a surface area on which your game interacts. It can be sized to fit directly into a window in your application or it can be large and scrollable.

The Game

The Silverlight game I have built for this book is an online multi-player adventure game. In this game, you start off as a level-one character and work your way up by gaining experience. Experience is gained by fighting creatures and players, questing, and other such means. Once you reach the maximum level, you have the option to become a wizard. Wizards are elite players who are able to create (using the Map Editor) and rule over their own maps in the game.

Sound familiar? This game theme is based on the old text-based games called MUDs (Multi-User Dungeons). Back in the early 90s, I developed and ran one of the oldest MUDs, called *Tsunami*. Believe it or not, this game is still up and running today (although I am no longer involved). You can find it at http://tsunami.thebigwave.net.

Note

Since the game is multi-player, it is built around a client-server model. For security purposes, all game logic, map details, and so on, are stored and managed by the server application. The client is programmed in such a way that it is simply an interface to the game. That is, the client's primary task is to record input, relay it to the server, and render what the server tells the client to render. The client can in no way manipulate any of the data in the game. For example, the client should not be able to check a file to see what tiles are walkable on a map; that has to be done on the server. Otherwise, players could manipulate the files so they could walk anywhere they want. Although it may be more CPU and network traffic efficient to have the client process game logic and data, you will leave your game vulnerable to hacks, which I can almost guarantee will happen if your game is met with any kind of success.

This game is made up three separate applications:

- **Map Editor**—Used to make the game maps, including custom maps created by players for their domains. The source for this application, including the website needed to host the editor, is in a file called mapeditor.zip.
- **Client**—Application run by players to connect to the server, process input, and render the game UI. The source for this application is in a file called client.zip.
- **Server**—Application that manages player connections and the game world data. The source for this application is in a file called server.zip.

The source code for all three applications is too large to describe and fit into one book. Rather than listing all the code, I will be covering snippets of code that represent the key components to building the game. You can download the entire source for these applications at http://code.msdn.microsoft.com/Silverlight.

Artwork

Since artwork is so essential to building maps, I thought I would give you pointers on where you can obtain some rather awesome artwork and how you can convert the 3D models to 2D sprites. If you are anything like me (a pure developer), you might find obtaining modern, high-quality artwork for your game to be a rather disheartening venture. I can't count the hours I spent scouring the Internet for art resources. Fortunately, I was lucky enough to find a great developer store at GarageGames (http://www.garagegames.com). On this site, you will find a variety of art packs created by third parties, individuals, and companies. If you wish to use any of the art in your game, you must first purchase it from the site. The prices, in my opinion, are very reasonable for what you get.

Figure 5.1
GarageGames Art Packs

Figure 5.1 shows just a few of the many art packs available to you.

These packages come with pretty much everything you need to decorate your world. Examples include trees, fences, buildings, creatures, plants, and more. Figure 5.2 shows an assortment of objects from these packs.

Converting 3D Models to Sprites

Because Silverlight does not yet support 3D models, we will be working with 2D sprites to display all our objects in the game. Sprites, rendered as bitmap images, are pretty much anything you see drawn in the game, whether it be a tree, a creature, a rock, or the ground floor. All the images in Figure 5.2 can be rendered as sprites.

Silverlight supports PNG and JPG image formats. In my games, I have chosen to go exclusively with PNG files because of their support for transparency. *PNG*, which stands for Portable Network Graphics, employs what is called lossless data compression, which is a class of algorithm used for data compression. The next section shows you how to make transparent PNG images.

Figure 5.2
Assortment of Artwork from GarageGames.com

With the exception of the 2D Fantasy Character Pack, you will probably notice that the artwork that comes with these packages is stored as a Torque Game Engine 3D model. In order to use these models in your game, you will need a tool that will convert these 3D models into transparent 2D sprites in PNG format.

To accomplish this, I use a tool by EnvyGames (http://www.envygames.com) called SpriteWorks. SpriteWorks requires that the following be installed before you can run it:

- Microsoft Visual Studio 2008 or Microsoft Visual C# Express 2008
- Microsoft XNA 3.0

To install Visual C# Express and XNA for free, search for them by name at http://www.microsoft.com/downloads.

SpriteWorks supports a variety of 3D model formats including DirectX .X files and Torque 3D models. In addition to generating single stand-alone images, SpriteWorks supports generating animation frames from Torque animation sequence files. To get an idea of what an animation sequence would look like in a single image file, look at Figure 5.3. You will see a total of eight frames that make up an attack in the southwestern direction.

Figure 5.3
Animation Sequence File

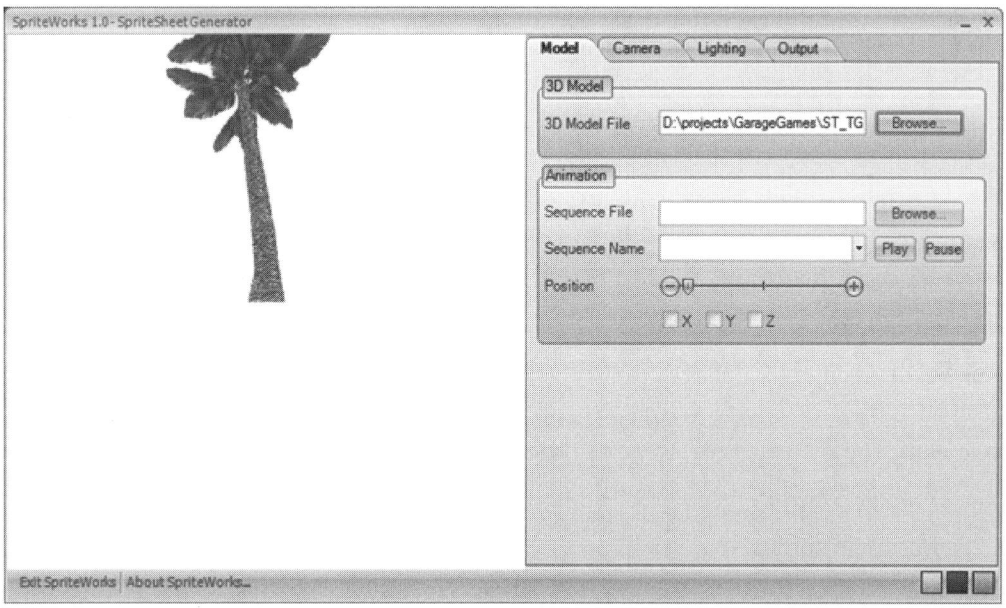

Figure 5.4
Opening a Model

Once you have this tool installed, launch it. Under the Model tab, click the Browse button to open your 3D model. In Figure 5.4, I have opened a Torque 3D model of a palm tree.

As you can see from Figure 5.4, the palm tree needs to be centered and angled correctly. You can modify these and other camera settings via the Camera tab. For my palm tree, I have changed the Y Rotation to be 50 degrees since my game

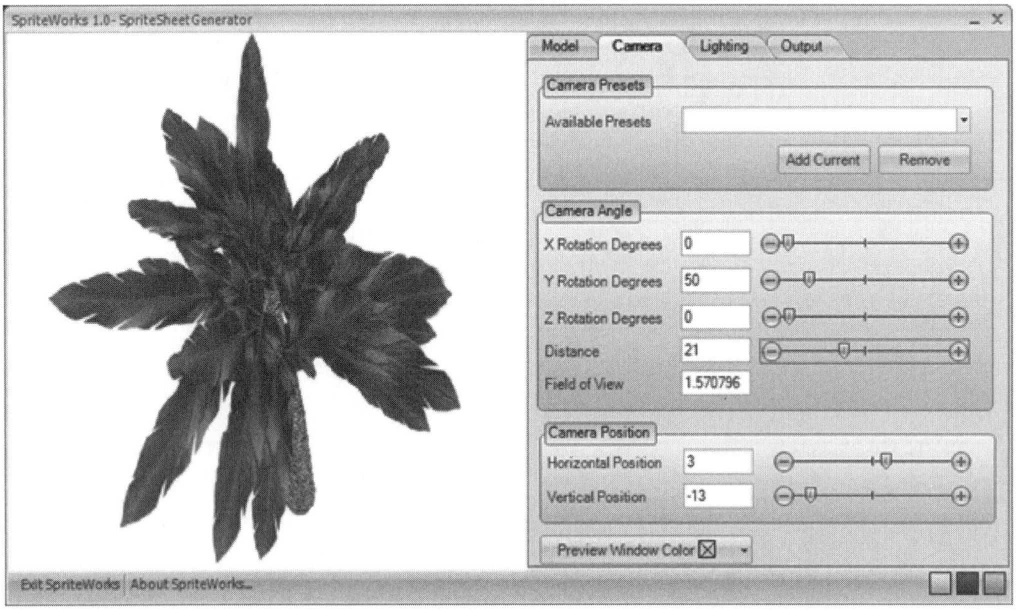

Figure 5.5
Camera Settings

is represented by a bird's eye view of the world. Additionally, I have updated the vertical position and the distance to center and sized it correctly. Figure 5.5 shows the result.

Once everything is sized and positioned correctly and you are ready to create the transparent PNG file, click on the Output tab. As seen in Figure 5.6, you will need to specify the output file. Also, update the Sprite Sheet Width and Height to be the size you want for the image.

To generate an animation sequence, I have imported a model of a goblin and I have loaded and set the animation sequence to be Axe Swing under the Model tab. In Figure 5.7, you will see you can also preview the animation.

When I generate the animation, I get the complete sequence created into a single PNG image file, similar to what I showed back in Figure 5.3.

Coordinate System

Every game needs to deal with coordinates and positioning. Silverlight coordinates work in two dimensions running vertically along the Y axis and horizontality along the X axis. The origin (0,0) is the upper-left corner of your screen. As shown in Figure 5.8, from the origin, X increases to the right and

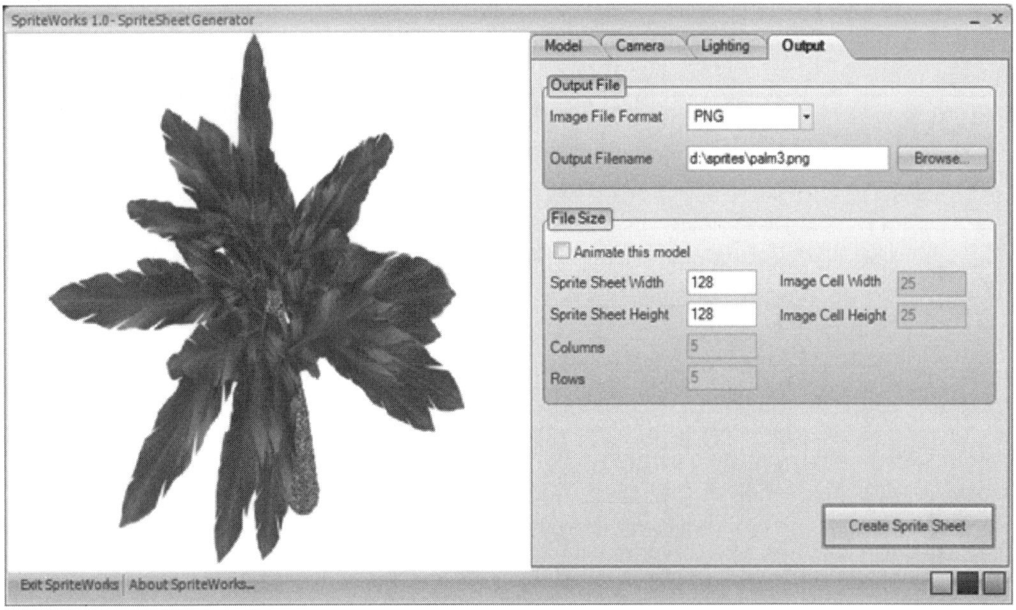

Figure 5.6
Saving the File

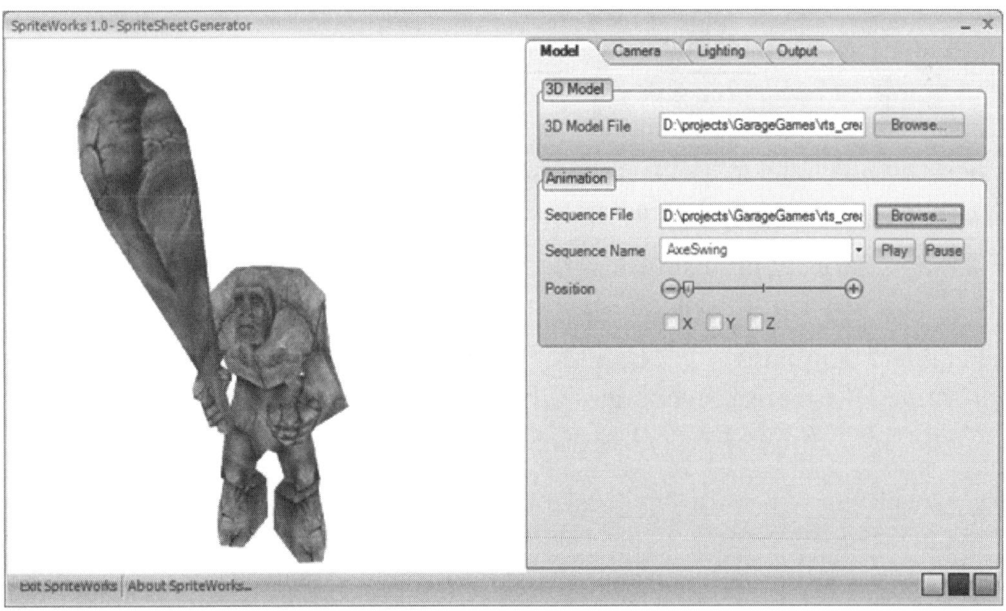

Figure 5.7
Animation Sequence

Figure 5.8
Silverlight Coordinate System

Y increases down. In my game, the upper-left corner of all the maps is at the origin, so all coordinates are positive.

The Map Editor

The maps used in your game will provide the users with the overall look and feel of the game and will often give your customers the first impression of your game. To give a good impression, you will want to have an attractive environment that is rich and fully interactive. To accomplish this, I have created a Map Editor that can be used to create individual maps for your game.

The Map Editor is built using Silverlight and includes a wide variety of features. These features, which I will be covering in detail, include the following:

- **Object templates**—The base template for all objects that can appear in your game. These objects contain all the generic data needed to render and animate the object if necessary.
- **Opacity masks**—Opacity masks are used on terrain tiles for impressive tile-transition effects.
- **Preview window**—Previews the selected template you are painting with.
- **Object placement**—Draw, Drag/Drop, Fill, and Delete.

- **Object editing**—Objects added to the game can be fully customized by changing their properties—for example, a creature's strength, a potion's potency, a weapon's damage, and so on.
- **Collision detection**—Each object in the template can have a polygon that represents its collision zone.
- **Triggers**—Triggers cause events to fire when walked on. For example, triggers can activate traps, warp a player to another map, play a music file, and so on.
- **Save and load**—Silverlight 3 introduced the `SaveFileDialog`, which allows you to save files anywhere on your computer. Maps are created and stored in XML format and can be directly loaded into your game.
- **Terrain editing**—The Map Editor allows you to place tiles on different layers.
- **Map generation**—Create maps of any height and width. In addition, you can specify the radius of each tile.
- **Preview mode**—Walk around your map in preview mode.

Figure 5.9 shows a screenshot of the Map Editor.

Object Templates

An object template is a base representation of any object in the game. It contains static commonalities such as width, height, and the list of images that are needed to render the object. On the left side of the Map Editor is a tree view called Object Templates. This tree view contains all the templates that are available in the game. They are sorted by type as follows:

- **Terrain objects**—These are the ground objects that make up the floor of your game. Each terrain object is laid out and positioned across a grid in your map. Terrain tiles cannot move but there are special cases where you will want them to animate (such as water tiles).
- **Creature objects**—These are all the living animals and creatures of your game. Most likely these will be the most complex objects you will need to deal with.

Figure 5.9
Map Editor

- **Map objects**—Static objects that are always in the same position and in the same state when you first load the map. Examples include trees, statues, rocks, fences, signs, houses, and so on. Although these objects are static, you can and should make them interactive. For example, trees should sway in the wind, fences and doors could open, and so on.
- **Game objects**—Dynamic objects that are created in-game that can be used, consumed, and destroyed. Examples include weapons, armor, potions, bags, and so on. Often, players can pick up these objects and use them for a wide variety of purposes.
- **Effect objects**—Effects are there for visual purposes only. They are used when casting spells, burning fire, and so on.

Once you add any of these template objects to the map, they become discrete objects. From there, you can extend the properties of the object to make it something unique. For example, you can add a dragon to the game and then change its properties such as its level, hit points, and so on.

In my game, object templates are stored in a database. They are imported via a web service call by the server and the Map Editor. As an alternative to storing the templates in a database, you could store them in a file such as an XML file, but as your game grows, it will become harder to manage them. The next chapter shows you the code needed to import these objects from the web service.

Opacity Masks

On the left side of the Map Editor is an additional tree control called Opacity Masks that lists all the available opacity masks. Figure 5.10 shows this tree control.

An opacity mask allows you to specify the transparency level of the pixels in your image. This is done by setting the alpha value of the color that corresponds to each pixel. The complete color of a pixel is represented by its alpha, red, green, and blue values in that order. The notation is AARRGGBB where A=alpha, R=red, G=green, and B=blue. The values can be anywhere from 0-255 decimal or 0-FF hex. For opacity, you only have to set the alpha values. That is, setting either the red, green, or blue values will have no effect on the transparency.

Figure 5.11 shows an image of a dragon on top of green grass. The following code associates an opacity mask with the dragon image. At FF, there is no transparency,

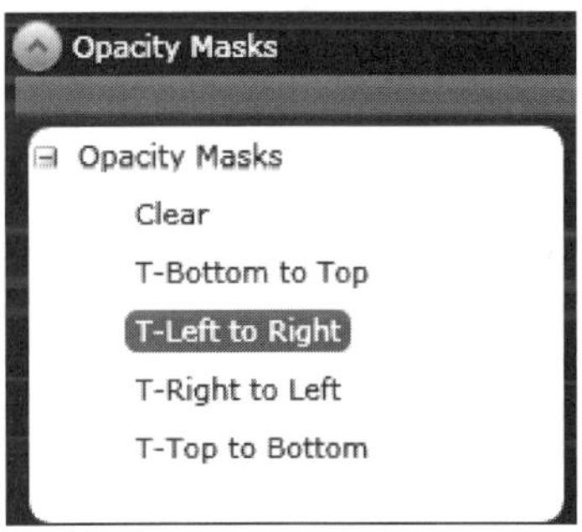

Figure 5.10
Opacity Masks Tree Control

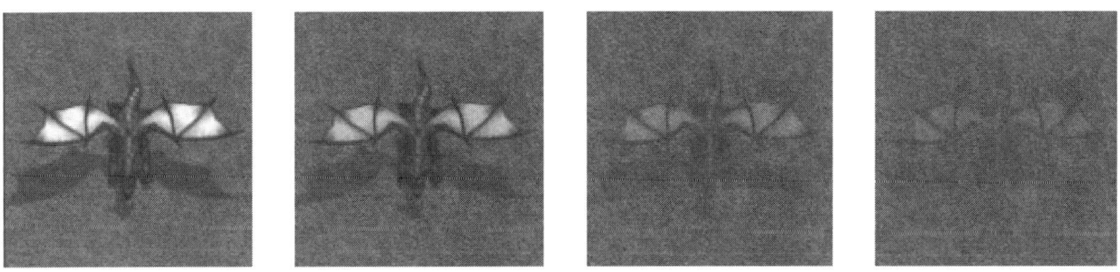

Figure 5.11
Increased Transparency

as seen in the first frame. If you were to decrease the alpha value from FF to 00, you would see the dragon slowly fading away as you saw in the other three frames. This trick can be used for a wide variety of effects such as a creature turning invisible.

```
<Image Source="grass.png"></Image>
<Image Source="dragon.png">
    <Image.OpacityMask>
        <SolidColorBrush Color="#FF000000" ></SolidColorBrush>
    </Image.OpacityMask>
</Image>
```

You can also create realistic terrain tile-transition effects using opacity. Figure 5.12 shows the result of two tiles positioned next to each other without an opacity mask applied. As you can see, the straight line does not give a very realistic transition effect.

By applying an opacity mask, as seen in Figure 5.13, you can get a much more realistic transition effect.

So how does this work? To accomplish this, I rendered two images on top of each other and applied an opacity mask to the top layer, as seen in Figure 5.14.

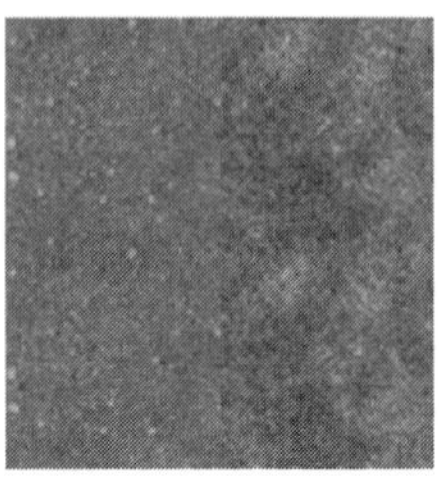

Figure 5.12
No Opacity Mask

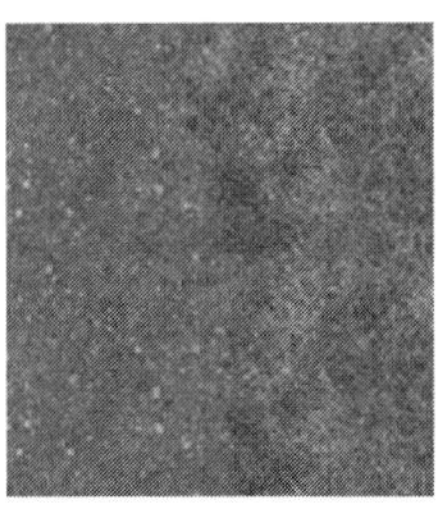

Figure 5.13
Opacity Mask Applied

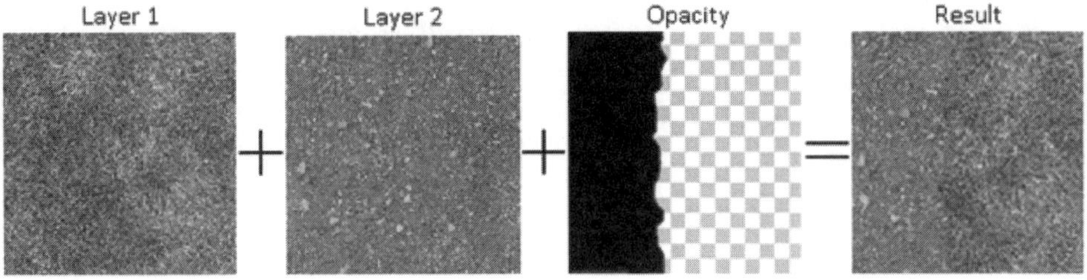

Figure 5.14
Applying Opacity to Layers

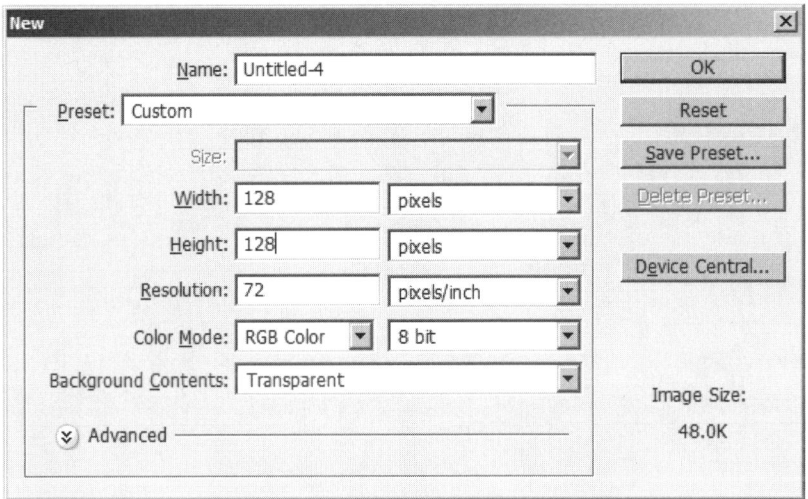

Figure 5.15
New Document

The code needed to create this is as follows:

```
<Image Source="grass.png"></Image>
<Image Source="dirt.png" >
    <Image.OpacityMask >
        <ImageBrush ImageSource="opacityMask.png"></ImageBrush>
    </Image.OpacityMask>
</Image>
```

You can create your own opacity masks by using a tool such as Adobe Photoshop. If you have this tool, or a tool that does something similar, follow these steps to create an opacity mask.

To start, create a new document equal to the exact width and height of a single tile in your game. As shown in Figure 5.15, set the Color Mode to 8-bit and the Background Contents to Transparent.

Next, select the Gradient tool in the Photoshop toolbar, as seen in Figure 5.16. In Photoshop, this tool is combined with the Paint Bucket tool on the toolbar.

Once the Gradient tool is selected, go to the top toolbar and display the Gradient List. This window is shown in Figure 5.17. Select Foreground to Transparent and change your Foreground color to Black.

Finally, Shift-click with your mouse and drag the Gradient tool from the top-left corner to the bottom-right corner, as seen in Figure 5.18. Experiment with different angles and repeat motions to add strength. Also, experiment with using the Eraser tool to cut out distinct patterns and shapes.

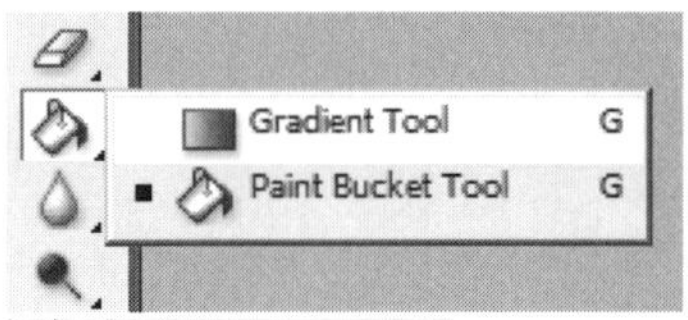

Figure 5.16
Gradient Tool

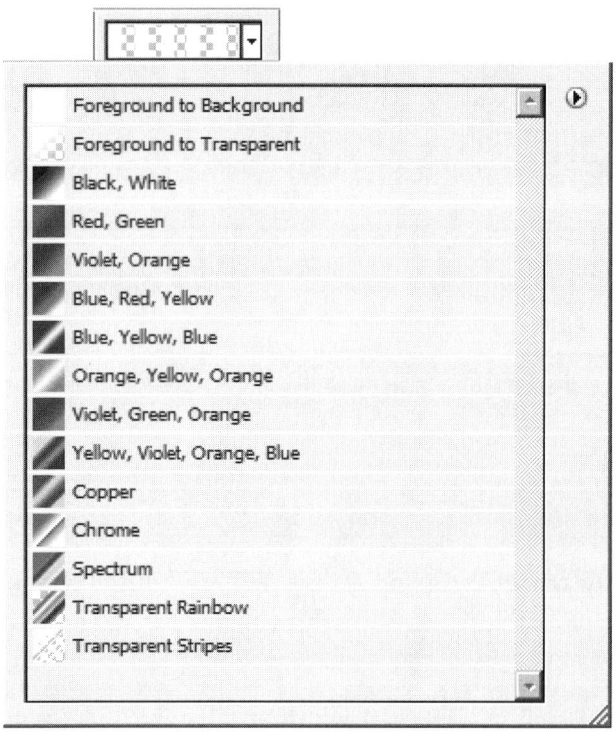

Figure 5.17
Gradient List

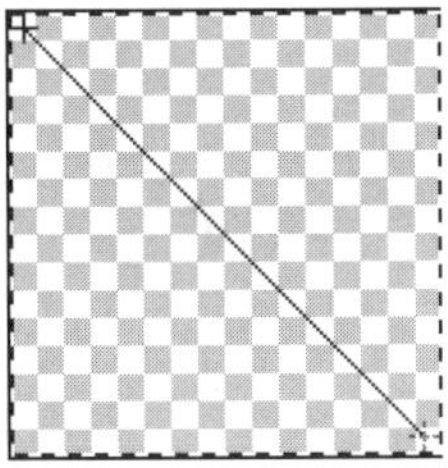

Figure 5.18
Using the Gradient Tool

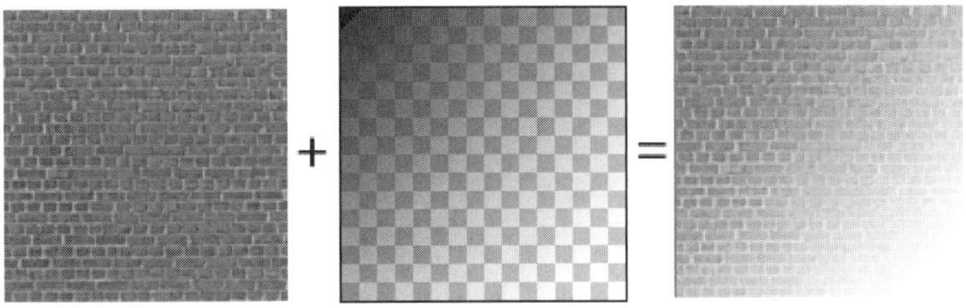

Figure 5.19
Mask Applied to Brick Tile

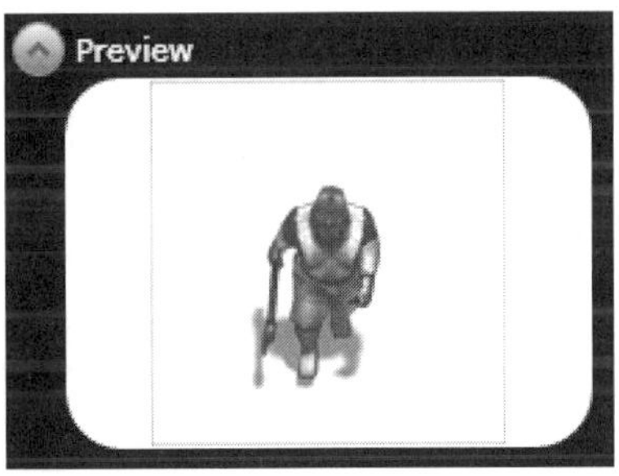

Figure 5.20
Preview Window

In Figure 5.19 I have combined the resulting mask with an image of a brick tile.

Preview Window

The preview window in the lower-left corner of the Map Editor shows you what template you have selected for painting the world. It does not show you the object you have selected in the map. Use the toolbar to select the method of painting you wish to use. Fill only works for terrain objects. The preview window is shown in Figure 5.20.

Object Placement

To place objects on the map, simply select the template you want to use from the Object Templates tree (see Figure 5.21). Click the Draw button in the toolbar and from there you can click anywhere on the map canvas to create the object. Each time you click on the canvas, you will generate a new object. If you wish to reposition an object, click on the Arrow button in the toolbar. From there, select the object you wish to move and, while holding down the left mouse button, move the object to its new position. Release the mouse button when you are ready to drop and place the object.

Object Editing

Once an object is selected, you can set its custom properties through the Property Grid. Changes made in the Grid are validated and instantly applied to the selected object. When the map is saved, the unique properties applied to each object are saved with the map.

Collision Detection

Each object has one or more rectangles that represent the region within the sprite that collision detection should check against. When the object is selected, you will notice it is surrounded by a red rectangle. This rectangle shows you the total width and height of the image or frame. The collision region for the sprite is

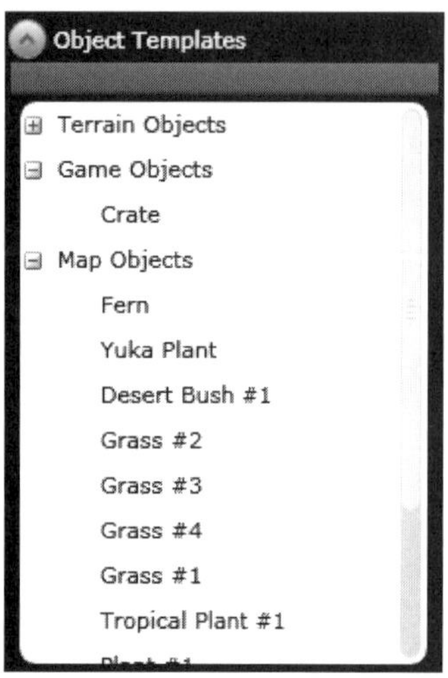

Figure 5.21
Object Templates

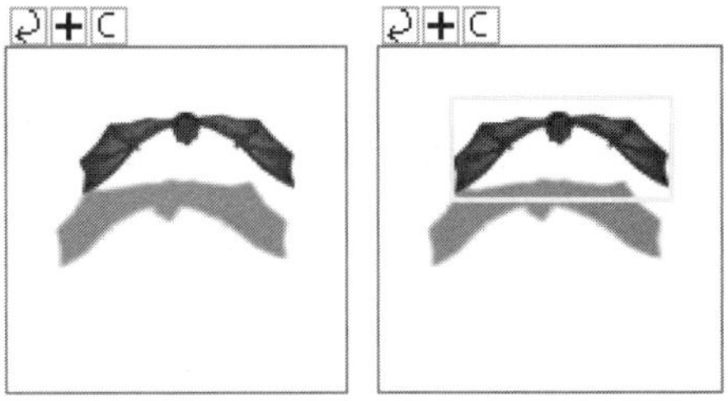

Figure 5.22
Collision Rectangle

represented by a yellow rectangle. Clicking on the C button (third from the left) will toggle the display of this collision rectangle, as seen in Figure 5.22.

Some objects are oddly shaped and do not fit well into a single rectangle. For that reason, each object can have whatever number of collection rectangles is desired.

To check if a point where you have clicked on the map intersects an object, you simply have to see if the coordinates fall within the boundaries of the collision rectangle. The following code shows you how to do so:

```
internal bool DetectCollision(Point pt, Rectangle collisionRect)
{
    double x = (double) collisionRect.GetValue(Canvas.TopProperty);
    double y = (double) collisionRect.GetValue(Canvas.LeftProperty);

    return(pt.X >= x && pt.Y >= y && pt.X < (x + collisionRect.ActualWidth)
                    && pt.Y < (y + collisionRect.ActualHeight));
}
```

Triggers

Triggers are events applied to invisible objects that get fired, resulting in a specified action. They can be fired when one of the following happens:

- A creature walks within a given range of the object.
- A creature walks on top of the object.

Triggers can span any width and height on the map and they can be applied to a game creature and/or a player. In addition, when configured, you can specify the chance the trigger will have of occurring. Examples of usages include the following:

- A player or creature walks to the edge of a map and is transported into a new map.

- A player enters a dungeon, thus kicking off the dungeon theme song.
- A player approaches a specific gravestone, causing an aggressive ghost to spawn.

Save and Load

Support for the `SaveFileDialog` was introduced with the release of Silverlight 3. Rather than giving you a name of a file to save to, it gives you a pointer to a stream. Using the `SaveFileDialog` method, you can save maps locally to a file such as an XML file. My Map Editor also supports saving and loading maps through a web service. In a multi-player game, I want the server, not the client, to be loading the maps. When a client enters a map, the server will send the map data to the client over the network. I will be covering how to use web services in Chapter 6, "Object Management."

The best way to save and load from XML is to use a LINQ (language integrated query). This component can be found in System.Xml.Linq.dll. You will need to add a reference to this DLL if you want to use LINQ in your project. I have found that reading XML data via LINQ is much simpler and more straightforward than other techniques such as using XMLReader.

The following function demonstrates using LINQ to save data to a file. To illustrate it, I have shown a snippet of the code from `SaveMap()` that saves some of the key data about the map.

```
public void SaveMap()
{
    SaveFileDialog sfd = new SaveFileDialog();
    sfd.Filter = "map files (*.xml)|*.xml|All files (*.*)|*.*";
    sfd.ShowDialog();
    System.IO.Stream stream = sfd.OpenFile();
    if (null != stream)
    {

        XDocument document = new XDocument();

        document.Declaration = new XDeclaration("1.0", "utf-8", "true");

        XElement rootElement = new XElement("Map");
        document.Add(rootElement);
```

```
        XElement childElement = new XElement("MapName");
        childElement.Value = _mapName;
        rootElement.Add(childElement);

        childElement = new XElement("WidthInTiles");
        childElement.Value = Convert.ToString(_terrainWidthInTiles);
        rootElement.Add(childElement);

        childElement = new XElement("HeightInTiles");
        childElement.Value = Convert.ToString(_terrainHeightInTiles);
        rootElement.Add(childElement);

        childElement = new XElement("TileRadius");
        childElement.Value = Convert.ToString(_terrainTileRadius);
        rootElement.Add(childElement);

        childElement = new XElement("LayerCount");
        childElement.Value = Convert.ToString(Consts.TerrainLayerCount);
        rootElement.Add(childElement);

        document.Save(stream);

        stream.Flush();
        stream.Close();
    }
}
```

Each XML node is represented by an `XElement`. The entire document is represented by `XDocument`. Make certain to call `stream.Flush()` or the file may not be written.

Creating Transparent Images

When you're using GIF images, transparency is very straightforward since you can just specify what color you want to represent the transparency. However, Silverlight does not support the GIF format, which leaves us with the PNG format. When you're using PNG files, you need to use a tool that will essentially "clear" out the sections you want to be transparent. To accomplish this task using a program like Photoshop, for example, follow these steps.

Start by opening an image like the one in Figure 5.23.

In Photoshop, there is a Magic Wand tool that you can use to select the background color. Click this tool then click on the background of your image. The entire background is outlined, as you can see in Figure 5.24.

Figure 5.23
Non-Transparent Image

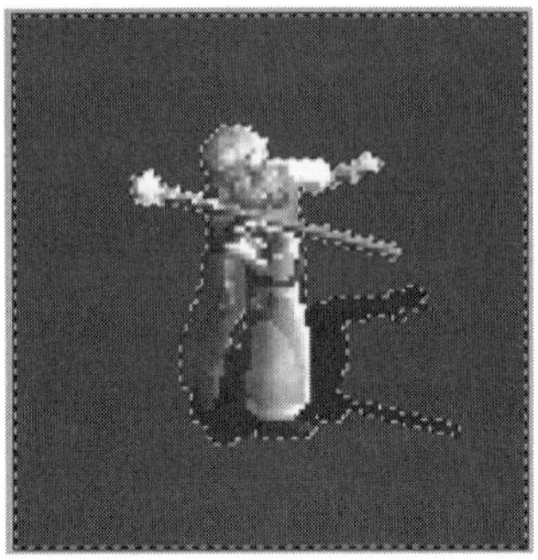

Figure 5.24
Background Selected

Figure 5.25
Transparent Image

With the background selected, press the Delete key to remove it. The result is a transparent image, as seen in Figure 5.25.

You should now save this image as a PNG file. The areas of the image that you removed using the Magic Wand tool will now render as transparent.

Summary

This chapter covered the tools you can use to build worlds in Silverlight. It also discussed some of the artwork available to you that you can integrate into your game at a very low cost as well as ways to apply opacity masks to create terrain-transition effects. The next chapter covers the ways you can manage world objects through a web service.

CHAPTER 6

Object Management

Web Services

Silverlight applications often need to store data on a back-end server. This data can be anything from specific data about a customer to a player's high score. In the case of the game here, both the client and the game Map Editor leverage what is called a WCF-based web service to load and save the game data from a server. WCF, which stands for Windows Communication Foundation, is a framework that applications can use to communicate with each other. It was created in order to unify a variety of communication systems into a single model. Because WCF is part of the .NET framework, .NET applications such as Silverlight can fully leverage it. WCF is located in `System.ServiceModel.dll`.

So why use WCF? Consider some of these advantages:

- WCF is significantly higher performing, running around 25-50% faster on average compared to other existing distribution systems. For more details on the performance, see http://msdn.microsoft.com/en-us/library/bb310550.aspx.
- The throughput of WCF is inherently scalable from a single processor to a quad processor.

- The WCF model unifies the feature wealth of ASMX, WSE, Enterprise Services, MSMQ, and remoting. This way, developers only have to master a single programming model.
- WCF can be hosted in IIS servers, Windows services, and standalone apps like Windows forms and console apps.
- WCF can have messages sent in a variety of channels, including HTTP, TCP, MSMQ, and named pipe.
- WCF provides a `DataContractSerializer`, which allows complex data types and private attributes to be serialized and sent.

In order to demonstrate web services in action, I will now step you through what's needed to create and communicate with one from Silverlight. To add a web service to your project in Visual Studio, right-click on your web project and choose Add New Item from the context menu. Make certain you do this from your website project and not your Silverlight application since the web service needs to be added to your website. This will bring up the Add New Item dialog box shown in Figure 6.1.

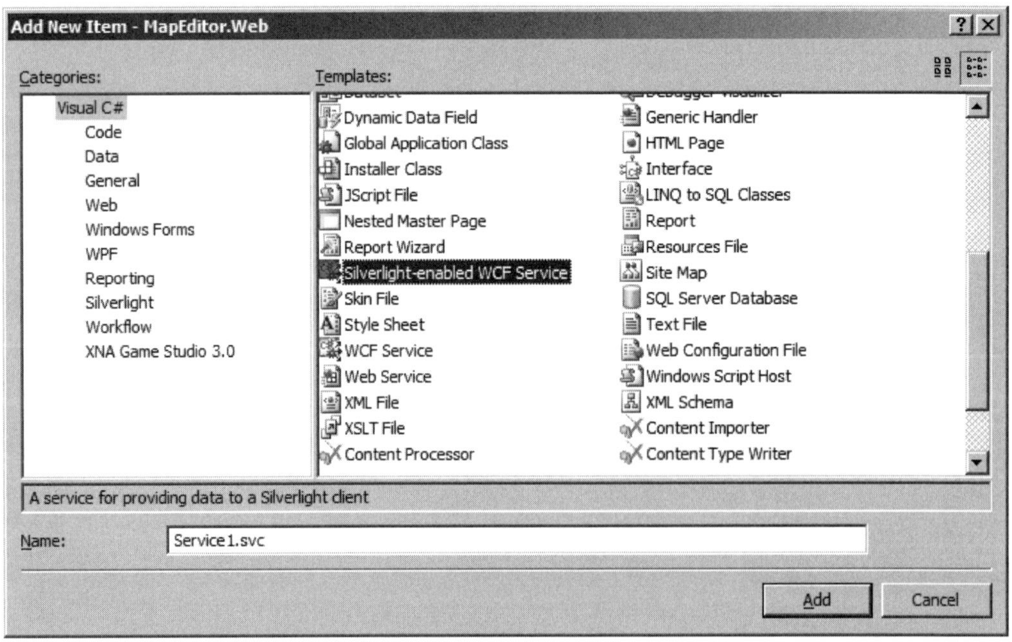

Figure 6.1
Add New Item Dialog Box

Under Templates, select Silverlight-Enabled WCF Service. You may have noticed that there is also a normal WCF Service template to choose from. Although this one is a valid option, the Silverlight-enabled WCF service has already been pre-configured with some added ASP.NET compatibility support.

Before you click the Add button, give the service a descriptive name. For example, I named the service that handles my Map Editor data `MapEditorService`. Once you're ready, click the Add button. This will add an implementation of a WCF service to your website. By default, the web service contains one method found in MapEditorService.svc.cs called `DoWork()`, as seen here:

```
public class MapEditorService
{
    [OperationContract]
    public void DoWork()
    {
    }
}
```

Any method that you want to be callable from your Silverlight application must be prefaced with the attribute `[OperationContract]`.This attribute will cause the method to be exposed as a service operation. Before your Silverlight application can reference the web service, you must first build the website project. Once you have built your project, right-click on the Silverlight application project, this time in the Solution Explorer, and choose Add Service Reference. Click the Discover button to find your web service. The web service will appear in the Services window, as shown in Figure 6.2

Select your service, pick a good name for the namespace, and click the OK button when you are ready. If you see the error shown in Figure 6.3, it's because you did not build your project before attempting to add a service reference to it.

At this point, you will have a service reference declared that you can use to directly call methods on your web service. Since Silverlight follows an asynchronous model, all calls made to the web service are made asynchronously. In order to call the `DoWork()` method in the web service, you need to add some code.

In the first line of code, you must create a reference to the web service client object. Next, since the call is asynchronous, specify the callback function that is to be called when the call is complete. Finally, make the asynchronous call to `DoWork()`.

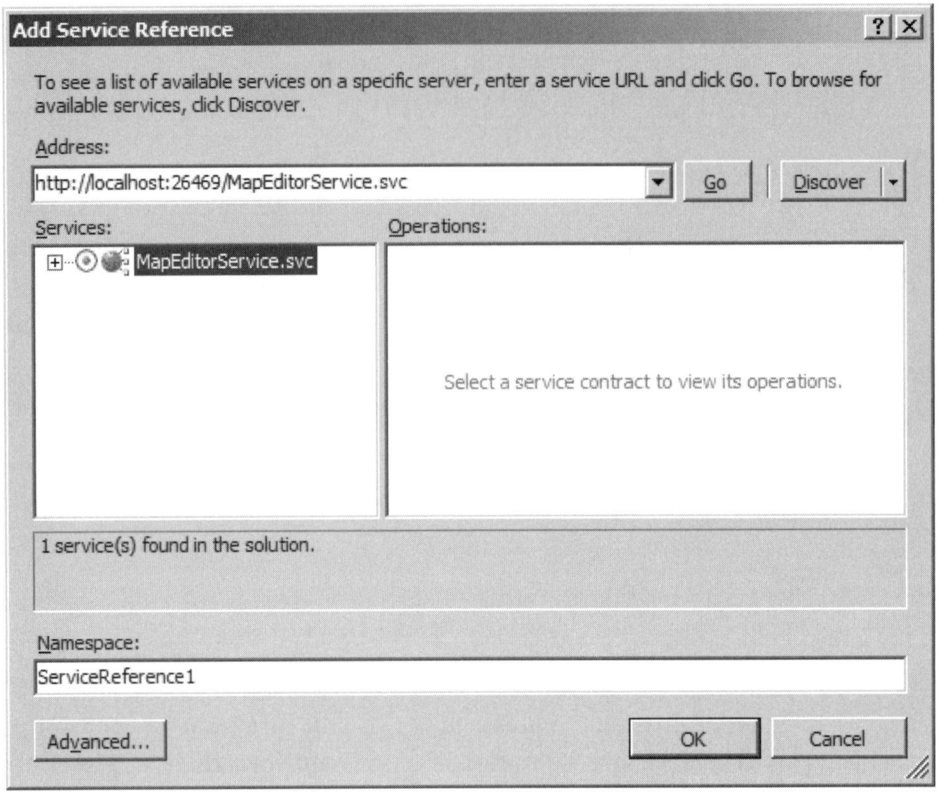

Figure 6.2
Add Service Reference

Figure 6.3
Error from Not Building a Project First

```
public void WebServiceTest()
{
    ServiceReference1.MapEditorServiceClient client =
        new MySLApp.ServiceReference1.MapEditorServiceClient();
```

```
    client.DoWorkCompleted +=
        new EventHandler<System.ComponentModel.AsyncCompletedEventArgs>
        (client_DoWorkCompleted);
    client.DoWorkAsync();
}

void client_DoWorkCompleted(object sender,
     System.ComponentModel.AsyncCompletedEventArgs e)
{
}
```

To further illustrate this process, I will show you how to create a method that returns data. To begin, add the following function to your web service file MapEditorService.svc.cs. This function will return a string to the Silverlight application. Make certain to include the `[OperationContract]` attribute so the method will be visible as a web service method.

```
[OperationContract]
public string GetData()
{
    return "Hello World";
}
```

When you're ready, build your project so that the service reference will pick up on the change. In order for your Silverlight application to pick up on this change, you need to right-click on your service reference in the Solution Explorer of your Silverlight application and choose Update Service Reference. This will bring up the dialog box shown in Figure 6.4, which generates the service reference client code.

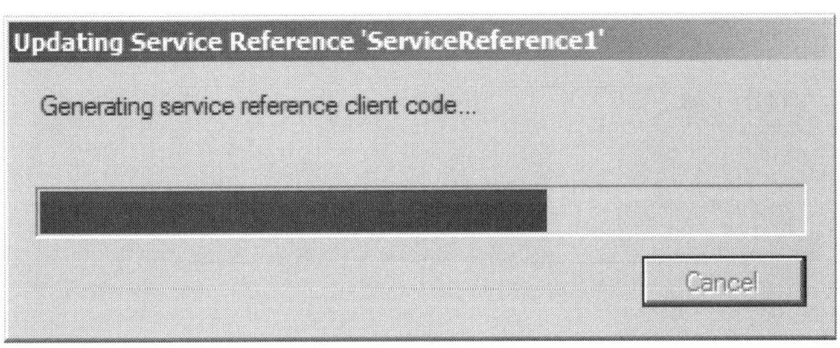

Figure 6.4
Updating Service Reference

Once the generation is complete, you can reference the new method:

```
public void TestWebServiceRead()
{
    ServiceReference1.MapEditorServiceClient client =
      new MySLApp.ServiceReference1.MapEditorServiceClient();

    client.GetDataCompleted +=
      new EventHandler<MySLApp.ServiceReference1.
      GetDataCompletedEventArgs>(client_GetDataCompleted);
    client.GetDataAsync();
}

void client_GetDataCompleted(object sender,
     MySLApp.ServiceReference1.GetDataCompletedEventArgs e)
{
    string result = (string) e.Result;
}
```

The data returned from the web service is contained in `e.Result`. You will need to typecast the data in order to convert it. In the previous code, the data is type-casted to be a string.

So what if you want to return an array of data? The following methods found in MapEditorService.svc.cs demonstrate two ways to return multiple data items:

```
[OperationContract]
public string[] GetDataArray()
{
    string[] data = new string[2];
    data[0] = "Hello";
    data[1] = "There";
    return data;
}
[OperationContract]
public List<string> GetDataCollection()
{
    List<string> data = new List<string>();
    data.Add("Hello");
    data.Add("There");
    return data;
}
```

In order to intercept this data from your Silverlight application, you will need to convert the data into an ObservableCollection. An ObservableCollection is essentially a class that represents a dynamic data collection. The following code shows you how to convert the result returned from the web service into an ObservableCollection.

```
System.Collections.ObjectModel.ObservableCollection<string> data;
data = e.Result;
```

So far, I have shown you how to retrieve data from a web service. Writing to a web service is just as straightforward. The following method from MapEditorService.svc.cs in the web service will save a player's passwords to the backend store on the server:

```
[OperationContract]
public void SavePassword(int playerID, string password)
{
    // Add code to save password to your back-end store
    // (SQL, etc).
}
```

To call the SavePassword() method, simply create the client as usual and call the async method SavePasswordAsync(). I also added a listener to the event Save-PasswordComplete() so that I know when the operation is complete.

```
public void TestWebServiceWrite(int playerID, string password)
{
    ServiceReference1.MapEditorServiceClient client =
    new MySLApp.ServiceReference1.MapEditorServiceClient();
    client.SavePasswordCompleted += new EventHandler<System.ComponentModel.
          AsyncCompletedEventArgs>(client_SavePasswordCompleted);
    client.SavePasswordAsync(playerID, password);
}

void client_SavePasswordCompleted(object sender,
        System.ComponentModel.AsyncCompletedEventArgs e)
{

}
```

Loading Object Templates

Now that you are familiar with how to use web services from Silverlight, I will be showing you the code needed to load the various types of objects described in Chapter 5, "Creating the World," from the web service.

To accomplish this, I have created a class called `ObjectTemplateManager`. This class has the two following members:

```
public static List<ObjectBase> ObjectTemplates = new List<ObjectBase>();
private static ObjectLoadComplete OnLoadComplete;
```

The first one, `ObjectTemplates`, represents the complete list of all object templates. It is a static object that can be referenced from anywhere in the application. The second property, `OnLoadComplete`, is a delegate callback that will communicate when loading is complete. This is required because loading is done asynchronously and the application needs to know when loading has finished.

The function you call to load objects is `LoadObjectTemplates()` and is declared as such:

```
public static void LoadObjectTemplates(ObjectLoadComplete onLoadComplete)
{
    OnLoadComplete = onLoadComplete;

    ServiceReference1.MapEditorServiceClient client =
      new MapEditor.ServiceReference1.MapEditorServiceClient();
    client.GetBaseObjectsCompleted +=
      new EventHandler<MapEditor.ServiceReference1.
      GetBaseObjectsCompletedEventArgs>(client_GetBaseObjectsCompleted);
    client.GetBaseObjectsAsync();
}
```

Once the data has been retrieved from the web service, the callback `client_GetBaseObjectsCompleted` is then called.

```
private static void client_GetBaseObjectsCompleted(object sender,
      MapEditor.ServiceReference1.GetBaseObjectsCompletedEventArgs e)
{
    foreach (ServiceReference1.BaseObject baseObj in e.Result)
    {
        switch (baseObj.ObjType)
        {
            case ServiceReference1.ObjectType.Creature:
```

```
                CreateCreatureTemplate(baseObj);
                break;
            case ServiceReference1.ObjectType.Effect:
                CreateEffectTemplate(baseObj);
                break;
            case ServiceReference1.ObjectType.Game:
                CreateGameTemplate(baseObj);
                break;
            case ServiceReference1.ObjectType.Map:
                CreateMapTemplate(baseObj);
                break;
            case ServiceReference1.ObjectType.Terrain:
                CreateTerrainTemplate(baseObj);
                break;
        }
    }
    OnLoadComplete();
}
```

In this function, you must enumerate through all the objects and create a new object template based upon its type. Each one of these templates is represented by its own class, which inherits from a base class called `ObjectBase`.

For example, in the `ObjectTemplateManager` class, the method to create a creature template is as follows:

```
private static void CreateCreatureTemplate(ServiceReference1.BaseObject baseObj)
{
    ObjectCreature creatureObj = new ObjectCreature(0, 0);
    creatureObj.ObjectName = baseObj.Name;
    creatureObj.IsWalkable = baseObj.Walkable;
    creatureObj.SetWidth(baseObj.Width);
    creatureObj.SetHeight(baseObj.Height);

    foreach (MapEditor.ServiceReference1.ObjectImage objectImg in baseObj.
                                    ObjImages)
    {
        creatureObj.AddImageFrame((Enums.Direction)objectImg.Direction,
            (Enums.AnimationType)objectImg.AnimationType,
            objectImg.FrameCount, objectImg.FramesPerRow, objectImg.ImageUrl);
    }

    ObjectTemplates.Add(creatureObj);
}
```

ObjectBase Class

The base class, called ObjectBase, is a Silverlight user control that consists of its XAML file ObjectBase.xaml and its code-behind file ObjectBase.xaml.cs. The ObjectBase class is declared to be an abstract class because the class is meant only to be a base class of one of the parent classes. The parent classes are all the different types of objects that can be in the game. Those objects, defined in Chapter 5, include Terrain, Creature, Map, Game, and Effect.

The abstract modifier prevents the class from being instantiated by itself. This is because the ObjectBase class is only used to handle the common functionality across all objects. Here is the class declaration of the ObjectBase control as is used in the Map Editor:

```
public abstract partial class ObjectBase : UserControl
{
    public string Description = Consts.Unknown;
    public string ObjectName = Consts.Unknown;
    public bool IsWalkable = true;
    public int BaseObjectID = Consts.None;

    public ObjectBase(double x, double y, int baseObjID)
    {
        InitializeComponent();

        BaseObjectID = baseObjID;

        this.SetValue(Canvas.LeftProperty, x);
        this.SetValue(Canvas.TopProperty, y);
    }

    public void SetWidth(double width)
    {
        this.Width = width;
        SelectionRect.Width = width;
        CollisionRect.Width = width;
        ObjClip.Rect = new Rect(0,0,this.Width,this.Height);
    }

    public void SetHeight(double height)
    {
        this.Height = height;
        SelectionRect.Height = height;
```

```
        CollisionRect.Height = height;
        ObjClip.Rect = new Rect(0, 0, this.Width, this.Height);
    }

    internal bool DetectCollision(Point pt, ref Point selectionPoint)
    {
        double x = (double)CollisionRect.GetValue(Canvas.TopProperty);
        double y = (double)CollisionRect.GetValue(Canvas.LeftProperty);

        bool collide = pt.X >= x && pt.Y >= y && pt.X <
           (x + CollisionRect.ActualWidth) && pt.Y <
           (y + CollisionRect.ActualHeight);

        if (true == collide)
        {
            selectionPoint.X = pt.X-x;
            selectionPoint.Y = pt.Y-y;
        }

        return collide;
    }

    public abstract ObjectBase Clone(int maxRadius);
    public abstract void Deselect();
    public abstract ObjectBase Select();
}
```

And the following is the object XAML:

```
<UserControl x:Class="MapEditor.ObjectBase"
    xmlns="http://schemas.microsoft.com/winfx/2006/xaml/presentation"
    xmlns:x="http://schemas.microsoft.com/winfx/2006/xaml">

    <Canvas x:Name="ParentCanvas" Background="Transparent" >
        <Canvas x:Name="ObjectCanvas" Canvas.ZIndex="110">
            <Canvas.Clip>
                <RectangleGeometry x:Name="ObjClip" Rect="0,0,128,128"/>
            </Canvas.Clip>
        </Canvas>
        <Rectangle x:Name="CollisionRect" Stroke="Yellow"
             StrokeThickness="0.3" Visibility="Collapsed"
             Width="128" Height="128"></Rectangle>
        <Rectangle x:Name="SelectionRect" Stroke="Gray"
```

```
            Canvas.ZIndex="1" StrokeThickness="0.3"  Width="128"
            Height="128"></Rectangle>
    </Canvas>
</UserControl>
```

Setting the parent `Canvas` as transparent enables the child `Canvas` to receive mouse events. Anything common to all objects is placed in this base class. For example, everything has a name and a description. In addition, you may want to know if the game object can be walked on. For example, a tree cannot be walked on by a creature, so you will want to set `walkable` to `false` in that case. Any function that should be implemented by the parent class should be labeled as `abstract`. This will force the parent class to implement the method. The functions `OnDeselect()` and `Select()` are called when the object is deselected and selected. The function `Clone()` is called to create a copy of the object.

Terrain Objects

Terrain objects are objects used to paint the ground floor of your map. One terrain object represents one tile on the map. From a Z-ordering perspective, the terrain is always on the bottom of all other object types (Z-order is used to specify the order that overlapping objects are drawn.) The positioning of terrain objects is constricted to a grid layout, with each grid cell having a radius in width and height. Each grid cell can contain only one terrain object. By default, the Map Editor allows each terrain object to have two image layers. However, the layer depth can be customized to any desired depth from the Map Editor. Terrain objects are made up of multiple layers of images with an optional opacity mask that is used to blend layers together. These images are usually seamless rectangle textures of dirt, grass, road, and so on. It's important that the images are seamless so they can be connected to one other without having an obvious transition border between them. Figure 6.5 shows some examples of seamless terrain images.

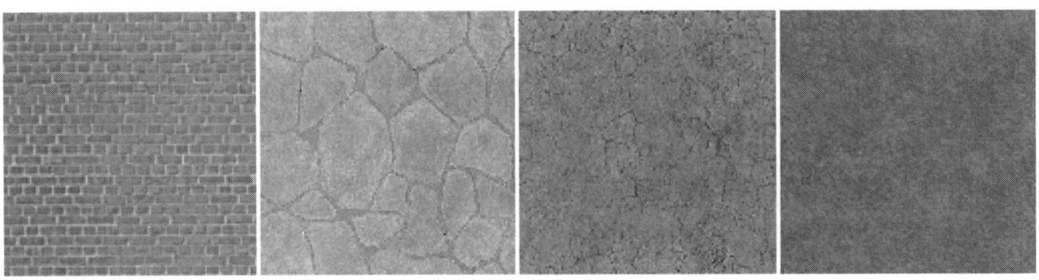

Figure 6.5
Terrain Objects

The following code from ObjectTerrain.cs represents the class for the terrain object:

```
public class ObjectTerrain : ObjectBase
{
    private Image[] _layers;
    private int[] _baseObjectIDs;
    private int[] _opacityIDs;
    private double _radius = 0;

    public ObjectTerrain(double x, double y, int radius,
           int layerCount, int baseObjID)
        : base(x, y, baseObjID)
    {
        ObjectCanvas.Children.Clear();
        _radius = radius;
        SelectionRect.Width = _radius;
        SelectionRect.Height = _radius;
        ParentCanvas.Width = _radius;
        ParentCanvas.Height = _radius;

        _baseObjectIDs = new int[layerCount];
        _opacityIDs = new int[layerCount];
        _layers = new Image[layerCount];
        for (int i = 0; i < layerCount; i++)
        {
            _layers[i] = new Image();
            ObjectCanvas.Children.Add(_layers[i]);
            _baseObjectIDs[i] = Consts.None;
            _opacityIDs[i] = Consts.None;
        }
    }

    public void ClearLayers()
    {
        for (int i = 0; i < _layers.Length; i++)
        {
            ObjectCanvas.Children.Remove(_layers[i]);
            _layers[i] = new Image();
            ObjectCanvas.Children.Add(_layers[i]);
            _baseObjectIDs[i] = Consts.None;
            _opacityIDs[i] = Consts.None;
        }
    }
```

```
public Image GetLayerImage(int layer)
{
    return _layers[layer];
}

public int GetLayerBaseObjectID(int layer)
{
    return _baseObjectIDs[layer];
}

public int GetLayerOpacityID(int layer)
{
    return _opacityIDs[layer];
}

public void ApplyOpacityMask(int layer, Image opacityImage)
{
    ImageBrush imgBrush = new ImageBrush();
    imgBrush.ImageSource = Utils.LoadImage
                       (Utils.GetImageFileName(opacityImage));

    _layers[layer].OpacityMask = imgBrush;
}

public void SetLayer(int layer, int baseObjectID, string fileName)
{
    _layers[layer].Visibility = Visibility.Collapsed;
    _layers[layer].Source = Utils.LoadImage(fileName);
    _layers[layer].ImageOpened +=
           new EventHandler<RoutedEventArgs>(Image_ImageOpened);

    _baseObjectIDs[layer] = baseObjectID;
}

private void LoadImage(string fileName)
{
    Image img = new Image();
    Uri uri = new Uri(fileName, UriKind.Relative);
    img.Source = new System.Windows.Media.Imaging.BitmapImage(uri);
    img.ImageOpened += new EventHandler<RoutedEventArgs>(Image_ImageOpened);
}

void Image_ImageOpened(object sender, RoutedEventArgs e)
```

```
    {
        Image img = (Image)sender;
        if (_radius != 0)
        {
            BitmapImage bi = (BitmapImage)img.Source;
            if (bi.PixelWidth != _radius)
                img.Height = _radius;
            if (bi.PixelWidth != _radius)
                img.Width = _radius;
        }
        img.Visibility = Visibility.Visible;
    }

    public override ObjectBase Clone(int maxRadius)
    {
        ObjectTerrain terrainObj = new ObjectTerrain(0, 0,
                                        maxRadius, _layers.Length, BaseObjectID);

        terrainObj.Description = Description;
        terrainObj.ObjectName = ObjectName;
        terrainObj.IsWalkable = IsWalkable;

        for (int i = 0; i < _layers.Length; i++)
        {
            if (_layers[i] != null)
                terrainObj.SetLayer(i,_baseObjectIDs[i],
                                    ((BitmapImage)_layers[i].Source).
                                    UriSource.OriginalString);
        }
        return (ObjectBase)terrainObj;
    }

    public override void Deselect()
    {
        SelectionRect.Stroke = null;
        if(Consts.ShowGrid)
            SelectionRect.Stroke = new SolidColorBrush(Colors.White);
    }
    public override ObjectBase Select()
    {
        SelectionRect.Stroke = new SolidColorBrush(Colors.Red);
        return (ObjectBase)this;
    }
}
```

In the constructor of the `ObjectTerrain`, you must specify the X and Y location of the terrain as well as its unique identifier, which is passed on the base constructor. You also set the radius as well as the number of layers you want to be on the map. Setting the radius tells you the width and the height of the tile. Because tiles cannot overlap, you must check if the image is larger or smaller than the radius and automatically resize it, if necessary, to fit the radius. Because this is an expensive operation that can affect the performance of your game, it's important that your game images are sized in advance to the exact dimensions you plan to use.

When loading an image, you must set its visibility to be `false` until it has completely loaded. An image's actual size is not known until the event `ImageOpened` is called. If you were to check the `ActualWidth` or `ActualHeight` properties before this event is called, they would be most likely set to `NaN`, which means "not set." Once you know the real size of the image, you can size it the appropriate dimensions and then set it to `visible`. If you set the image to `visible` beforehand, you would see the resizing of the image on the screen.

Creature Objects

Creature objects represent every living entity in the game. They can perform a wide variety of actions, making animation a sometimes complex and daunting task. There are a number of possible features to consider but it is recommended that you keep the list simple for your first iteration. For example, because Silverlight does not yet support 3D, these examples don't implement the ability for creatures to wear clothing and armor or wield weapons (since doing so would be a very time-consuming task). These examples do, however, support seven types of creature actions, including walking, idling, running, attacking, flying, dying, and getting hit. To accomplish these actions, I have a separate PNG file pre-rendered for each of the possible eight directions and for each possible action. The directions include north, northeast, east, southeast, south, southwest, west, and northwest. Each PNG file has the frames needed to render the complete animation sequence.

To illustrate this process, Figure 6.6 shows the frames needed for a dwarf attacking to the east.

For one character to have all directions represented for all actions, you need a total of eight directions times seven actions (56 individual files). It is not required

Figure 6.6
Creature Object

that each creature have every action animated. For example, not all creatures can fly nor can all creatures run. You need to include only the frames you wish to support.

Each image can have any number of frames to represent the complete animation sequence for a given direction. Also, the frames that represent the creature can be of any size and any count of frames per row. Chapter 7 discusses how to animate objects and their frames.

Each creature is represented in a class called `ObjectCreature`, which inherits from the base class `ObjectBase`. By default, each creature has the following properties (not including its animation tracking properties):

- Name—The name of the creature
- Description—The description of the creature
- Health—Total number of hit points.
- Mana—Total number of spell points
- Dexterity—Affects the creature's ability to dodge
- Strength—Affects attack power
- Agility—Affects critical hit chance
- Stamina—Affects health

- Intelligence—Affects spell damage and mana
- Armor—Affects physical damage taken
- Resilience—Affects total damage and chance to be critically hit
- Mana Regen—The rate of mana regeneration every second
- Gold—The number of gold coins this creature is carrying
- Silver—The number of silver coins this creature is carrying
- Copper—The number of copper coins this creature is carrying

The following two classes are used to represent the creatures. These classes reside in ObjectCreature.cs. Chapter 7, "Animation," covers how the animation works with complex objects like creatures.

```
public class ObjectFrames
{
    public Image[] DirectionFrames;
    public int FramesPerRow = 0;
    public int FrameCount = 0;
}

public class ObjectCreature : ObjectBase
{
    public int Level;

    // Base Stats
    public int Health;        // Total number of hit points.
    public int Mana;          // Total number of spell points.
    public int Dexterity;     // Affects changes to dodge.
    public int Strength;      // Affects attack power.
    public int Agility;       // Affects critical hit chance.
    public int Stamina;       // Affects overall health.
    public int Intelligence;  // Affects spell damage and mana.

    // Stats from Gear Worm
    public int Armor;         // Affects physical damage taken.
    public int Resilience;    // Affects total damage and chance
                              // to be critically hit.
    public int ManaRegen;     // Affects mana regeneration.
```

```
// Money changes everything.
public int Gold;
public int Silver;
public int Copper;

public ObjectFrames WalkingFrames   = new ObjectFrames();
public ObjectFrames FlyingFrames    = new ObjectFrames();
public ObjectFrames AttackingFrames = new ObjectFrames();
public ObjectFrames HitFrames       = new ObjectFrames();
public ObjectFrames DyingFrames     = new ObjectFrames();
public ObjectFrames IdlingFrames    = new ObjectFrames();
public ObjectFrames RunningFrames   = new ObjectFrames();

private ObjectFrames _currentObjectFrames;
private int _currentFrameIndex = 0;
private Enums.Direction _currentDirection = Enums.Direction.South;

private bool _repeatAnimation = false;
private Enums.AnimationType _currentAnimation = Enums.AnimationType.Walk;
DispatcherTimer _timer = new DispatcherTimer();

private Button NextAnimation = new Button();
private Button NextDirection = new Button();

public ObjectCreature(double x, double y, int baseObjID)
    : base(x, y, baseObjID)
{
    _timer.Interval = new TimeSpan(0, 0, 0, 0, 100);
    _timer.Tick += new EventHandler(HeartBeat);

    NextDirection.Content = "D";
    NextDirection.SetValue(Canvas.TopProperty, (double)-20);
    NextDirection.Click += new RoutedEventHandler(NextDirection_Click);
    NextDirection.Visibility = Visibility.Collapsed;
    ParentCanvas.Children.Add(NextDirection);

    NextAnimation.Content = "A";
    NextAnimation.SetValue(Canvas.TopProperty, (double)-20);
    NextAnimation.SetValue(Canvas.LeftProperty, (double)20);
    NextAnimation.Click += new RoutedEventHandler(NextAnimation_Click);
    NextAnimation.Visibility = Visibility.Collapsed;
    ParentCanvas.Children.Add(NextAnimation);
}
```

```
void NextDirection_Click(object sender, RoutedEventArgs e)
{
    AnimateNextDirection();
}

void NextAnimation_Click(object sender, RoutedEventArgs e)
{
    AnimateNextAnimation();
}

private void UpdateAnimationFrame()
{
    int row = _currentFrameIndex / _currentObjectFrames.FramesPerRow;
    int column = _currentFrameIndex -
               (row * _currentObjectFrames.FramesPerRow);

    _currentObjectFrames.DirectionFrames[(int)_currentDirection].
         SetValue(Canvas.LeftProperty, (double)-(column*this.Width));
    _currentObjectFrames.DirectionFrames[(int)_currentDirection].
         SetValue(Canvas.TopProperty, (double)-(row*this.Height));
    if (++_currentFrameIndex == _currentObjectFrames.FrameCount)
    {
        if (true == _repeatAnimation)
            _currentFrameIndex = 0;
        else
            _timer.Stop();
    }
}

void HeartBeat(object sender, EventArgs e)
{
    UpdateAnimationFrame();
}

public void SetAnimationDelay(int milliseconds)
{
    _timer.Interval = new TimeSpan(milliseconds);
}

public void Animate(Enums.Direction direction,
        Enums.AnimationType animationType, bool repeatAnimation)
{
    _timer.Stop();
```

```
if (null != _currentObjectFrames && null
        != _currentObjectFrames.DirectionFrames)
{
    Image currentImage = _currentObjectFrames.DirectionFrames
                        [(int)_currentDirection];
    if (currentImage != null)
    {
        if (ObjectCanvas.Children.Contains(currentImage))
            ObjectCanvas.Children.Remove(currentImage);
    }
}

_currentObjectFrames = null;
_currentFrameIndex = 0;

_currentDirection = direction;
_currentAnimation = animationType;

switch (_currentAnimation)
{
    case Enums.AnimationType.Walk:
        _currentObjectFrames = WalkingFrames;
        break;
    case Enums.AnimationType.Fly:
        _currentObjectFrames = FlyingFrames;
        break;
    case Enums.AnimationType.Attack:
        _currentObjectFrames = AttackingFrames;
        break;
    case Enums.AnimationType.Hit:
        _currentObjectFrames = HitFrames;
        break;
    case Enums.AnimationType.Death:
        _currentObjectFrames = DyingFrames;
        break;
    case Enums.AnimationType.Idle:
        _currentObjectFrames = IdlingFrames;
        break;
    case Enums.AnimationType.Run:
        _currentObjectFrames = RunningFrames;
        break;
}
```

```
            if (null != _currentObjectFrames && null
                    != _currentObjectFrames.DirectionFrames)
            {
                if (null != _currentObjectFrames.DirectionFrames
                          [(int)_currentDirection])
                {
                    _repeatAnimation = repeatAnimation;
                    _currentFrameIndex = 0;

                    ObjectCanvas.Children.Add(_currentObjectFrames.
                                DirectionFrames[(int)_currentDirection]);
                    _timer.Start();
                }
            }
        }

        public Enums.AnimationType CurrentAnimation
        {
            get { return _currentAnimation; }
            set
            {
                _currentAnimation = value;
            }
        }

        public Enums.Direction CurrentDirection
        {
            get { return _currentDirection; }
            set
            {
                _currentDirection = value;
            }
        }

        private void LoadImageFrame(ref ObjectFrames frames,
                    int framesPerRow, int frameCount,
                    Enums.Direction direction, string str)
        {
            if (null == frames.DirectionFrames)
               frames.DirectionFrames = new Image[8];

            Image img = new Image();
            img.Source = Utils.LoadImage(str);
```

```
        frames.DirectionFrames[(int)direction] = img;
        frames.FramesPerRow = framesPerRow;
        frames.FrameCount = frameCount;
    }

    public void AddImageFrame(Enums.Direction direction,
                Enums.AnimationType animationType, int frameCount,
                int framesPerRow, string src)
    {
        switch (animationType)
        {
            case Enums.AnimationType.Walk:
                LoadImageFrame(ref WalkingFrames, framesPerRow,
                                frameCount, direction, src);
                break;
            case Enums.AnimationType.Fly:
                LoadImageFrame(ref FlyingFrames, framesPerRow,
                                    frameCount, direction, src);
                break;
            case Enums.AnimationType.Attack:
                LoadImageFrame(ref AttackingFrames, framesPerRow,
                                    frameCount, direction, src);
                break;
            case Enums.AnimationType.Hit:
                LoadImageFrame(ref HitFrames, framesPerRow, frameCount,
                                    direction, src);
                break;
            case Enums.AnimationType.Death:
                LoadImageFrame(ref DyingFrames, framesPerRow, frameCount,
                                    direction, src);
                break;
            case Enums.AnimationType.Idle:
                LoadImageFrame(ref IdlingFrames, framesPerRow, frameCount,
                                    direction, src);
                break;
            case Enums.AnimationType.Run:
                LoadImageFrame(ref RunningFrames, framesPerRow,
                                    frameCount, direction, src);
                break;


        }
    }
```

```
public void SetFrames(ref ObjectFrames destFrames, ref ObjectFrames srcFrames)
{
    if (null != srcFrames.DirectionFrames)
    {
        destFrames.DirectionFrames = new Image[srcFrames.DirectionFrames
                                     .Length];

        for (int i = 0; i < srcFrames.DirectionFrames.Length; i++)
        {
            string fileName = Utils.GetImageFileName
                            (srcFrames.DirectionFrames[i]);
            destFrames.DirectionFrames[i] = new Image();
            destFrames.FramesPerRow = srcFrames.FramesPerRow;
            destFrames.DirectionFrames[i].Source = Utils.LoadImage(fileName);
            destFrames.FrameCount = srcFrames.FrameCount;
        }
    }
}

public void AnimateNextAnimation()
{
    int animation = (int) _currentAnimation;
    animation++;
    if (animation == (int)Enums.AnimationType.End)
        animation = 0;

    Animate(_currentDirection, (Enums.AnimationType) animation, true);
}

public void AnimateNextDirection()
{
    int direction = (int)_currentDirection;
    direction++;
    if (direction == (int)Enums.Direction.End)
        direction = 0;

    Animate((Enums.Direction) direction, _currentAnimation, true);
}

public override ObjectBase Clone(int maxRadius)
{
    ObjectCreature creatureObject = new ObjectCreature (0, 0, BaseObjectID);
    creatureObject.Width = this.Width;
```

```
        creatureObject.Height = this.Height;

        SetFrames(ref creatureObject.AttackingFrames, ref AttackingFrames);
        SetFrames(ref creatureObject.DyingFrames, ref DyingFrames);
        SetFrames(ref creatureObject.FlyingFrames, ref FlyingFrames);
        SetFrames(ref creatureObject.HitFrames, ref HitFrames);
        SetFrames(ref creatureObject.WalkingFrames, ref WalkingFrames);
        SetFrames(ref creatureObject.IdlingFrames, ref IdlingFrames);
        SetFrames(ref creatureObject.RunningFrames, ref RunningFrames);

        return creatureObject;
    }

    public override void Deselect()
    {
        NextAnimation.Visibility = Visibility.Collapsed;
        NextDirection.Visibility = Visibility.Collapsed;
        SelectionRect.Stroke = null;
    }

    public override ObjectBase Select()
    {
        NextAnimation.Visibility = Visibility.Visible;
        NextDirection.Visibility = Visibility.Visible;
        SelectionRect.Stroke = new SolidColorBrush(Colors.Red);

        return (ObjectBase)this;
    }
}
```

Map Objects

Map objects are static objects that are always in the same position and in the same state when you first load the map. Depending upon your game, players can often interact with these types of objects, but for the most part these objects cannot be consumed or destroyed since they will always reappear whenever the map is loaded.

Examples of map objects include trees, boulders, plants, houses, signs, and so on. Figure 6.7 shows an example of a temple that can be declared as a map object.

The following code represents the `ObjectMap` class used by the Map Editor. This code resides in the file ObjectMap.cs.

Figure 6.7
Map Object

```
public class ObjectMap: ObjectBase
{
    private Image[] _frames;
    public double AnimationDelayInMS = 0;
    public bool RepeatAnimation = false;
    public bool Animate = false;
    public bool IsAnimating = false;
    public int MaxRadius = 0;

    public ObjectMap(double x, double y, int frameCount,
                    int baseObjID) : base(x,y,baseObjID)
    {
        ObjectCanvas.Children.Clear();

        _frames = new Image[frameCount];
        for (int i = 0; i < frameCount; i++)
        {
            _frames[i] = new Image();
            ObjectCanvas.Children.Add(_frames[i]);
        }
    }

    public void SetImage(int frame, string fileName)
    {
        _frames[frame].Source = Utils.LoadImage(fileName);
```

```
    _frames[frame].Visibility = Visibility.Collapsed;
    _frames[frame].ImageOpened +=
                    new EventHandler<RoutedEventArgs>(Image_Image
                    Opened);
}

void Image_ImageOpened(object sender, RoutedEventArgs e)
{
    Image img = (Image)sender;
    BitmapImage bi = (BitmapImage)img.Source;

    int width = bi.PixelWidth;
    int height = bi.PixelHeight;

    if (MaxRadius != 0)
    {
        if (bi.PixelWidth > MaxRadius)
        {
            img.Height = MaxRadius;
            width = MaxRadius;
        }
        if (bi.PixelWidth > MaxRadius)
        {
            img.Width = MaxRadius;
            height = MaxRadius;
        }
    }
    img.Visibility = Visibility.Visible;

    SetWidth(width);
    SetHeight(height);

}

public void ShowFrame(int frame, Visibility visibility)
{
    _frames[frame].Visibility = visibility;
}

public override ObjectBase Clone(int maxRadius)
{
    ObjectMap mapObject = new ObjectMap(0,0,_frames.Length, BaseObjectID);
   // mapObject.InitializeImages(_frames.Length);
```

```
            for (int i = 0; i < _frames.Length; i++)
            {
                mapObject.SetImage(i, ((BitmapImage)_frames[0].Source)
                                        .UriSource.OriginalString);
            }
            mapObject.MaxRadius = maxRadius;
            mapObject.RepeatAnimation = false;
            mapObject.Animate = Animate;
            mapObject.ShowFrame(0, Visibility.Visible);
            mapObject.AnimationDelayInMS = AnimationDelayInMS;
            mapObject.Description = Description;
            mapObject.ObjectName = ObjectName;
            mapObject.IsWalkable = IsWalkable;

            return (ObjectBase)mapObject;
        }

        public override void Deselect()
        {
            SelectionRect.Stroke = null;
        }
        public override ObjectBase Select()
        {
            SelectionRect.Stroke = new SolidColorBrush(Colors.Red);
            return (ObjectBase)this;
        }

    }
```

Game Objects

Game objects are the most complex objects in the game. Depending upon its type, a game object can be used, worn, wielded, traded, consumed, and more. Because of the complexity, they need to be very flexible to accommodate just about any possible action.

Examples of game objects include swords, armor, potions, scrolls, food, drink, and so on.

At the base level is the common functionality that can be shared across all game objects. The following code represents the base class for game objects.

```
public class ObjectGame: Object
{

    private Image[] _frames;
    public double AnimationDelayInMS = 0;
    public bool RepeatAnimation = false;
    public bool Animate = false;
    public bool IsAnimating = false;
    public int MaxRadius = 0;

    public ObjectGame(double x, double y, int frameCount, int baseObjID)
        : base(x, y, baseObjID)
    {
        ObjectCanvas.Children.Clear();

        _frames = new Image[frameCount];
        for (int i = 0; i < frameCount; i++)
        {
            _frames[i] = new Image();
            ObjectCanvas.Children.Add(_frames[i]);
        }
    }

    public void SetImage(int frame, string fileName)
    {
        _frames[frame].Source = Utils.LoadImage(fileName);
        _frames[frame].Visibility = Visibility.Collapsed;
        _frames[frame].ImageOpened +=
                        new EventHandler<RoutedEventArgs>(Image_ImageOpened);
    }

    void Image_ImageOpened(object sender, RoutedEventArgs e)
    {
        Image img = (Image)sender;
        BitmapImage bi = (BitmapImage)img.Source;

        int width = bi.PixelWidth;
        int height = bi.PixelHeight;

        if (MaxRadius != 0)
        {
            if (bi.PixelWidth > MaxRadius)
            {
```

```
                img.Height = MaxRadius;
                width = MaxRadius;
            }
            if (bi.PixelWidth > MaxRadius)
            {
                img.Width = MaxRadius;
                height = MaxRadius;
            }
        }
        img.Visibility = Visibility.Visible;

        SetWidth(width);
        SetHeight(height);

    }

    public void ShowFrame(int frame, Visibility visibility)
    {
        _frames[frame].Visibility = visibility;
    }

    public override ObjectBase Clone(int maxRadius)
    {
        GameObjectGame gameObject =
            new ObjectGame(0, 0, _frames.Length, BaseObjectID);
        // mapObject.InitializeImages(_frames.Length);

        for (int i = 0; i < _frames.Length; i++)
        {
            gameObject.SetImage
                        (i, ((BitmapImage)_frames[0].Source).
                            UriSource.OriginalString);
        }
        gameObject.MaxRadius = maxRadius;
        gameObject.RepeatAnimation = false;
        gameObject.Animate = Animate;
        gameObject.ShowFrame(0, Visibility.Visible);
        gameObject.AnimationDelayInMS = AnimationDelayInMS;
        gameObject.Description = Description;
        gameObject.ObjectName = ObjectName;
        gameObject.IsWalkable = IsWalkable;
```

```
            return (ObjectBase)gameObject;
        }

        public override void Deselect()
        {
            SelectionRect.Stroke = null;
        }
        public override ObjectBase Select()
        {
            SelectionRect.Stroke = new SolidColorBrush(Colors.Red);
            return (ObjectBase)this;
        }
    }
```

Parent classes for each game object will represent the specifics needed for the object. For example, weapons are represented by `ObjectWeapon`. In a weapon you will have various attributes such as the hit power for the weapon, its current durability, the type of weapon it is (knife, sword, axe, and so on), and more. The class for the weapon, located in ObjectWeapon.cs, looks something like this:

```
public class ObjectWeapon: GameObject
{
    public int HitPower;
    public int Durability;
    public WeaponType weaponType;

    public ObjectWeapon(double x, double y, int frameCount, int baseObjID)
        : base(x, y, frameCount, baseObjID)
    {
    }
}
```

Summary

This chapter covered in-depth how to leverage web services to retrieve and store data. In addition, it discussed the object structure used in RPG-type games where the base class is represented by the `ObjectBase` class and all the parent object classes such as `ObjectCreature`, `ObjectMap`, and so on inherit from this base class. The next chapter will discuss how animation works in Silverlight. It discusses the various types of timers and shows you how to animate the `ObjectCreature` that was discussed in this chapter.

CHAPTER 7

Animation

Animation is used extensively to enhance websites by making them more interactive and appealing. It also adds necessary visual cues to help guide users. For game development, animation is almost always a requirement. There are many different approaches to animating content with Silverlight. This chapter explores the three animation timers available to you:

- `DispatcherTimer`
- `Storyboard` timer
- `CompositionTarget.Rendering`

This chapter covers techniques for animating frames. Since animation is often the bottleneck of any application, the chapter concludes with some performance tips, including ways you can monitor and analyze your application's performance. The chapter also covers how to enable hardware acceleration for your Silverlight plug-ins and controls.

DispatcherTimer

The `DispatcherTimer` is part of the `System.Windows.Threading` namespace. It is a fairly straightforward timer that runs on a specified interval of time. The interval is a `TimeSpan` that allows you to indicate the delta between each call to your ticking function.

Creation is fairly simple. The following example creates a timer that is called every 500 milliseconds.

```
DispatcherTimer dt = new DispatcherTimer();
dt.Interval = new TimeSpan(0, 0, 0, 0, 500);
dt.Start();
dt.Tick +=new EventHandler(dt_Tick);

void dt_Tick(object sender, EventArgs e)
{
        // Do your work here.
}
```

In addition to `Start()`, you can also call `Stop()` to stop the timer when you are ready for the timer to exit. You can also determine whether the timer is enabled through the property `IsEnabled`.

The Storyboard Timer

The `Storyboard` timer is part of the `System.Windows.Media.Animation` namespace. It's primarily used to animate properties belonging to controls over a given timeline. Overall, it's much more flexible than the `DispatcherTimer` and includes advantages such as the following:

- The `Storyboard` is handled on a separate thread that is not affected by the UI thread that the `DispatcherTimer` is on.
- The `DispatcherTimer` is a lower resolution timer than the timer behind the `Storyboard` class, which can cause loss in fidelity.
- The `Storyboard` execution is more stable across the different supported OSes and web browsers.
- In addition to creating `Storyboard` timers in procedural code like you would the `DispatcherTimer`, you can also create them as a resource in your XAML, thereby using them to animate the properties of other controls.

Only static members of the `Storyboard` are guaranteed to be thread-safe. For instance members, you may need to guard against any possible conflicts. Also, make sure you do not call `Storyboard` members within the constructor of your page because this will cause the animation to silently fail, which can happen if thepage is not yet fully loaded. Animations should be started after the page is loaded. For example:

```
public MainPage()
{
    InitializeComponent();

    this.Loaded += new RoutedEventHandler(MainPage_Loaded);
}

void MainPage_Loaded(object sender, RoutedEventArgs e)
{
    myStoryboard.Begin();
}
```

To declare a `Storyboard` timer in your XAML, you need to place it in the `Resources` section. For example:

```
<Canvas x:Name="LayoutRoot" Background="White">
    <Canvas.Resources>
        <Storyboard x:Name="myStoryboard"/>
    </Canvas.Resources>
</Canvas>
```

A number of properties are available for your storyboard. These include the following:

- `Storyboard.TargetName`—This property allows you to specify which object you want to animate. For example, the following code shows you how to target an `Image` control.

  ```
  <Canvas.Resources>
      <Storyboard Storyboard.TargetName="MyImage"></Storyboard>
  </Canvas.Resources>

  <Image x:Name="MyImage"></Image>
  ```

- `Storyboard.TargetProperty`—This property allows you to specify which property on the control you want to animate. For example, to animate the width of an image, you could use this code:

  ```
  <Canvas.Resources>
      <Storyboard Storyboard.TargetName="MyImage"
              Storyboard.TargetProperty="Width">
      </Storyboard>
  </Canvas.Resources>

  <Image x:Name="MyImage"></Image>
  ```

- `AutoReverse`—When set to `true`, the animation will reverse itself along the specified timeline back to the beginning value.
- `BeginTime`—If you do not want the animation to instantly start, you can specify the amount of the delay you want by setting this property.
- `Duration`—This property is used to specify the length of time that the animation will run.
- `FillBehavior`—This property allows you to indicate how the timeline will act once it reaches the end. By default, this is set to `HoldEnd`, which causes the object to keep its value at the end. The only other option is `Stop`, which will cause the object to revert back to the beginning value.
- `RepeatBehavior`—Use this property to define the repeating behavior of the timeline. There are three possible uses this property can be set to. These include the following:
  - `Iteration`—Any integer value followed by the character `x` that specifies the number of times the animation should repeat. For example, to repeat two times, you specify `RepeatBehavior="2x"`.
  - `TimeSpan`—The length of time the animation is active. Its format is *`[days]. hours:minutes:seconds[.fractionSeconds]`*. *`Days`* and *`fraction Seconds`* are optional. For example, to cause the animation to repeat for five seconds, you would specify `RepeatBehavior="0:0:05"`.
  - `Forever`—Specifying the string `Forever` will cause the animation to repeat forever. For example, `RepeatBehavior="Forever"`.
- `SpeedRatio`—The rate at which the animation occurs over the timeline. By default, the ratio is set to 1 for normal speed. You can double the speed by setting it to 2 or slow it down by half by setting it to 0.5.

In addition to these previous properties, the following methods are commonly used with the `Storyboard` timer:

- `Begin`—Starts the animation.
- `CheckAccess`—Returns `true` if the thread you are on has access to the `Storyboard`.
- `GetCurrentState`—Returns the current `ClockState` for the given `Storyboard`. The `ClockState` can tell you if the animation is `Active`, `Filling`, or `Stopped`.

- GetCurrentTime—Returns a TimeSpan that indicates the current time of the Storyboard. If the Storyboard is stopped, the return value is null.
- Pause—Pauses the animation. All children of the storyboard are also paused.
- Resume—Resumes an animation that was paused.
- Seek—Moves the Storyboard animation to a specified location in the timeline. This method takes a TimeSpan as a parameter. The change does not occur until the next tick has occurred. In the following example, the timeline is advanced by two seconds:

  ```
  myStoryboard.Seek(new TimeSpan(0, 0, 2));
  ```

- SeekAlignedToLastTick—Same as Seek except that the change is made immediately.
- SkipToFill—Moves the current time to the very end of the timeline. This operation is not valid if RepeatBehavior is set to Forever. If AutoReverse is true, the current time is moved to the start of the Storyboard, where it ends.
- Stop—Stops the animation. Note that this method does not cause the Completed event to fire.

There are a variety of animation types you can apply to a Storyboard, including the following:

- DoubleAnimation
- PointAnimation
- ColorAnimation

These animations all use *linear interpolation,* which means their values are evenly spaced across a timeline from one value to another. For example, if you were going from position 0 to position 100 in four seconds, at one second you will be at 25 and at two seconds you will be at 50, and so on. The starting and ending values are designated by the properties From and To. For example, From="0" To="100" Duration="0:0:2" would take the animation from 0 to 100 in two seconds.

DoubleAnimation

DoubleAnimation will animate a property of type Double. *Doubles* are numbers that can have decimal points like floats. The starting value is specified with the

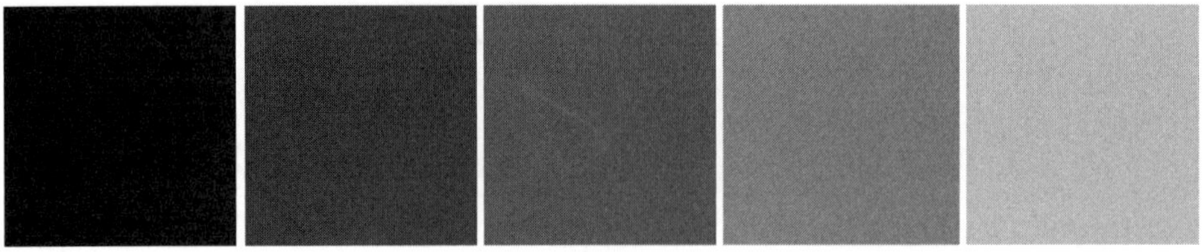

Figure 7.1
Animating Opacity

From property and the finishing value is specified with the To property. The following example animates the Opacity property of a rectangle. The Duration is set to one second. This will cause the rectangle to gradually become less opaque over the one-second period, as shown in Figure 7.1.

Here's the XAML:

```
<Canvas.Resources>
   <Storyboard x:Name="myStoryboard">
     <DoubleAnimation Storyboard.TargetName="myRect"
        Storyboard.TargetProperty="Opacity" From="1.0" To="0.0" Duration="0:0:1">
     </DoubleAnimation>
   </Storyboard>
</Canvas.Resources>

<Rectangle Loaded="myRect_Loaded" x:Name="myRect" Fill="Black"
        Width="100" Height="100">
</Rectangle>
```

Here's the code-behind:

```
private void myRect_Loaded(object sender, RoutedEventArgs e)
{
    myStoryboard.Begin();
}
```

Notice that the example targets the rectangle object by setting Storyboard.TargetName. It targets the property in the rectangle you want to animate by setting Storyboard.TargetProperty. From is the value you want the property to start off at and To is the value you want the property to end up at. In this case, the property in question is the Opacity property.

You can also create a lot of other cool effects such as making objects spin and rotate. To rotate an image along its Y axis, you simply need to target the object's

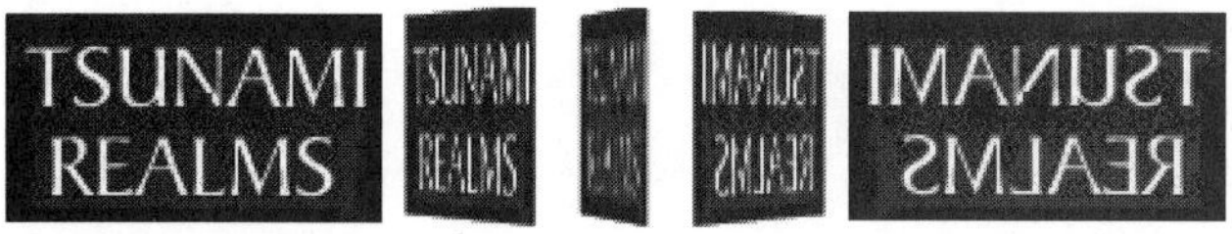

Figure 7.2
Animating RotationY

RotationY property of its PlaneProjection. The following code demonstrates this process, with the result shown in Figure 7.2.

Here's the XAML:

```
<Canvas.Resources>
    <Storyboard x:Name="myStoryboard">
      <DoubleAnimation Storyboard.TargetName="MyProj"
         Storyboard.TargetProperty="RotationY" From="0" To="360"
         RepeatBehavior="Forever" Duration="0:0:10">
        </DoubleAnimation>
    </Storyboard>
</Canvas.Resources>

<Image Canvas.Left="50" ImageOpened="Image_ImageOpened"
      Canvas.Top="50" Source="TR.jpg">
    <Image.Projection>
      <PlaneProjection x:Name="MyProj" RotationY="0"></PlaneProjection>
    </Image.Projection>
</Image>
```

Here's the code-behind:

```
private void Image_ImageOpened(object sender, RoutedEventArgs e)
{
    myStoryboard.Begin();
}
```

Notice that RepeatBehavior is set to Forever, meaning the image will spin non-stop.

PointAnimation

Whereas DoubleAnimation targets double values, PointAnimation targets point values. The following code animates the center point of an ellipse, moving its center from 100,100 to 400,400 on the screen, as shown in Figure 7.3.

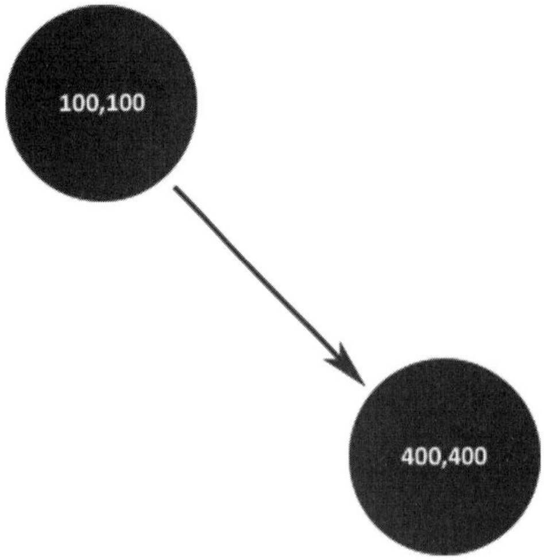

Figure 7.3
Animating the Center Point

Here's the XAML:

```
<Canvas.Resources>
    <Storyboard x:Name="myStoryboard">
        <PointAnimation
         Storyboard.TargetProperty="Center"
         Storyboard.TargetName="MyEllipse"
         Duration="0:0:5"
         From="100,100"
         To="400,400"/>
    </Storyboard>
</Canvas.Resources>

<Path Stroke="Black">
    <Path.Data>
        <GeometryGroup>
          <EllipseGeometry x:Name="MyEllipse" RadiusX="50"
            RadiusY="50" Center="100,100" ></EllipseGeometry>
        </GeometryGroup>
    </Path.Data>
</Path>
```

ColorAnimation

`ColorAnimation` allows you to target and animate values of type `Color`. This can be useful in many cases, such as to gradually change the colors of buttons when the mouse hovers over it.

Figure 7.4
Animating a Color Value

The following code shows you how to gradually change the color of the text in a button from black to white when the mouse hovers over it. This happens over a two-second period and the result can be seen in Figure 7.4. When the mouse leaves the button area, the color returns to black over the same two-second period. This example typecasts the `TargetProperty` as `(ForeGround).(SolidColor Brush.Color)`.

Here's the XAML:

```
<Canvas.Resources>
    <Storyboard x:Name="MouseColorEnter">
      <ColorAnimation Duration="00:00:02" To="#000000"
         Storyboard.TargetName="MyButton"
         Storyboard.TargetProperty="(Foreground).(SolidColorBrush.Color)"/>
    </Storyboard>
      <Storyboard x:Name="MouseColorLeave">
         <ColorAnimation Duration="00:00:02" To="#FFFFFF"
         Storyboard.TargetName="MyButton"
         Storyboard.TargetProperty="(Foreground).(SolidColorBrush.Color)" />
    </Storyboard>
</Canvas.Resources>

<Button FontSize="50" Content="ClickMe" x:Name="MyButton"
    MouseEnter="MyButton_MouseEnter" MouseLeave="MyButton_MouseLeave">
</Button>
```

Here's the code-behind:

```
private void MyButton_MouseEnter(object sender, MouseEventArgs e)
{
    MouseColorEnter.Begin();
}

private void MyButton_MouseLeave(object sender, MouseEventArgs e)
{
    MouseColorLeave.Begin();
}
```

Key Frames

So far, the chapter has shown you animations that take you from one value to another. An alternative method that gives you more control but adds more complexity is the use of key frames. *Key frames* allow you to more closely control the actual values across the timeline because you can state the actual values you want at specific times. The added variance allows you to create much more powerful animations.

There are three key-frame types available:

- `LinearDoubleKeyFrame`—Animates a double value using linear interpolation. This means the animation will smoothly transition between values.
- `DiscreteDoubleKeyFrame`—Animates a double value using discrete values. This means the animation will jump between positions.
- `SplineDoubleKeyFrame`—Animates a double value using splined interpolation. This key frame makes use of a `KeySpline`. (To understand better how this works, review the term Bezier curve at http://en.wikipedia.org/.) Essentially, it has a starting point (always 0), an ending point (always 1), and two control points. You set the two control points using the `KeySpline`. The result is a curve that represents the rate of change for the animation.

The following example shows a storyboard that targets and animates two separate properties of an image of a mage simultaneously. It uses the `LinearDoubleKeyFrame` animation to specify where to position the mage at specific time intervals. The mage travels in a square pattern over the specified timeline. Also, the example sets the storyboard's `RepeatBehavior` to `Forever` so that it repeats non-stop. Figure 7.5 shows the results.

Here's the XAML:

```
<Canvas.Resources>
    <Storyboard RepeatBehavior="Forever" x:Name="MageSB">
        <DoubleAnimationUsingKeyFrames
            Storyboard.TargetName="MyMage"
            Storyboard.TargetProperty="(Canvas.Left)">
            <LinearDoubleKeyFrame KeyTime="00:00:02" Value="100"/>
            <LinearDoubleKeyFrame KeyTime="00:00:04" Value="200"/>
            <LinearDoubleKeyFrame KeyTime="00:00:08" Value="200"/>
```

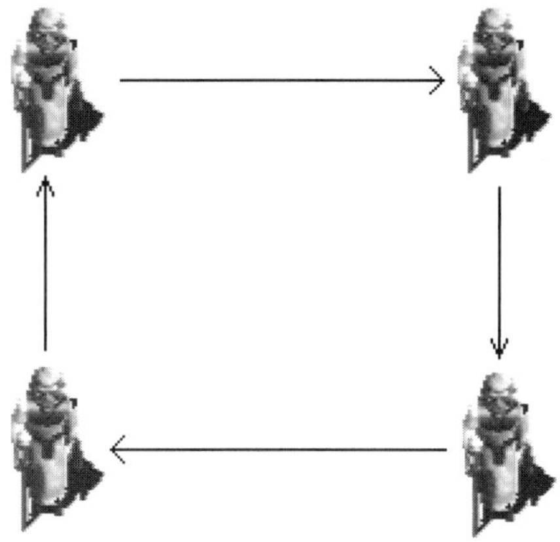

Figure 7.5
Key-Frame Animations

```
            <LinearDoubleKeyFrame KeyTime="00:00:10" Value="100"/>
            <LinearDoubleKeyFrame KeyTime="00:00:12" Value="0"/>
        </DoubleAnimationUsingKeyFrames>

        <DoubleAnimationUsingKeyFrames
            Storyboard.TargetName="MyMage"
            Storyboard.TargetProperty="(Canvas.Top)">
            <LinearDoubleKeyFrame KeyTime="00:00:04" Value="0"/>
            <LinearDoubleKeyFrame KeyTime="00:00:06" Value="100"/>
            <LinearDoubleKeyFrame KeyTime="00:00:08" Value="200"/>
            <LinearDoubleKeyFrame KeyTime="00:00:12" Value="200"/>
            <LinearDoubleKeyFrame KeyTime="00:00:14" Value="100"/>
            <LinearDoubleKeyFrame KeyTime="00:00:16" Value="0"/>
        </DoubleAnimationUsingKeyFrames>
    </Storyboard>
</Canvas.Resources>

<Image Source="Mage.png" ImageOpened="MyMage_ImageOpened"
                                    x:Name="MyMage"></Image>
```

Here's the code-behind:

```
private void MyMage_ImageOpened(object sender, RoutedEventArgs e)
{
    MageSB.Begin();
}
```

CompositionTarget.Rendering

This timer gets fired once before each frame of your application is rendered in the browser. Because of this, this timer stays in sync with your current frame rate. Once layout is computed, the event gets fired right before the objects in your Silverlight composition tree are rendered. If you modify layout within this event, layout will once again be computed before rendering.

This is a great timer to use with custom rendering and animation. It's the timer used here for MainGameLoop. To set up a MainGameLoop with this timer, you essentially do the following:

```
CompositionTarget.Rendering += new EventHandler(MainGameLoop);
void MainGameLoop(object sender, EventArgs e)
{
    // Perform your game updates/animations here.
}
```

When you are done using this event, make certain to unregister it in order to unload it. This event will continue to fire even if the object is no longer in the visual tree. Also, you should keep this event firing only when you have work going on in it; otherwise, you are wasting valuable CPU resources. To unregister the event, simply make this call:

```
CompositionTarget.Rendering -= new EventHandler(MainGameLoop);
```

Frame-Based Animation

In 2D games where 3D models are not an option, frame-based animation is the way to go. This essentially involves flipping through pre-rendered frames of an image to create the illusion that the object is moving. For example, to animate a dragon flying west, you could load the image shown in Figure 7.6.

To animate this image, you flip through one sub-image at a time over a given timeline. Because Silverlight does not provide an easy way to extract sub-images from images, the best way to animate the frames is using clipping. Silverlight provides a property called Clip that can be set to any object. When Clip is set, Silverlight will only render pixels that are contained within the confines of the clip region. A clip region can be an ellipse, rectangle, line, or path. To animate through each frame, you simply need to move the part of the image you want visible to the clip region to encapsulate only the frame you want rendered at the time.

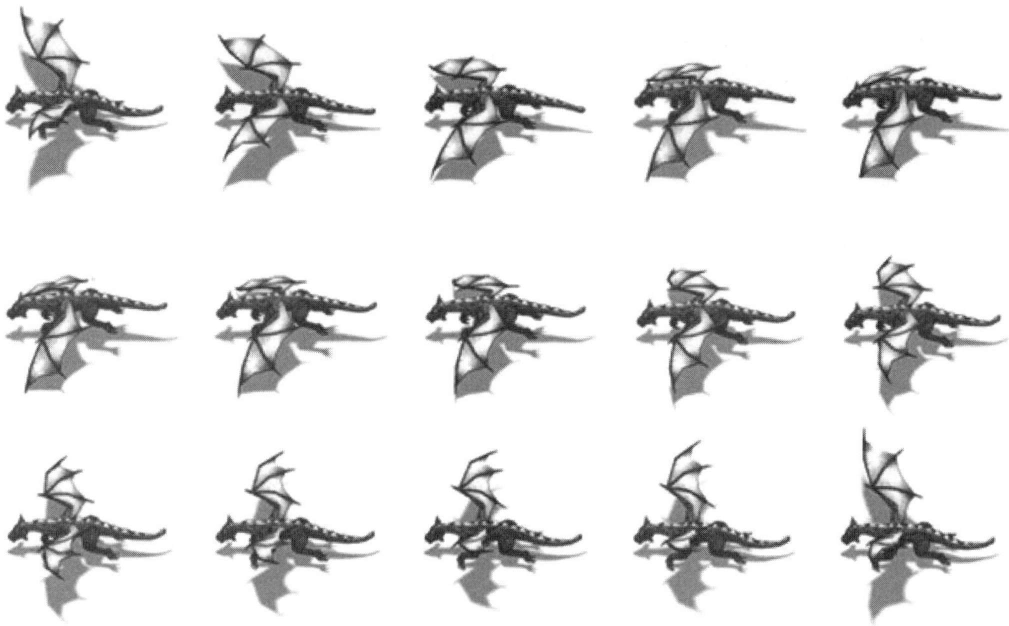

Figure 7.6
Frame-Based Animation

For example, Figure 7.7 shows an image of a temple before it's clipped.

Applying the following clip to the image will result in Figure 7.8. The `Rect` being specified takes the first two paired values to be the left and top coordinates and the second two paired values to be the width and height of the clip region.

```
<Image Source="temple.png">
    <Image.Clip>
        <RectangleGeometry Rect="0,0,128,128" ></RectangleGeometry>
    </Image.Clip>
</Image>
```

An ellipse clip, as shown in the following code, would result in Figure 7.9.

```
<Image Source="temple.png">
    <Image.Clip>
        <EllipseGeometry RadiusX="75" RadiusY="75" Center="122,122">
</EllipseGeometry>
    </Image.Clip>
</Image>
```

Figure 7.7
Temple Without Clipping

Figure 7.8
Rectangle Clip

Figure 7.9
Ellipse Clip

To demonstrate this process, let's walk through how you animate creatures for your game. Creature animation can be the most daunting and complex process in the game. For most games, you will want to render the creature in all eight directions: north, northeast, east, southeast, south, southwest, west, and northwest. You will also want your creatures to have a variety of actions including but not limited to walking, flying, attacking, hitting, dying, idling, and running. That's a total of seven actions times eight directions, for a total of 56 images needed to support a single creature!

To handle this process, a class called `ObjectFrames` that resides in the file ObjectCreature.cs was created. This object contains all the frames for a given action.

```
public class ObjectFrames
{
    public Image[] DirectionFrames;
    public int FramesPerRow = 0;
    public int FrameCount = 0;
}
```

This class also tracks the number of frames in a given row and the total frame count. For example, Figure 7.10 has `FramesPerRow=4` and `FrameCount=8`.

In the `ObjectCreature` class, the program declares separate `ObjectFrames` objects for each of the possible action types.

Figure 7.10
Single Direction

```
public ObjectFrames WalkingFrames = new ObjectFrames();
public ObjectFrames FlyingFrames = new ObjectFrames();
public ObjectFrames AttackingFrames = new ObjectFrames();
public ObjectFrames HitFrames = new ObjectFrames();
public ObjectFrames DyingFrames = new ObjectFrames();
public ObjectFrames IdlingFrames = new ObjectFrames();
public ObjectFrames RunningFrames = new ObjectFrames();
```

To determine which animation is currently the active animation for the creature, this example uses an object to track it as well as the current frame, current direction, and current animation type.

```
private ObjectFrames _currentObjectFrames;
private int _currentFrameIndex = 0;
private Enums.Direction _currentDirection = Enums.Direction.South;
private Enums.AnimationType _currentAnimation = Enums.AnimationType.Walk;
```

`Enums.Direction` is an `enum` that represents each possible direction:

```
public enum Direction
{
    North = 0,
    NE = 1,
    East = 2,
    SE = 3,
    South = 4,
    SW = 5,
    West = 6,
    NW = 7,
    End=8,
};
```

`Enums.AnimationType` is an `enum` that represents all the possible animation types:

```
public enum AnimationType
{
    Unknown=-1,
    Walk=0,
    Fly=1,
    Attack=2,
    Hit=3,
    Death=4,
    Idle=5,
    Run=6,
    End=7,
}
```

You will want some animations such as Idling to be repeated non-stop. For this purpose, you can add a variable to track if the animation should be repeated.

```
private bool _repeatAnimation = false;
```

Each creature has its own living "heartbeat." This HeartBeat is essentially a DispatcherTimer that gets fired once every 1/10 of a second. On the client side, you can use this HeartBeat to update the creature's animation frames.

```
public CreatureObject(double x, double y, int baseObjID)
    : base(x, y, baseObjID)
{
    _timer.Interval = new TimeSpan(0, 0, 0, 0, 100);
    _timer.Tick += new EventHandler(HeartBeat);
}
void HeartBeat(object sender, EventArgs e)
{
    UpdateAnimationFrame();
}
```

The method UpdateAnimationFrame will take the _currentObjectFrame, determine what row and column the current frame is in, and move the object to be centered in the frame you want to render. Once the frame index is equal to the total frame count, you must stop the timer unless you need to repeat the animation.

```
private void UpdateAnimationFrame()
{
   int row = _currentFrameIndex / _currentObjectFrames.FramesPerRow;
   int column = _currentFrameIndex - (row * _currentObjectFrames.FramesPerRow);

   _currentObjectFrames.DirectionFrames[(int)_currentDirection].
   SetValue(Canvas.LeftProperty, (double)-(column*this.Width));

   _currentObjectFrames.DirectionFrames[(int)_currentDirection].
   SetValue(Canvas.TopProperty, (double)-(row*this.Height));
       if (++_currentFrameIndex == _currentObjectFrames.FrameCount)
        {
        if (true == _repeatAnimation)
            _currentFrameIndex = 0;
        else
            _timer.Stop();
    }
}
```

Finally, to set which animation you want, you just call the method `Animate()` and specify the direction, type, and whether you want the animation to be repeated. The `ObjectCanvas` is the map canvas where all objects are placed. You will need to remove from the canvas any previously used frame before adding a new one.

```
public void Animate(Enums.Direction direction,
    Enums.AnimationType animationType, bool repeatAnimation)
{
    _timer.Stop();

    if (null != _currentObjectFrames && null !=
              _currentObjectFrames.DirectionFrames)
    {
        Image currentImage =
            _currentObjectFrames.DirectionFrames[(int)_currentDirection];
        if (currentImage != null)
        {
            if (ObjectCanvas.Children.Contains(currentImage))
                ObjectCanvas.Children.Remove(currentImage);
        }
    }

    _currentObjectFrames = null;
    _currentFrameIndex = 0;
    _currentDirection = direction;
    _currentAnimation = animationType;

    switch (_currentAnimation)
    {
        case Enums.AnimationType.Walk:
            _currentObjectFrames = WalkingFrames;
            break;
        case Enums.AnimationType.Fly:
            _currentObjectFrames = FlyingFrames;
            break;
        case Enums.AnimationType.Attack:
            _currentObjectFrames = AttackingFrames;
            break;
        case Enums.AnimationType.Hit:
            _currentObjectFrames = HitFrames;
            break;
        case Enums.AnimationType.Death:
```

```
                _currentObjectFrames = DyingFrames;
                break;
            case Enums.AnimationType.Idle:
                _currentObjectFrames = IdlingFrames;
                break;
            case Enums.AnimationType.Run:
                _currentObjectFrames = RunningFrames;
                break;
        }
        if (null != _currentObjectFrames && null != _currentObjectFrames.DirectionFrames)
        {
            if (null != _currentObjectFrames.DirectionFrames[(int)_currentDirection])
            {
                _repeatAnimation = repeatAnimation;
                _currentFrameIndex = 0;

                ObjectCanvas.Children.Add(_currentObjectFrames.DirectionFrames
                                          [(int)_currentDirection]);
                _timer.Start();
            }
        }
    }
```

Performance Tips

To conclude, this chapter covers ways you can improve application performance. Monitoring your application's performance is extremely important, especially when it comes to games. No one wants to play a game that is slow or visually lagging. Silverlight supports a few features to help you track and improve your application's performance.

FPS

Frames per second (FPS) shows you how many frames your browser is rendering every second. This will give you a good indication of the overall performance of your application. Obviously, the higher the value, the better. To track this data, the Silverlight control in your website has a property called `EnableFrameRateCounter` that will show the frames-per-second counter in your browser's status bar. (In some browsers, this may need to be enabled in the browser's settings.) By default, the max frame rate is 60, which typically yields the best results. However, you can change this by setting an additional property called `MaxFrameRate`.

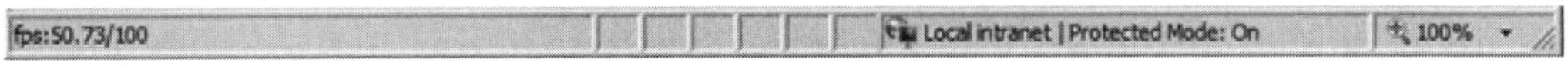

Figure 7.11
Enabling FPS

For example, the following would result in Figure 7.11:

```
<asp:Silverlight EnableFrameRateCounter="true" MaxFrameRate="100"...>
```

EnableRedrawRegions

`EnableRedrawRegions` is available to help you see what is being redrawn each frame. It uses color rectangles to highlight the regions that are redrawn. This is a great setting to use if you want to further investigate performance bottlenecks.

There is a profiling tool called *Xperf* that you can use to analyze the performance of your Silverlight application. For example, you can track CPU and disk usage over time. This tool can be installed from http://msdn.microsoft.com/en-us/library/cc305187.aspx.

Image Size

Make certain to display your media and images at the original size and avoid resizing them while rendering. This will save on bandwidth and interpolation of every pixel each frame. Also, running Silverlight with `Windowless = false` is faster than `Windowless=true`. Because running in `Windowless` mode is computationally expensive, set it to `true` only if you need to overlay HTML content on top of your Silverlight application.

Hardware Acceleration

With Silverlight 3 came the option to enable hardware acceleration. This is a huge win for media-intensive applications such as games. This is accomplished through what is called GPU (Graphics Processing Unit) acceleration. The GPU is a processor on your graphics card that is primarily used for calculating floating-point operations. It contains a number of graphic primitives that can greatly save CPU time.

By default, this option is disabled, and it must be enabled at both the plug-in level and the individual control level. To enable it on your Silverlight plug-in, you will simply need to set `EnableGPUAcceleration` to `true`. For ASPX pages, this is done via this attribute:

```
<asp:Silverlight ID="Silverlight1" EnableGPUAcceleration="true"
                 runat="server" Source="~/MyApp.xap"
                 MinimumVersion="3.0.40307.0" Width="100%"
                 Height="100%" />
```

For HTML, you will need to add the following `param` to the `<object>` tag:

```
<param name="EnableGPUAcceleration" value="true" />
```

Next, you must enable it on each control you want GPU acceleration applied to (see Figure 7.12). This is done by setting `CacheMode="BitmapCache"`. Here's an example of enabling it on an `Image` control:

```
<TextBlock CacheMode="BitmapCache" Text="Hello There"></TextBlock>
```

`BitmapCache` is currently the only type of GPU acceleration that Silverlight provides. Behind the scenes, Silverlight takes the control and all its children elements and it caches them as bitmaps once they have been rendered. Once these controls are cached, your application can just display them, which allows it to bypass the expensive rendering phase.

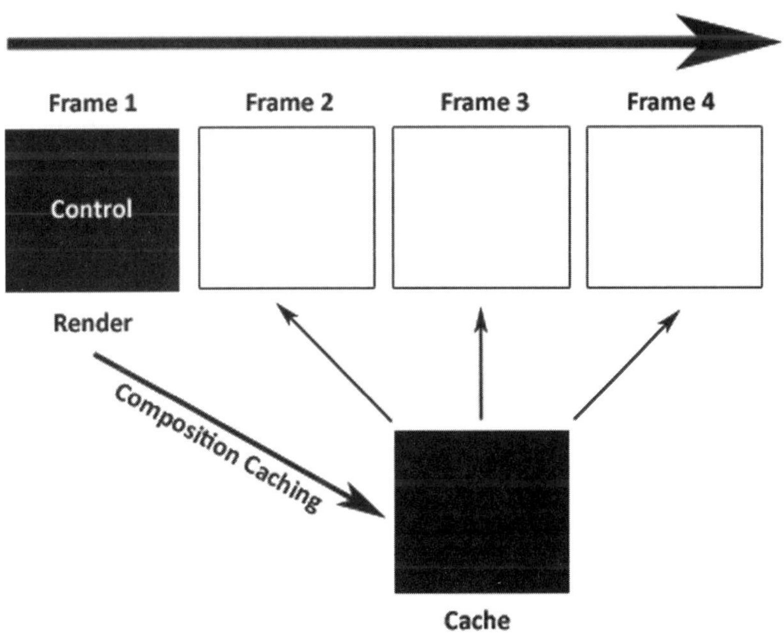

Figure 7.12
GPU Acceleration

So when should you use this feature? This feature is best suited for expensive scenarios such as transformations (translating, rotating, stretching, and so on), as well as for clipping and blending. You will need to make certain not to misuse this feature; otherwise, it can have the reverse effect and actually hurt your performance. You're best off reducing the total number of rendering surfaces you have in your application.

If you want to see what is being cached when you run your application, you can accomplish this by adding the attribute `EnableCacheVisualization` to your Silverlight control. For example:

```
<asp:Silverlight EnableCacheVisualization="true" ID="Silverlight1"
    EnableGPUAcceleration="true" runat="server"
    Source="~/ClientBin/MyAPp.xap" MinimumVersion="3.0.40307.0"
    Width="100%" Height="100%" />
```

This will cause uncached controls to appear tinted. Everything untinted is cached.

For the Mac platform, this feature is currently supported only in full-screen mode. For Windows, it is supported in both full-screen and non-full screen modes.

Summary

This chapter discussed the various timers available for you to perform animation in your game. These timers included the `DispatcherTimer`, the `Storyboard` timer, and the `CompositionTarget.Rendering` event. It also showed you how to use these timers to animate a creature in your game. Finally, this chapter concluded with performance tips that will help you optimize your game for speed. The next chapter discusses how to create a UI for your game.

CHAPTER 8

The Client UI

This chapter explores the ways to create the UI for your game. It covers grid controls as well as custom buttons and dialog boxes used to create the UI for the client application. It concludes with styles and skins that can give your controls a common theme.

Using `Grid` Controls

Grids are an important part of any UI because they allow you to accurately set the position and layout of the controls in your UI. Similar to tables, grids are broken up into *x* number of rows and columns. The following is an example of how to declare a `Grid` control that has two rows and two columns, with each cell having a width and height of 100 pixels.

```
<Grid x:Name="LayoutRoot" Background="Black">
    <Grid.ColumnDefinitions>
        <ColumnDefinition Width="100"/>
        <ColumnDefinition Width="100"/>
    </Grid.ColumnDefinitions>
    <Grid.RowDefinitions>
        <RowDefinition Height="100"/>
        <RowDefinition Height="100"/>
    </Grid.RowDefinitions>
</Grid>
```

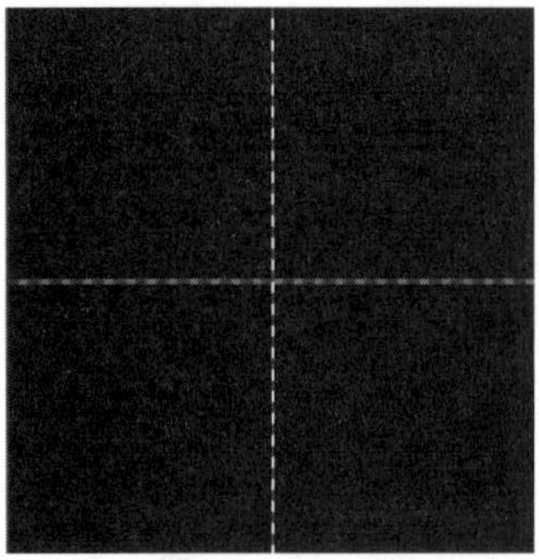

Figure 8.1
Grid Control

The Grid control has a property called ShowGridLines that creates dotted lines around each cell (see Figure 8.1). By setting this to true, you can see how the table lays out. You can use only dotted lines because this property is intended for debugging and testing purposes. If you want actual lines for the cells, you should stylize the elements in the cells to have borders.

To keep rows or columns spaced proportionally, you can set Width="*" or Height="*". Those cells set to * will have the remaining space in the grid row or column distributed evenly among them. If you use stars, make certain to set the grid's width and height so that it knows how much overall space is available for each cell. For example:

```
<Grid x:Name="LayoutRoot" Background="Black" ShowGridLines="True"
        Width="200" Height="200">
<Grid.ColumnDefinitions>
        <ColumnDefinition Width="*"/>
        <ColumnDefinition Width="*"/>
    </Grid.ColumnDefinitions>
    <Grid.RowDefinitions>
        <RowDefinition Height="*"/>
        <RowDefinition Height="*"/>
    </Grid.RowDefinitions>
</Grid>
```

To assign controls to individual cells, you simply have to specify which row and which column you want them to belong to. This is done via the properties Grid.Row and Grid.Column, which are set to zero by default. To put a Button control in each of the four cells declared previously, you would do this:

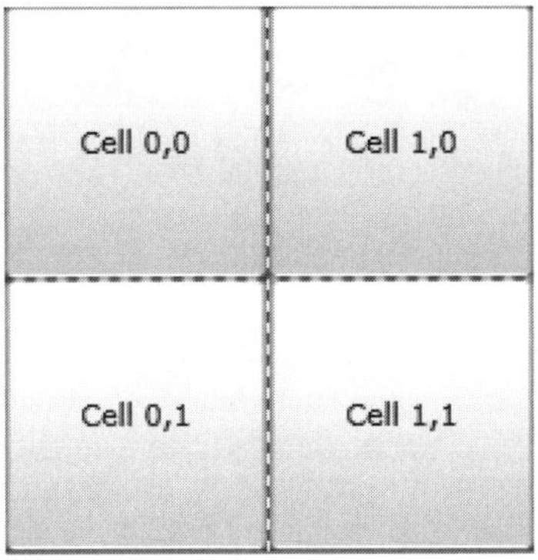

Figure 8.2
Grid Control with Content

```
<Button Content="Cell 0,0"/>
<Button Grid.Column="1" Content="Cell 1,0"/>
<Button Grid.Row="1" Content="Cell 0,1"/>
<Button Grid.Row="1" Grid.Column="1" Content="Cell 1,1"/>
```

The result is what you see in Figure 8.2.

By default, controls contained within grid cells are scaled and stretched to fit the entire region of the cells. You can prevent this stretching by hard-coding the width and height value. Also, for image controls, you can set `Stretch=None` to prevent the image from taking up the entire cell.

```
<Button Width="60" Height="30" Content="Cell 0,0"/>
<Button Width="60" Height="30" Grid.Column="1" Content="Cell 1,0"/>
<Button Width="60" Height="30" Grid.Row="1" Content="Cell 0,1"/>
<Button Width="60" Height="30" Grid.Row="1" Grid.Column="1" Content="Cell 1,1"/>
```

This code results in what you see in Figure 8.3.

You will notice in Figure 8.3 that the controls are vertically and horizontally aligned to the center. This can be modified by setting the properties `VerticalAlignment` and `HorizontalAlignment`. Options include `Left`, `Right`, `Top`, `Bottom`, `Center`, and `Stretch`. For example:

```
<Button VerticalAlignment="Bottom" Width="60" Height="30" Content="Cell 0,0"/>
<Button HorizontalAlignment="Right" Width="60" Height="30" Grid.Column="1"
        Content="Cell 1,0"/>
<Button VerticalAlignment="Top"  Width="60" Height="30" Grid.Row="1"
        Content="Cell 0,1"/>
<Button HorizontalAlignment="Left" Width="60" Height="30" Grid.Row="1"
        Grid.Column="1" Content="Cell 1,1"/>
```

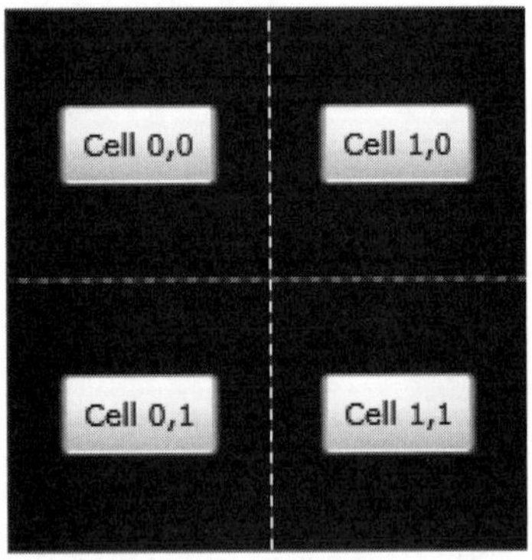

Figure 8.3
Sizing Controls in a Grid

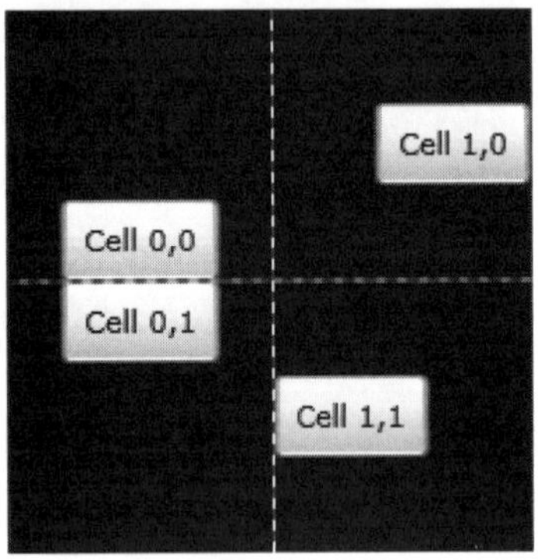

Figure 8.4
Grid Alignment

This code will result in Figure 8.4.

You can nest `Grid` controls within `Grid` controls, similarly to how you can have tables within tables. To illustrate this, the next example breaks up cell (1,1) into four new cells. To do this, you must simply specify which parent grid row and column the child grid belongs to.

```
<Grid x:Name="LayoutRoot" Background="Black" ShowGridLines="True">
    <Grid.ColumnDefinitions>
        <ColumnDefinition Width="100"/>
        <ColumnDefinition Width="100"/>
    </Grid.ColumnDefinitions>
    <Grid.RowDefinitions>
        <RowDefinition Height="100"/>
        <RowDefinition Height="100"/>
    </Grid.RowDefinitions>
```

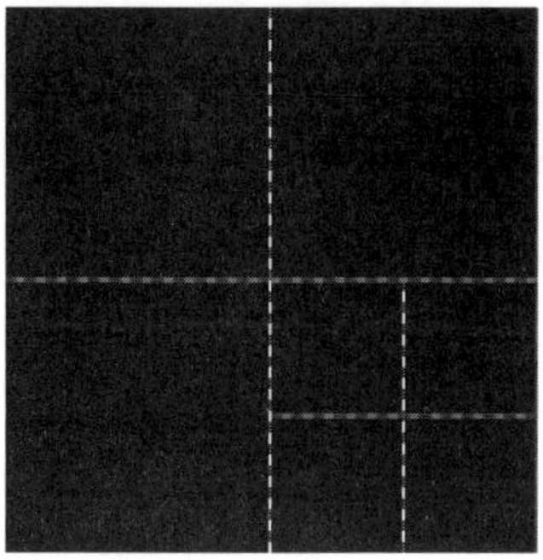

Figure 8.5
Nested Grids

```
    <Grid Grid.Row="1" Grid.Column="1" ShowGridLines="True">
        <Grid.ColumnDefinitions>
            <ColumnDefinition Width="50"/>
            <ColumnDefinition Width="50"/>
        </Grid.ColumnDefinitions>
        <Grid.RowDefinitions>
            <RowDefinition Height="50"/>
            <RowDefinition Height="50"/>
        </Grid.RowDefinitions>
    </Grid>
</Grid>
```

The result can be seen in Figure 8.5.

Creating Buttons

Buttons are used extensively in almost any kind of game. They can be used to activate spells, open dialog boxes, or for whatever other purpose you can imagine. Because there are so many possibilities for buttons, I have created a generic Silverlight user control that can represent most any type of button. This control does not contain an actual Silverlight button control but rather contains an image that represents the button as well as a rectangle that is used to place a fading highlight effect over the button when it is clicked.

The following code shows the XAML that represents each button object:

```
<UserControl x:Class="Client.ButtonBase"
    xmlns="http://schemas.microsoft.com/winfx/2006/xaml/presentation"
    xmlns:x="http://schemas.microsoft.com/winfx/2006/xaml" >
```

```
    <Canvas x:Name="ButtonObject" MouseLeftButtonDown=
                                   "Canvas_MouseLeftButtonDown"
        MouseMove="Object_MouseMove" MouseLeftButtonUp=
                                       "Object_MouseLeftButtonUp" >
        <Image x:Name="ButtonImage" Source="Images/Spells/Fireball.png"
        ImageOpened="Image_ImageOpened"></Image>
        <Rectangle x:Name="ClickRect" Width="50" Height="50" Fill="Green"
        Visibility="Collapsed" Opacity="0.5">
        </Rectangle>
    </Canvas>
</UserControl>
```

You will notice that the previous XAML tracks the mouse button down, up, and move events for the object. The down event is obvious since you will want to know when the button is being clicked. However, in the case where you want to enable drag/drop so users can re-position the buttons in your game, you also need to track the mouse up and mouse move events. A public property called `EnableDragDrop` can be set to enable or disable drag/drop for the button.

Check for `Shift+MouseLeftButtonDown` to start the drag/drop process. This is done by checking the `Keyboard.Modifiers` like so:

```
ModifierKeys keys = Keyboard.Modifiers;
bool shiftKey = (keys & ModifierKeys.Shift) != 0;

if (true == shiftKey)
{
    // Process drag/drop
}
```

It's important when tracking a drag/drop that you first call `CaptureMouse()` for the control. This way, if the mouse gets outside of the bounds of the control, you will still be able to track the mouse movement. When drag/drop is released, you will want to call `ReleaseMouseCapture()`.

The following is the code-behind for this button control:

```
public partial class ButtonBase : UserControl
{
    private DispatcherTimer _selectionTimer;
    private OnButtonClicked OnClicked = null;
    private bool _dragDropping = false;
    private double _dragDropOffsetX = 0;
    private double _dragDropOffsetY = 0;
```

```
private double _imageWidth;
private double _imageHeight;
private int _buttonID;

public bool EnableDragDrop = true;

public ButtonBase()
{
    InitializeComponent();

    _selectionTimer = new DispatcherTimer();
    _selectionTimer.Interval = new TimeSpan(0, 0, 0, 0, 50);
    _selectionTimer.Tick += new EventHandler(timer_Tick);
}

public void SetCallback(OnButtonClicked onClicked, int buttonID)
{
    OnClicked = onClicked;
    _buttonID = buttonID;
}

private void timer_Tick(object sender, EventArgs e)
{
    ClickRect.Opacity -= 0.1;
    if (ClickRect.Opacity <= 0)
    {
        ClickRect.Visibility = Visibility.Collapsed;
        _selectionTimer.Stop();
    }
}

public Color FillColor
{
    set
    {
        ClickRect.Fill = new SolidColorBrush(value);
    }
}

public void MoveTo(double x, double y)
{
    this.SetValue(Canvas.LeftProperty, x);
```

```
        this.SetValue(Canvas.TopProperty, y);
    }

    public void SetImage(string resource)
    {
        Uri uri = new Uri(resource, UriKind.Relative);
        BitmapImage bi = new System.Windows.Media.Imaging.BitmapImage(uri);
        ButtonImage.Source = bi;
    }

    private void Canvas_MouseLeftButtonDown(object sender, MouseButtonEventArgs e)
    {
        ModifierKeys keys = Keyboard.Modifiers;
        bool controlKey = (keys & ModifierKeys.Control) != 0;

        if (true == controlKey)
        {
            if (true == EnableDragDrop)
            {
           ButtonObject.CaptureMouse();
           _dragDropOffsetX = e.GetPosition(ButtonImage).X;
           _dragDropOffsetY = e.GetPosition(ButtonImage).Y;
           _dragDropping = true;

}
        }
        else
        {
            Click();
        }
    }

    private void Object_MouseLeftButtonUp(object sender, MouseButtonEventArgs e)
    {
        _dragDropping = false;
        ButtonObject.ReleaseMouseCapture();
    }

    private void Object_MouseMove(object sender, MouseEventArgs e)
    {
        if (true == _dragDropping)
        {
```

```
            double x = e.GetPosition(null).X - _dragDropOffsetX;
            double y = e.GetPosition(null).Y - _dragDropOffsetY;

            if (x < 0) x = 0;
            if (y < 0) y = 0;

            if (x > Consts.AppWidth - _imageWidth)
                x = Consts.AppWidth - _imageWidth;
            if (y > Consts.AppHeight - _imageHeight)
                y = Consts.AppHeight - _imageHeight;

            MoveTo(x, y);

        }
    }

    private void Click()
    {
        ClickRect.Opacity = 0.5;
        ClickRect.Visibility = Visibility.Visible;
        _selectionTimer.Start();
        if (null != OnClicked)
            OnClicked(_buttonID);
    }

    private void Image_ImageOpened(object sender, RoutedEventArgs e)
    {
        ClickRect.Width = ButtonImage.ActualWidth;
        ClickRect.Height = ButtonImage.ActualHeight;

        _imageWidth = ButtonImage.ActualWidth;
        _imageHeight = ButtonImage.ActualHeight;
    }
}
```

In the previous code you will notice a few things:

- The button needs to be aware of the game's window size so that its position during drag/drop is constrained to the borders of the application. In addition, the button needs to know its own width and height so it can determine how far to the right and bottom of the screen it can go without being pushed off the edge of the screen.

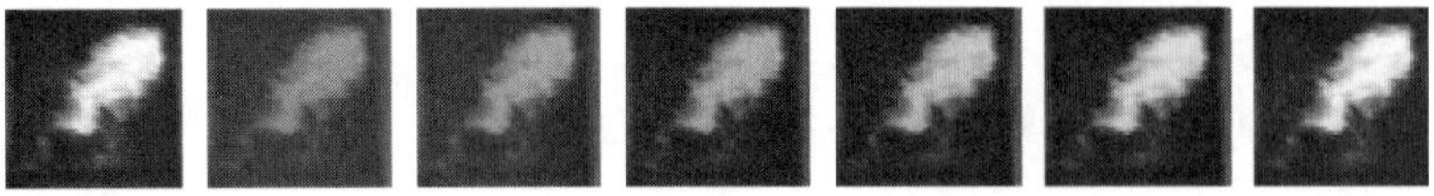

Figure 8.6
Button-Click Animation

- When you click the button, it kicks off a timer that will start by showing the highlight over the button. Every 50 milliseconds, it will reduce the opacity until it is less than zero. At this time, the timer is stopped. Figure 8.6 shows the transitions as they occur for each frame.
- A public property called `FillColor` allows you to change the highlight color you want over your button when it's clicked.
- You can change the image of the button by calling `SetImage()` and passing the resource filename.
- When positioning the button outside of the drag/drop operation, make certain to call `MoveTo()` so that both the image and the highlighting rectangle are moved.

Finally, you must call `SetCallback()` with the callback function and a unique identifier. When the button is clicked, the callback function is called with the ID passed as its parameter. To create a callback function, you simply need to declare a `delegate` function.

```
public delegate void OnButtonClicked(int ID);
```

The following is an example of how to create the button and how to process the event when clicked:

```
ButtonBase fireballSpell = new ButtonBase();
fireballSpell.SetImage("images/spells/fireball.png");
fireballSpell.EnableDragDrop = true;
fireballSpell.MoveTo(100,100);
fireballSpell.SetCallback(new OnButtonClicked(OnButtonClicked),
                          Consts.FireballSpell);
LayoutRoot.Children.Add(fireballSpell);

protected internal void OnButtonClicked(int buttonID)
{
    switch (buttonID)
```

```
    {
        case Consts.FireballSpell:
            CastFireball();
            break;
    }
}
```

Creating Dialog Boxes

Dialog boxes are used for a wide variety of purposes such as obtaining information from the user, displaying data, and more. This section shows you how to create a base dialog control that you can expand upon to create customized dialog boxes.

There are two different types of dialog boxes:

- **Modal**—A dialog box that forces users to interact with it and close it before they can access the parent application.
- **Modeless**—A free-floating dialog box that can stack with other modeless dialogs.

In order to make a dialog box modal, this example creates a transparent (non-visible) rectangle that takes up the entire background of your application. This prevents users from clicking on anything except the dialog box. By default, the dialog box is set to `Modal`, but you can change it to `Modeless` by calling `SetMode()`.

The following XAML represents the common base dialog box control.

```
<UserControl x:Class="Client.DlgCommon"
    xmlns="http://schemas.microsoft.com/winfx/2006/xaml/presentation"
    xmlns:x="http://schemas.microsoft.com/winfx/2006/xaml">

    <Canvas>
        <Rectangle x:Name="BkgCover" HorizontalAlignment="Stretch" Width="5000"
              Height="5000" VerticalAlignment="Stretch" Fill="White" Opacity="0"/>

        <Canvas x:Name="DlgWindow" Width="250" Height="250">
            <Grid>
                <Grid.ColumnDefinitions>
                    <ColumnDefinition Width="225"/>
                    <ColumnDefinition Width="25"/>
                </Grid.ColumnDefinitions>
```

```
<Grid.RowDefinitions>
    <RowDefinition Height="25"/>
    <RowDefinition Height="2"/>
    <RowDefinition Height="190"/>
    <RowDefinition Height="2"/>
    <RowDefinition Height="25"/>
</Grid.RowDefinitions>

<Border Grid.RowSpan="5" Grid.ColumnSpan="3" CornerRadius="5"
    BorderBrush="Black" BorderThickness="1" >
    <Border.Background>
        <LinearGradientBrush StartPoint="0,0.5" EndPoint="1,0.5">
            <GradientStop Color="#E1E1E1" Offset="0">
            </GradientStop>
            <GradientStop Color="#EFEFEF" Offset="1">
            </GradientStop>
        </LinearGradientBrush>
    </Border.Background>
</Border>

<Border x:Name="TitleBar" Margin="3" Grid.Row="0"
         Grid.ColumnSpan="2"  MouseMove="TitleBar_MouseMove"
         MouseLeftButtonUp="TitleBar_MouseLeftButtonUp"
         MouseLeftButtonDown="TitleBar_MouseLeftButtonDown">
    <Border.Background>
        <LinearGradientBrush StartPoint="0,0.5" EndPoint="1,0.5">
            <GradientStop Color="Black" Offset="0"></GradientStop>
            <GradientStop Color="DarkGray" Offset="1">
            </GradientStop>
        </LinearGradientBrush>
    </Border.Background>

</Border>

<Image x:Name="CloseHighlight" Stretch="None" Grid.Column="1"
              Source="images/close.png"/>

<Rectangle Grid.Row="1" Grid.ColumnSpan="2" Fill="#6000"
                    Canvas.Top="26" />
<Rectangle Grid.Row="1" Grid.ColumnSpan="2" Fill="#3FFF"
                    Canvas.Top="27" />
```

```
                <TextBlock Text="Title" Foreground="White" Margin="5"
                                       IsHitTestVisible="False"
                                       x:Name="TitleText" Grid.Column="0" />

                <StackPanel Grid.Row="3" Grid.ColumnSpan="2" Orientation
                                       ="Vertical" >
                    <Rectangle Height="1" Fill="#6000" />
                    <Rectangle Height="1" Fill="#3FFF" />
                </StackPanel>

                <StackPanel  Grid.Row="4" Orientation="Horizontal" >
                    <Button Margin="4,0,0,4" Click="Button_Click_OK"
                         Width="60" Height="20"  Content="OK"/>
                    <Button Margin="4,0,0,4" Click="Button_Click_Cancel"
                        Width="60" Height="20"  Content="CANCEL"/>
                </StackPanel>
            </Grid>
        </Canvas>
    </Canvas>
</UserControl>
```

Essentially, what you are looking at is (in order of the controls as they appear in the XAML):

- A rectangle, named `BkgCover`, that prevents users from clicking on anything behind the dialog box if you are in `Modal` mode. In `Modeless` mode, the visibility of this rectangle is set to `Collapsed`.
- A `Border` control that represents the gray gradient background of the dialog box. Notice that `CornerRadius` is set to 5. This gives the dialog box's edges a slight curve.
- A `Border` control, named `TitleBar`, that represents the title bar of the dialog box. This control monitors for mouse clicks so that you can drag/drop the control around your application in a similar way to how I did the `Button` base control.
- An `Image` control that represents the Close button in the upper-right corner of the dialog box.
- A horizontal line created by combining two rectangles that are one pixel high.

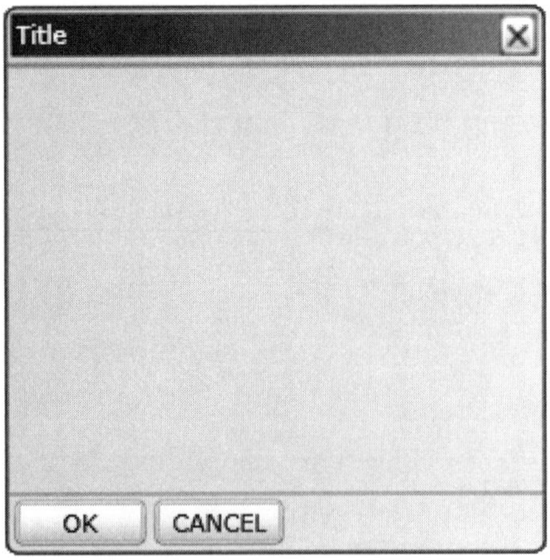

Figure 8.7
Common Base Dialog Box

- A text box used to store the title of the dialog box.
- A `Rectangle` control that places a highlight over the Close button when the mouse hovers over it.
- Two buttons for OK and Cancel.

All these controls are laid out in a grid. A screenshot representation of this dialog box is seen in Figure 8.7.

The following code represents the code-behind for the dialog box:

```
public partial class DlgCommon : UserControl
{
    private bool _dragDropping = false;
    private double _dragDropOffsetX = 0;
    private double _dragDropOffsetY = 0;
    private OnDialogButtonClicked _onClicked = null;
    public bool EnableDragDrop = true;
    private DialogResult _dialogResult = DialogResult.OK;

    public DlgCommon(string title)
    {
        InitializeComponent();

        SetTitle(title);
        this.KeyDown += new KeyEventHandler(DlgBase_KeyDown);
    }
```

```
void DlgBase_KeyDown(object sender, KeyEventArgs e)
{
    if (e.Key == Key.Escape && null != _onClicked)
        _onClicked(DialogResult.Cancel);
}

public void SetCallback(OnDialogButtonClicked onClicked)
{
    _onClicked = onClicked;
}

public void SetMode(DialogType type)
{
    if (type == DialogType.Modal)
        BkgCover.Visibility = Visibility.Collapsed;
    else
        BkgCover.Visibility = Visibility.Visible;
}

public void SetTitle(string text)
{
    TitleText.Text = text;
}

private void TitleBar_MouseLeftButtonDown(object sender,
    MouseButtonEventArgs e)
{
    _dragDropOffsetX = e.GetPosition(DlgWindow).X;
    _dragDropOffsetY = e.GetPosition(DlgWindow).Y;

    _dragDropping = true;
    TitleBar.CaptureMouse();
    this.Opacity = 0.75;
}

private void TitleBar_MouseMove(object sender, MouseEventArgs e)
{
    if (true == _dragDropping)
    {
        double x = e.GetPosition(null).X - _dragDropOffsetX;
        double y = e.GetPosition(null).Y - _dragDropOffsetY;
```

```
            if (x < 0) x = 0;
            if (y < 0) y = 0;

            if (x > Consts.AppWidth - this.Width)
                x = Consts.AppWidth - this.Width;
            if (y > Consts.AppHeight - this.Height)
                y = Consts.AppHeight - this.Height;

            DlgWindow.SetValue(Canvas.LeftProperty, x);
            DlgWindow.SetValue(Canvas.TopProperty, y);
        }
    }

    private void TitleBar_MouseLeftButtonUp(object sender,
      MouseButtonEventArgs e)
    {
        _dragDropping = false;
        TitleBar.ReleaseMouseCapture();
        this.Opacity = 1.0;
    }


    private void Button_Click_OK(object sender, RoutedEventArgs e)
    {
        _onClicked(_DialogResult.OK);
    }

    private void Button_Click_Cancel(object sender, RoutedEventArgs e)
    {
        _onClicked(_DialogResult.Cancel);
    }
}
```

There are a few things to note about this code:

- When the dialog box is moving, its opacity is set to 0.5. This allows you to partially see the background elements behind the dialog box as you move it around the screen, giving it a cool visual effect.
- When the OK or Cancel button is clicked, the program returns the `DialogResult` through the `onClicked()` callback. `DialogResult` is an `enum` as follows:

```
public enum DialogResult
{
   OK=1,
   Cancel=2,
}
```

- Dragging and /dropping the dialog box works in the same way as the `ButtonBase` except that you have to grab the title bar of the dialog box to drag/drop it.

Normally, when a dialog box is closed, it just disappears. However, you can add some visually appealing effects through the use of storyboards and animation. For example, to make the dialog box rotate horizontally until it disappears, all you need to do is add the following XAML:

```
<Canvas.Resources>
    <Storyboard x:Name="DialogAnimation"
                        Completed="DialogAnimation_Completed"
        Storyboard.TargetName="CanvasProjection" Storyboard
           .TargetProperty="RotationY">
        <DoubleAnimation From="0" To="-90" Duration="0:0:0.5">
        </DoubleAnimation>
    </Storyboard>
</Canvas.Resources>

<Canvas.Projection>
    <PlaneProjection x:Name="CanvasProjection" RotationY="0">
    </PlaneProjection>
</Canvas.Projection>
```

The previous XAML sets up a storyboard animation that will rotate the dialog box's `PlaneProjection` along its Y axis from 0 to −90. To kick it off, you must call `DialogAnimation.Begin` from the OK or Cancel button event:

```
private DialogResult _dlgResult = DialogResult.OK;

private void Button_Click_OK(object sender, RoutedEventArgs e)
{
     _dlgResult = DialogResult.OK;
    DialogAnimation.Begin();
}
```

```
private void Button_Click_Cancel(object sender, RoutedEventArgs e)
{
    _dlgResult = DialogResult.Cancel;
    DialogAnimation.Begin();
}

private void DialogAnimation_Completed(object sender, EventArgs e)
{
    _onClicked(_dlgResult);
}
```

Figure 8.8 shows the resulting frames that occur when you click the OK or Cancel button.

You can copy, extend, and customize the base dialog box to fit your need for each type of dialog box you will have in your application. For example, to make a password dialog box, all you would need to do is follow these steps:

1. In the Solution Explorer, select DlgBase.xaml. Ctrl click and then drag/drop the control to create a new copy.

2. Rename the copy of DlgBase.xaml to DlgPassword.xaml.

3. Open DlgPassword.xaml.cs. Change the class name from `DlgBase` to `DlgPassword`. When you are typing, you will notice a red triangle under the new name. Hover your mouse over this triangle and click the drop-down button, as shown in Figure 8.9. Choose Rename DlgBase to DlgPassword. This changes all references of DlgBase to DlgPassword, including your XAML and code-behind files.

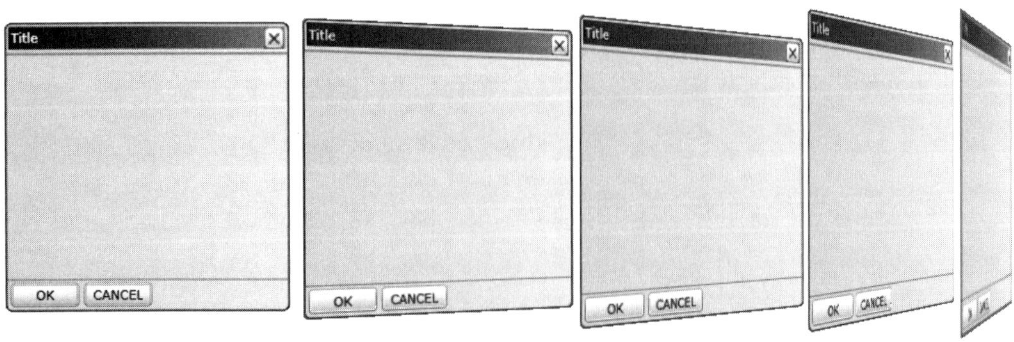

Figure 8.8
Rotation Effect

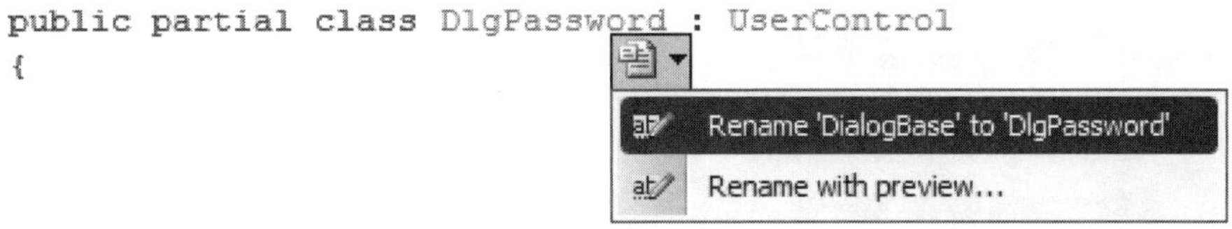

Figure 8.9
Renaming Across Files

4. Now that you have a new dialog box, add the following XAML to your DlgPassword.xaml file:

```
<Grid Grid.Row="2" Grid.ColumnSpan="2">

    <Grid.ColumnDefinitions>
        <ColumnDefinition Width="100"/>
        <ColumnDefinition Width="150"/>
    </Grid.ColumnDefinitions>
    <Grid.RowDefinitions>
        <RowDefinition Height="35"/>
        <RowDefinition Height="35"/>
    </Grid.RowDefinitions>

    <TextBlock Margin="5" Text="Name:"/>
    <TextBlock Margin="5" Grid.Row="1" Text="Password:"/>

    <TextBox Width="140" Height="25" Foreground="White"
             Background="Black" CaretBrush="White"  Grid.Column="1"/>
    <PasswordBox Width="140" Height="25" Grid.Row="1" Grid.Column="1"
             Foreground="White" Background="Black" CaretBrush="White" />

</Grid>
```

The dialog box with this new XAML is shown in Figure 8.10.

A couple things to take note of:

- The background of the text boxes is set to be black. Because of this, you need to change the `CaretBrush` and `Foreground` text to be white so that they can be seen against the black background. The ability to set the `CaretBrush` is a new feature of Silverlight 3.

Figure 8.10
Password Dialog Box

- For the Password text box, use a `PasswordBox` control. This way, the keys are masked by special characters. You can change the character that's displayed by setting the property `PasswordChar`. For example, `PasswordChar="*"`.

Using Styles

Styles allow you to control the look and feel of UI controls across your entire application. They are very useful if you want to apply a common theme or skin to your UI. Each individual control can be associated with a globally declared style. By having your controls set to a style, any change you make to the style will automatically be reflected on all the controls associated with that style.

To demonstrate this idea, the following example creates a separate style for each of the individual controls in the dialog box. The result of applying the styles is the dialog box shown in Figure 8.11.

Global styles are stored in your App.xaml file under the section `<App.Resources>`. When declaring a style, you should give it a name and set the `TargetType` to the type of the control you are declaring the style for. For example, the following style declaration targets a `Border` control.

```
<Application.Resources>
    <Style TargetType="Border" x:Name="DlgBackgroundStyle">
    </Style>
</Application.Resources>
```

Figure 8.11
Skinned Dialog Box

In order to make this style represent the complete new look for the background `Border` control for the dialog boxes, you need to target and set the individual properties. This is done by using a `Setter` for each of the properties. A `Setter` contains a property name and a value. The following code shows you how this is done:

```
<Style TargetType="Border" x:Name="DlgBackgroundStyle">
    <Setter Property="BorderBrush" Value="#4FFF"/>
    <Setter Property="CornerRadius" Value="5"/>
    <Setter Property="Background">
        <Setter.Value>
            <LinearGradientBrush EndPoint="0.5,1" StartPoint="0.5,0">
                <GradientStop Color="#FF202020" Offset="1"/>
                <GradientStop Color="#FF505050" Offset="0"/>
            </LinearGradientBrush>
        </Setter.Value>
    </Setter>
</Style>
```

To have the `Border` control target the style, you simply have to set `Style={StaticResource StyleName}`. For example:

```
<Border Style="{StaticResource DlgBackgroundStyle}"/>
```

This is a lot cleaner and more manageable than setting the individual properties in the control itself.

For any TextBlocks, you can create the following style:

```
<Style TargetType="TextBlock" x:Name="DlgTextBlockStyle">
    <Setter Property="FontFamily" Value="Arial"/>
    <Setter Property="Margin" Value="5"/>
    <Setter Property="Foreground" Value="White"/>
    <Setter Property="FontSize" Value="12"/>
    <Setter Property="IsHitTestVisible" Value="false"/>
</Style>
```

Similar to the Border control, you can now have TextBlocks target the style like this:

```
<TextBlock Style="{StaticResource DlgTextBlockStyle}"/>
```

Summary

This chapter covered the advantages of using the Grid control to lay out your UI elements. Using the Grid control is a much simpler and more manageable approach than hard-coding positions for every UI element. The same principle applies to using styles, which are great for defining the overall look and feel of your individual controls. Also discussed were techniques for capturing the mouse to allow for dragging/dropping controls in your application. Now that you have a UI in place, the next chapter covers how to hook your client application up with a server to make your game multi-player.

Chapter 9

Networking Support: Making It Multi-Player!

Silverlight has built-in support for socket programming using TCP/IP as its protocol. UDP is currently not supported at this stage in Silverlight. This chapter covers code for a sample client/server implementation that will help you begin to make your game multi-player. Everything you need to get your Silverlight clients talking with a server is included.

Policy Server

When a Silverlight client application using a socket connection tries to connect to a server application, it will first attempt to connect to a policy server on the same host in order to download the policy file. If the policy server is not up and running on port 943, the connection to the host server will fail. The policy server is responsible for transmitting the client access policy file (clientaccesspolicy.xml) to all Silverlight client applications. This file tells the client which ports and domains are available for connection on the host. This is needed for security purposes to prevent denial-of-service attacks, DNS rebinding attacks, and reverse tunnel attacks. Having the policy system in place helps to mitigate these types of attacks.

The client access policy file (clientaccesspolicy.xml) looks like this:

```
<?xml version="1.0" encoding="utf-8" ?>
<access-policy>
  <cross-domain-access>
```

```
    <policy>
      <allow-from>
        <domain uri="http://www.silverlightdev.net"/>
      </allow-from>
      <grant-to>
        <socket-resource port="4502-4534" protocol="tcp"/>
      </grant-to>
    </policy>
  </cross-domain-access>
</access-policy>
```

The `allow-from` lists all domains that the client can use to access resources. Because Silverlight supports cross-domain connectivity, your Silverlight application can access resources from locations other than the original host. The example here puts the URI to be the server where the game resides, which makes it more secure.

The `grant-to` element defines all the server resources this policy affects. The example here uses only the `socket` resource.

Figure 9.1 illustrates the connection process.

For simplicity's sake, to demonstrate how the policy server works, this example creates a console application. For a real-life application, you should refactor this code into a Windows service. To create the policy server, follow these steps:

1. In Visual Studio, create a new C# console application and give it a name such as `PolicyServer`.

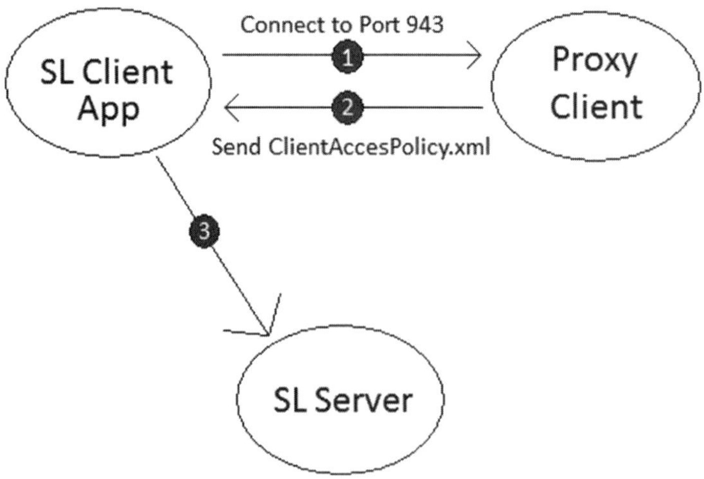

Figure 9.1
Proxy Server

2. Open the file program.cs.
3. Add the following code, but in `main()`, modify the path to point to the location where you have stored clientaccesspolicy.xml:

```
// Encapsulate and manage state for a single connection from a client
   class PolicyConnection
   {
     private Socket _connection;
     private byte[] _buffer; // buffer to receive the request from the client
     private int _received;
     private byte[] _policy; // the policy to return to the client

     // the request that we're expecting from the client
     private static string _policyRequestString = "<policy-file-request/>";

     public PolicyConnection(Socket client, byte[] policy)
     {
        _connection = client;
        _policy = policy;

        _buffer = new byte[_policyRequestString.Length];
        _received = 0;
        try
        {
            // receive the request from the client
            _connection.BeginReceive(_buffer, 0,
                    _policyRequestString.Length, SocketFlags.None,
              new AsyncCallback(OnReceive), null);
        }
         catch (SocketException)
          {
            _connection.Close();
          }
        }

     // Called when you receive data from the client
     private void OnReceive(IAsyncResult res)
    {
        try
        {
          _received += _connection.EndReceive(res);
```

```
        // if you haven't gotten enough for a full request yet, receive again
        if (_received < _policyRequestString.Length)
          {
            _connection.BeginReceive(_buffer,
            _received, _policyRequestString.Length - _received,
               SocketFlags.None, new AsyncCallback(OnReceive), null);
            return;
          }

         // make sure the request is valid
          string request = System.Text.Encoding.
             UTF8.GetString(_buffer, 0, _received);
          if (StringComparer.InvariantCultureIgnoreCase.
             Compare(request, _policyRequestString) != 0)
          {
             _connection.Close();
             return;
          }

        // send the policy
        Console.Write("Sending policy...\n");
        _connection.BeginSend(_policy, 0, _policy.Length, SocketFlags.None,
             new AsyncCallback(OnSend), null);
         }
         catch (SocketException)
         {
             _connection.Close();
         }
}

  // called after sending the policy to the client; close the connection.
  public void OnSend(IAsyncResult res
    {
      try
      {
          _connection.EndSend(res);
      }
       finally
         {
          _connection.Close();
       }
  }
}
```

```
class PolicyServer
{
   private Socket _listener;
   private byte[] _policy;

   // pass in the path of an XML file containing the socket policy
   public PolicyServer(string policyFile)
   {

      // Load the policy file
      FileStream policyStream = new FileStream(policyFile, FileMode.Open);

      _policy = new byte[policyStream.Length];
      policyStream.Read(_policy, 0, _policy.Length);
      policyStream.Close();


     // Create the Listening Socket
     _listener = new Socket(AddressFamily.InterNetwork, SocketType.Stream,
         ProtocolType.Tcp);

     _listener.SetSocketOption(SocketOptionLevel.Tcp, (SocketOptionName)
         SocketOptionName.NoDelay, 0);

     _listener.Bind(new IPEndPoint(IPAddress.Any, 943));
     _listener.Listen(10);

     _listener.BeginAccept(new AsyncCallback(OnConnection), null);
   }

   // Called when you receive a connection from a client
   public void OnConnection(IAsyncResult res)
   {
     Socket client = null;

     try
     {
         client = _listener.EndAccept(res);
     }
         catch (SocketException)
     {
         return;
      }
```

```
        // handle this policy request with a PolicyConnection
          PolicyConnection pc = new PolicyConnection(client, _policy);

          // look for more connections
          _listener.BeginAccept(new AsyncCallback(OnConnection), null);
    }

     public void Close()
     {
         _listener.Close();
     }
  }

  public class Program
  {
      static void Main()
      {
          Console.Write("Starting...\n");

          // Modify the path to be the place where you stored this file.
          PolicyServer ps = new
          PolicyServer(@"C:\projects\Server\PolicyServer\clientaccesspolicy.xml");
          System.Threading.Thread.Sleep(System.Threading.Timeout.Infinite);

      }
  }
```

The Server

As discussed, the server handles all the client connections and is responsible for maintaining and processing all the game data and its current state. The server listens to a given port for connections from a Silverlight client application. Once a connection is received with a valid name and password, the client is moved into the game.

The server doesn't have to have any fancy UI, so I have written it as a straightforward C# WinForms application. Since Silverlight only supports TCP/IP, you can use the .NET `TcpListener` class to listen for connections. This class allows you to listen for TCP connections from clients.

The network code for the server is lengthy, so I show only the applicable methods here. The rest of the code can be reviewed in the server project files.

To start the server, you need to instantiate an instance of the `TcpListener` object and pass it the port you want to use as the parameter. From there, the following three threads are created:

- `PollForConnections()`—Polls the port for any new incoming connections.
- `ProcessIncomingClientStreams()`—Processes data from all connected clients.
- `ProcessPackets()`—Processes all the packets that are stored in the queue.

The following is a quick breakdown of the properties belonging to the `Server` class:

- `_ tcpListener`—Object used to listen to the socket.
- `_ pollForConnectionsThread`—Thread used to poll for new connections.
- `_processPacketsThread`—Thread used to process queued packets.
- `_processIncomingClientStreams`—Thread used to check for incoming data from clients.
- `_keepAlive`—Flag used to determine if the server is up.
- `_packetQueue`—A queue of all packets waiting to be processed.
- `_clientUpdateEvent`—A callback event to the main thread to indicate a client change.
- `_nextID`—The next unique ID for a client.
- `_clients`—A dictionary object used to store all clients by their unique IDs.

The following code shows the class members declared for the class `Server` as well as the `StartServer()` and `StopServer()` methods.

```
public class Server
{
    private TcpListener          _tcpListener;
    private Thread               _pollForConnectionsThread = null;
    private Thread               _processPacketsThread = null;
    private Thread               _processIncomingClientStreams = null;
    private bool                 _keepAlive = true;
    private Queue                _packetQueue = new Queue();
    private EventHandler         _clientUpdateEvent;
    private int                  _nextID = 1;
```

```
private Dictionary<int, Client> _clients = new Dictionary<int, Client>();

public void StartServer()
{
    _keepAlive = true;

    try
    {
        _tcpListener = new TcpListener(Consts.Port);
        _tcpListener.Start();

        _pollForConnectionsThread = new Thread(
             new ThreadStart(PollForConnections));
        _pollForConnectionsThread.Name = "PollForConnectionsThread";
        _pollForConnectionsThread.Start();

        _processIncomingClientStreams =
             new Thread(new ThreadStart(ProcessIncomingClientStreams));
        _processIncomingClientStreams.Name = "ProcessIncomingClient
         Streams ";
        _ processIncomingClientStreams.Start();

        _processPacketsThread = new Thread(new ThreadStart(ProcessPackets));
        _processPacketsThread.Name = "ProcessPacketsThread";
        _processPacketsThread.Start();

    }
    catch (SocketException e)
    {
        StatusInfo.OutputText("Exception thrown " + e.Message);
    }
}

public void StopServer()
{
    _keepAlive = false;

    lock (_clients)
    {
        foreach (Client client in _clients.Values)
        {
            client.Close();
        }
```

```
        }
        if (null != _tcpListener)
        {
            _tcpListener.Stop();
            _tcpListener = null;
        }
        StatusInfo.OutputText("Server stopped.");
    }
}
```

As you can see, each client in the game is represented by its only class called `Client`. The `Client` class contains all the data needed to track the current state of the client. The following code shows a small snippet of what the `Client` class looks like. It includes the data that pertains to networking plus some other properties to give you an idea of what you will need to track for each client.

```
public class Client
{
    public string                Name;
    public int                   HitPoints = 100;
    public int                   SpellPoints = 100;
    public int                   CurrentX;
    public int                   CurrentY;
    public int                   DestX;
    public int                   DestY;
    public int                   CurrentMapID = 0;
    public int                   ClientID = -1;
    public bool                  IsDead = false;
    public bool                  IsConnected = true;
    public Enums.Direction       Direction = Enums.Direction.South;
    public Enums.ClientState     ClientState = Enums.ClientState.LoggingIn;
    public PacketManager         PacketMgr = new PacketManager();
    public TcpClient             TCPClient;
    public NetworkStream         Stream;
    public Socket                Socket;

    public Client(TcpClient tcpClient, NetworkStream ns)
    {
        TCPClient = tcpClient;
        Stream = ns;
    }

    public void Close()
```

```
    {
        Stream.Close();
        TCPClient.Close();
    }
}
```

Each one of the threads mentioned previously will loop infinitely until the `_keepAlive` flag is set to `false`. This flag gets set when the application is exiting or when the server is being manually shutdown. Also, these threads have a 100 millisecond `Sleep()` between processing to keep them from locking up the main process. The `Sleep()` method will suspend execution of the working thread until the specified amount of time has elapsed.

The first thread, `PollForConnections()`, loops until `_tcpListener.Pending()` returns `true`, which is used to indicate when a pending connection is available. Once a connection has been established and a new client object is formed, a unique ID for the client is set and the client is added to a dictionary list used to track all client connections. The client object itself is the dictionary value and the client ID is the dictionary key. To get the next ID, the program calls `GetNextID()`, which essentially cycles through up to `Int32.MaxValue` (2,147,483,647) and returns to zero once it reaches this value, as seen here:

```
private int GetNextID()
{
    _nextID++;
    // MaxValue =
    if (_nextID == Int32.MaxValue)
        _nextID = 0;

    return _nextID;
}
```

To accept a new connection, you call `_tcpListener.AcceptTcpClient()`. This returns a `TcpClient` object that contains the `NetworkStream` object needed to communicate with that client. The following code represents the thread `PollForConnections()`:

```
private void PollForConnections()
{
    StatusInfo.OutputText("Waiting for clients...");

    while (true == _keepAlive)
```

```
    {
        while (true == _keepAlive && false == _tcpListener.Pending())
        {
            System.Threading.Thread.Sleep(100);
        }
        if (true == _keepAlive)
        {
            TcpClient tcpClient = _tcpListener.AcceptTcpClient();
            NetworkStream ns = tcpClient.GetStream();
            Client newClient = new Client(tcpClient, ns);
            newClient.ClientID = GetNextID();
            _clients.Add(newClient.ClientID, newClient);
        }
    }
}
```

The next thread, `ProcessIncomingClientStreams`, loops through all known clients to determine if data is available on their `NetworkStream`. If there is data available, the program reads up to 1,024 bytes of the data and adds the data to the client's `PacketManager`, which is used to piece packets together. A single packet is not guaranteed to arrive in one piece, so you have to continue to append data until a complete packet is made. You can determine the length of a packet because the program sets the first four bytes of any given packet to represent the entire length of a packet. Once a complete packet has been formed, it is added to the packet queue, which is processed by the `ProcessPackets()` thread.

The only way to determine if a client has disconnected is to do an I/O operation such as a read or write. When you attempt to read and get zero bytes returned, you know the client has disconnected from the server. At this time, you should set the client's `IsConnected` flag to zero. If no client is connected, you must set the `cleanupRequired` flag to `true` and call `RemoveDisconnectedClients()` once the process has been completed. The following code shows `ProcessIncomingClientStreams()` and `RemoveDisconnectedClients()`:

```
private void ProcessIncomingClientStreams()
{
    byte[] data = new Byte[1024];
    int cleanupCounter = 0;

    while (true == _keepAlive)
    {
        lock (_clients)
```

```
        {
            foreach (Client client in _clients.Values)
            {
                if (false == client.IsConnected)
                {
                    cleanupCounter++;
                }
                else if (true == client.Stream.DataAvailable)
                {
                    int bytesRead = client.Stream.Read(data, 0, data.Length);
                    if (bytesRead == 0)
                    {
                        client.IsConnected = false;
                        cleanupCounter++;
                    }
                    else
                    {
                        if (true == client.PacketMgr.AddPacketData(data,
                        bytesRead))
                        {
                        AddPacketToQueue(new
                         Packet(client, client.PacketMgr.DequeuePacket()));
                        }
                    }
                }
            }
        }

        if (cleanupCounter > 0)
        {
            RemoveDisconnectedClients(cleanupCounter);
            cleanupCounter = 0;
        }
        System.Threading.Thread.Sleep(100);
    }
}

private void RemoveDisconnectedClients(int cleanupCounter)
{
    List<int> cleanupIDs = new List<int>();
    int cleanedCount = 0;

    foreach (Client client in _clients.Values)
```

```
    {
        if (client.IsConnected == false)
        {
            OnPlayerDisconnected(client);
            cleanupIDs.Add(client.ClientID);
            if (++cleanedCount == cleanupCounter)
                break;
        }
    }
    foreach (int ID in cleanupIDs)
    {
        _clients.Remove(ID);
    }
}


private void OnPlayerDisconnected(Client client)
{
    RemovePlayerFromMap(client);
    _clientUpdateEvent(null, null);
    StatusInfo.OutputText("Client disconnected: " +
        _clients.Count + " active connections.");
}
```

The final thread, `ProcessPackets()`, determines whether there are any packets on the packet queue. Queues store data as first in first out, which means the packets are processed in the order they are received.

When packets arrive through the `NetworkStream`, they are received as an array of bytes. As stated earlier, the first four bytes represent the length of the packet. The remaining bytes are converted into a string that contains the data for the packet. Each data item in the string is separated by a delimiter (a comma in the following example) so that it can be easily split up. A single packet can be represented by `packet type + "," + data + "," + data`, and so on. To split up a string that has data delimited by commas, you call `String.Split(new Char[] { ',' });`

The following code shows the `ProcessPacket()` thread. It includes some of the packet types so that you can see how they are processed:

```
private void ProcessPackets()
{
    while (true == _keepAlive)
    {
```

```
        while(_packetQueue.Count > 0)
        {
            lock(_packetQueue)
            {
                Packet packet = (Packet) _packetQueue.Dequeue();
                string[] identifiers = packet.PacketData.Split(new Char[]
                { ',' });
                switch (identifiers[0])
                {
                    case PacketManager.LOGIN:
                        ProcessLogin(packet.ClientObject,
                        identifiers[1], identifiers[2]);
                        break;
                    case PacketManager.CHAT_MESSAGE:
                        ReportChatToClients(packet.ClientObject,
                        identifiers[1]);
                        break;
                    case PacketManager.MOVE_TO:
                        packet.ClientObject.DestX = Convert.ToInt32
                        (identifiers[1]);
                        packet.ClientObject.DestY = Convert.ToInt32
                        (identifiers[2]);
                        ReportMoveToClients(packet.ClientObject);
                        break;
}
            }
        }
        System.Threading.Thread.Sleep(100);
    }
}
```

For the server to send packets to the client, it needs to call `NetworkStream.Write()` and `NetworkStream.Flush()`. The following code is the server's implementation of `SendPacket()`.

```
// Sends a packet to a given client's stream.
// If an exception is thrown then the client is considered disconnected.
public static bool SendPacket(NetworkStream ns, byte[] data)
{
    bool succeeded = true;

    try
    {
```

```
        int packetLength = data.Length + 4;
        byte[] dataLength = BitConverter.GetBytes(Convert.ToInt32
                             (data.Length));
        byte[] packet = new byte[packetLength];
        for (int i = 0; i < 4; i++)
            packet[i] = dataLength[i];
        for (int i = 4; i < packetLength; i++)
            packet[i] = data[i - 4];
        ns.Write(packet, 0, packet.Length);
        ns.Flush();
    }
    catch
    {
        succeeded = false;
    }

    return succeeded;
}
```

The PacketManager

The PacketManager is the class responsible for forming packets from bytes of data. The client and server applications share most of the code from the PacketManager since they need to be compatible.

When a client or server receives data, it calls PacketManager.AddPacketData(). This method determines whether you are creating a new packet or whether a packet is already in the process of being made and then it calls the appropriate method as shown. It returns true if a packet is ready for processing.

```
public bool AddPacketData(byte[] data, int dataLength)
{
    lock (this)
    {
        if (true == _packetStart)
        {
            ProcessPacketStart(data, 0, dataLength);
        }
        else
        {
            AddToPacket(data, 0, dataLength);
        }
```

```
    }
    return IsPacketAvailable();
}
```

`ProcessPacketStarts()` assumes the data is the start of a new packet if not the complete packet. It determines the length of the packet by looking at the first four bytes and converting them to an integer that represents the length.

```
private void ProcessPacketStart(byte[] data, int dataIndex, int dataLength)
{
    _packetStart = false;

    byte[] packetLength = new Byte[4];
    packetLength[0] = data[dataIndex];
    packetLength[1] = data[dataIndex + 1];
    packetLength[2] = data[dataIndex + 2];
    packetLength[3] = data[dataIndex + 3];
    _expectedLength = BitConverter.ToInt32(packetLength, 0);

    _packetData = new byte[_expectedLength];

    int bytesCopied = 0;
    while (bytesCopied < _expectedLength && bytesCopied < (dataLength - 4))
    {
        _packetData[bytesCopied] = data[dataIndex + bytesCopied + 4];
        bytesCopied++;
    }
    _currentLength = bytesCopied;

    if (_currentLength == _expectedLength)
            // did we get enough to create a full packet?
    {
        _processedPackets.Add(Encoding.UTF8.
                GetString(_packetData, 0, _expectedLength));
        if (bytesCopied + 4 < dataLength) // Is there more data to process?
            ProcessPacketStart(data, bytesCopied + 4 +
                                    dataIndex, dataLength - (bytesCopied + 4));
        else
        {
            Reset();
        }
    }
}
```

A call to Reset means you are expecting the next set of data to be the start of a new packet.

```
private void Reset()
{
    _packetStart = true;
    _currentLength = 0;
}
```

AddToPacket() is responsible for truncating data it receives onto the existing buffer of data that is forming the packet. It also determines whether a packet has been completely formed and then adds the packet to the main packet queue once it's ready. Any remaining data left unprocessed after a packet is formed is used to start the creation of a new packet by calling ProcessPacketStart(). The following code is the method for AddToPacket().

```
private void AddToPacket(byte[] data, int dataIndex, int dataLength)
{
    int bytesCopied = 0;
    while (_currentLength < _expectedLength && bytesCopied < dataLength)
    {
        _packetData[_currentLength] = data[dataIndex + bytesCopied];
        bytesCopied++;
        _currentLength++;
    }
    if (_currentLength == _expectedLength)
            // did we get enough to create a full packet?
    {
        _processedPackets.Add(Encoding.UTF8.GetString
                          (_packetData, 0, _expectedLength));

        if (bytesCopied < dataLength) // Is there more data to process?
            ProcessPacketStart(data, bytesCopied, (dataLength - bytesCopied));
        else
            Reset();
    }
}
```

The Client

On the Silverlight side of things is the client. The client uses the .NET framework class called Socket to communicate with the server. This class provides all the methods and properties you need for your network communication with the server. All data transfers are done asynchronously using the TCP/IP protocol.

To connect to the server, you simply call `Socket.ConnectAsync()` and pass a `SocketAsyncEventArgs` object that contains the following information about your connection:

- `RemoteEndPoint`—A `DnsEndPoint` object that represents the host or IP address and port number of the server
- `UserToken`—The socket object
- `Completed` —The event to call when the connection is complete

The following is the complete code for the `Connect()` method, including some of the class properties needed by the methods:

```
public class Network
{
    private Socket _clientSocket = null;
    private byte[] _sendBuffer = new byte[Consts.BufferSize];
    private byte[] _receiveBufffer = new byte[Consts.BufferSize];
    private bool _isConnected = false;
    private PacketManager _packetManager = new PacketManager();
    private string _userName = String.Empty;
    private string _userPassword = String.Empty;

    public EventHandler OnConnected;
    public EventHandler OnDisconnected;
    public EventHandler<ConnectionFailedEventArgs> OnConnectFailed;

    public void Connect(string name, string password)
    {
        try
        {
            if (false == _isConnected)
            {
                _userName = name;
                _userPassword = password;
                DnsEndPoint endPoint = new
            DnsEndPoint(Application.Current.Host.Source.Host, Consts.Port);

                _clientSocket = new Socket(AddressFamily.InterNetwork,
                   SocketType.Stream, ProtocolType.Tcp);
```

```
            SocketAsyncEventArgs args = new SocketAsyncEventArgs();
            args.UserToken = _clientSocket;
            args.RemoteEndPoint = endPoint;
            args.Completed += new EventHandler<SocketAsyncEventArgs>
            (OnConnect);
            _clientSocket.ConnectAsync(args);
            if (args.SocketError != SocketError.Success)
        {
                OnConnectFailed(this,
    new ConnectionFailedEventArgs(args.SocketError.ToString()));
}
            }
        }
        catch (Exception e)
        {
            ChatBox.AddMessage("Exception thrown in Client::Connect()"
            + e.Message);
        }
    }
}
```

The three callback events are used to communicate with the main thread of the client application about the state of the connection. This way, the main thread does not have to poll for the state but rather can wait until its event is fired.

Notice that `AddressFamily.InterNetwork` is specified as the host. This works fine if your client is connecting to a server on the same box where the client is running. You will want to change this to be the IP or host name where your server is located.

Once the connection is complete, a call to `OnConnect()` is made. In this function, you check if the connection to the server was successful. If it is, you immediately create and send the login packet, which specifies the user's name and password. Once the login is sent, you call `BeginReceive()`, which will begin monitoring for packets sent from the server.

```
private void OnConnect(object sender, SocketAsyncEventArgs args)
{
    try
    {
        _isConnected = (args.SocketError == SocketError.Success);
        if (true == _isConnected)
        {
            byte[] loginPacket = PacketManager.LoginPacket(_userName, _user
                                                            Password);
```

```
                SendPacket(loginPacket);
                BeginReceive();
            }
        }
        catch (Exception e)
        {
            ChatBox.AddMessage("Exception thrown in Client::OnConnect()" +
            e.Message);
        }
    }
```

In `BeginReceive()`, you create an instance of `SocketAsyncEventArgs` and specify the buffer to use for the data received and the function to call back when the read is complete. You must then call `ReceiveAsync()` on the client socket to start the read.

```
private void BeginReceive()
{
    try
    {
        SocketAsyncEventArgs args = new SocketAsyncEventArgs();
        args.SetBuffer(_receiveBufffer, 0, _receiveBufffer.Length);
        args.Completed += this.OnReceive;

        _clientSocket.ReceiveAsync(args);
    }
    catch (Exception e)
    {
        ChatBox.AddMessage("Exception thrown in Client::BeginReceive()" +
                                                e.Message);
    }
}
```

The callback function `OnReceive()` determines if the socket has been disconnected by determining whether the bytes transferred is set to zero. If not, and if there is no other socket error, you add the packet data to the `PacketManager` and continue to the next `BeginReceive()`. The following is the code for `OnReceive()`:

```
private void OnReceive(object sender, SocketAsyncEventArgs args)
{
    try
    {
        if (args.BytesTransferred == 0)
            Disconnect();
```

```
        else if (args.SocketError == SocketError.Success)
        {
            _packetManager.AddPacketData(args.Buffer, args.BytesTransferred);
            BeginReceive();
        }
        else
            Disconnect();
    }
    catch (Exception e)
    {
        ChatBox.AddMessage("Exception thrown in Client::OnReceive()" +
                                                          e.Message);
    }
}
```

Sending packets from the client to the server is very similar to sending packets from the server to the client. You again use the first four bytes of the packet to represent the length of the packet. Also, because the program uses a `Socket` object for the client instead of the `NetworkStream` used on the server, you have to call `Socket.SendAsync()` instead of `NetworkStream.Write()`. The following code shows the `SendPacket()` for the client:

```
public static void SendPacket(Socket client, byte[] data)
{
    try
    {
        // Add packet length
        int packetLength = data.Length + 4;
        byte[] dataLength = BitConverter.GetBytes(Convert.ToInt32(data.
                                                         Length));
        byte[] packet = new byte[packetLength];
        for (int i = 0; i < 4; i++)
            packet[i] = dataLength[i];
        // Add packet data
        for (int i = 4; i < packetLength; i++)
            packet[i] = data[i - 4];

        SocketAsyncEventArgs e = new SocketAsyncEventArgs();
        e.SetBuffer(packet, 0, packet.Length);

          // Starts an asynchronous request for a connection to the remote host.
        client.SendAsync(e);
    }
```

```
    catch (Exception e)
    {
        ChatBox.AddMessage("Exception thrown in PacketManager:SendPacket():
                                                        "+ e.Message);
    }
```

To disconnect from the server, you simply have to call `Socket.Shutdown()` as follows:

```
public void Disconnect()
{
    try
    {
        if (null != _clientSocket)
        {
            lock (_clientSocket)
            {
                _clientSocket.Shutdown(SocketShutdown.Both);
                _clientSocket.Close();
                _clientSocket = null;
                ChatBox.AddMessage("Connection closed.");
            }
        }
    }
    catch (Exception e) // throws if client process has already closed
    {
        ChatBox.AddMessage("Exception thrown in Client::Disconnect()" +
                                                    e.Message);
    }
    _isConnected = false;
}
```

Summary

This chapter discussed the requirements of the policy server that are used to send the Silverlight client the clientaccesspolicy.xml file, which contains information on what ports and domains the client can access. It also discussed the server and client code and a way to manage packets that are used for communicating data back and forth. The next chapter covers how to add sound, music, and video effects to your game.

CHAPTER 10

Sound, Music, and Video

No game is complete without some great sound effects and perhaps even a theme song to go with it. This chapter covers how to load and play sound and video files using a Silverlight object called `MediaElement`. The chapter covers the object called `MediaElement`, which is used to represent all sound and video, the file formats Silverlight supports, and a sample `SoundManager` class implementation, and then concludes with timeline markers, which are used to mark specific intervals in your media file.

Using `MediaElement`

Silverlight leverages an object called `MediaElement`, which is used to represent all sounds and video elements in your application. Adding a sound or video file to your game is as easy as adding one of these objects with the `Source` property pointing to the sound or video file you want to load.

Silverlight supports the following video formats (from MSDN–see http://msdn.microsoft.com/en-us/library/cc189080(VS.95).aspx):

- WMV1: Windows Media Video 7
- WMV2: Windows Media Video 8
- WMV3: Windows Media Video 9
- WMVA: Windows Media Video Advanced Profile, non-VC-1

- WMVC1: Windows Media Video Advanced Profile, VC-1
- H.264
  - Can only be used for progressive download, smooth streaming, and adaptive streaming
  - Supports base, main, and high profiles

For audio, Silverlight supports the following formats (from MSDN):

- WMA 7: Windows Media Audio 7
- WMA 8: Windows Media Audio 8
- WMA 9: Windows Media Audio 9
- WMA 10: Windows Media Audio 10
- AAC: Advanced Audio Coding
  - Can only be used for progressive download, smooth streaming, and adaptive streaming
  - AAC is the LC variety and supports sampling frequencies up to 48 kHz
- MP3: ISO/MPEG Layer-3
  - Input: ISO/MPEG Layer-3 data stream
  - Channel configurations: mono and stereo
  - Sampling frequencies: 8, 11.025, 12, 16, 22.05, 24, 32, 44.1, and 48 kHz
  - Bit rates: 8-320 Kbps, variable bit rate
  - Limitations: "free format mode" (see ISO/IEC 11172-3, sub clause 2.4.2.3) is not supported

The following XAML shows one way to declare a sound element:

```
<MediaElement x:Name="MyMedia" Source="Sound/Fireball.mp3" AutoPlay="True" />
```

Since `AutoPlay = true`, this sound element will automatically play when the application starts.

To do the same thing programmatically, you could use the following code:

```
MediaElement _startupSound = new MediaElement();
_startupSound.Source = new Uri("sound/Fireball.mp3", UriKind.Relative);
_startupSound.AutoPlay = true;
LayoutRoot.Children.Add(_startupSound);
```

Note that you have to add the MediaElement to your Silverlight tree; otherwise, it will not play. If you want to manually start a media file, you will need to wait until the event MediaOpened is fired before you can play it. Also, make certain to set AutoPlay=false since it is true by default.

For example:

```
MediaElement _startupSound = new MediaElement();
_startupSound.Source = new Uri("sound/Fireball.mp3", UriKind.Relative);
_startupSound.AutoPlay = false;
_startupSound.MediaOpened += new RoutedEventHandler(_startupSound_
                                                    MediaOpened);
LayoutRoot.Children.Add(_startupSound);

void _startupSound_MediaOpened(object sender, RoutedEventArgs e)
{
    _startupSound.Play();
}
```

When referencing sound files from your Silverlight application project, you will need to make certain they are either included in your Silverlight application or accessible on the web. With Silverlight, you cannot access files on the client machine that are not included in the application XAP. To ensure the media files are copied into your XAP, follow these steps:

1. Right-click on your Silverlight application in the Solution Explorer of Visual Studio and choose Add New Item.

2. Browse to the sound file (such as Fireball.mp3) and double-click to add it.

3. Select the media file and, under the Property grid for that file, set Build Action to Resource and Copy to Output Directory to Copy If Newer, as shown in Figure 10.1.

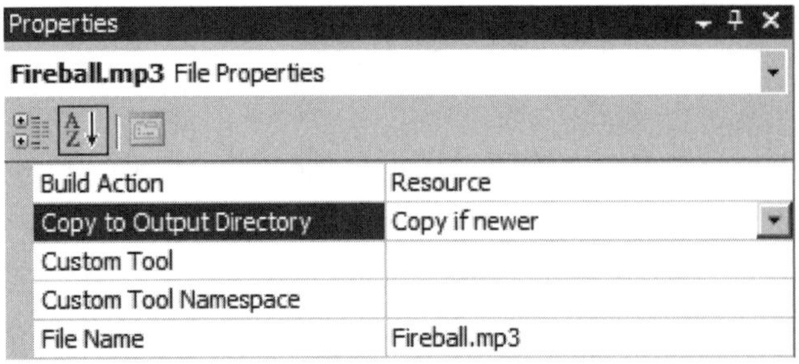

Figure 10.1
Media Element Properties

Because media files are large, the recommended approach is to put the media files on a server that your client application can access. This will greatly reduce the size of your XAP file that's downloaded when a client connects to the application.

In addition to `AutoPlay`, you might find some of the following `MediaElement` properties useful:

- `Balance`—Sets the ratio of volume across stereo speakers. This is a useful property if you want to simulate special effects such as people talking.
- `IsMuted`—Set this to `true` to silence the `MediaElement`.
- `Stretch`—This will cause video-type `MediaElements` to stretch to fill the entire `MediaElements` dimensions. Stretch can be set to `None`, `Uniform`, `UniformToFill`, and `Fill`. By default, `Stretch = Fill`.
- `Volume`—This property specifies the volume of the media sound. It is a float value that ranges from 0.0 to 1.0 with 1.0 being the maximum sound. By default, this is set to 0.5.

Since `MediaElement` is a `UIElement`, it inherits other useful properties (mostly for video) such as the ability to set opacity, clipping, and more.

The following include some of the many methods made available to you through the `MediaElement`:

- `Pause()`—Pauses the sound or video file at its current location. Make certain to check the property `CanPause` to ensure you are able to pause before proceeding. For example, streaming media cannot be paused.
- `Play()`—Play the sound or video file at its current location (wherever it was last paused). If it is already playing, this call is ignored.

- `Stop()`—Stop the sound or video file and reset the current location to be the beginning of the file.

To check to see what state a `MediaElement` is in, you can access the property `MediaElement.CurrentState`. The following are the possible states:

- `AcquiringLicense`—This state is only applicable when serving DRM-protected content. This state means the `MediaElement` is in the process of acquiring the license.
- `Buffering`—File is downloading the content for the media. Large media files will remain in this state for awhile.
- `Closed`—The `MediaElement` is empty and has no data.
- `Individualizing`—This state is also only applicable when serving DRM-protected content. This state means the `MediaElement` is in the process of ensuring the proper individualization components are installed.
- `Opening`—The `MediaElement` is in the process of opening the content from the URI specified in its `Source` property.
- `Paused`—The `MediaElement` is paused at a specific position in the file.
- `Playing`—The `MediaElement` is in the process of playing.
- `Stopped`—The `MediaElement` contains data but it is not playing and remains at position zero of the data file.

Using SoundManager

The `SoundManager` class handles the sound for the Silverlight client application in this example. This class is fairly straightforward; all you have to do is call `PlaySound` with the path to the media file you want to play. You can call this method multiple times and play as many sounds simultaneously as your game supports.

There are three event handlers that are important to listen for. The first one, as discussed previously, is `MediaOpened` and tells you when the media file is fully loaded and ready to play. Once this event is fired, you must call `Play()` on the `MediaElement` to start the sound. The next event is `MediaEnded`. You need to listen to this event so that you can remove the `MediaElement` from your Silverlight tree once it's completed (unless you have set the sound to repeat). The final event is called MediaFailed. If, for whatever reason, your media file fails to load, it's important to monitor for this exception; otherwise, your browser will throw an error.

In order to have a MediaElement repeat from the beginning, you must first call MediaElement.Stop() before you call MediaElement.Play(). Stop() causes the position to go back to zero; otherwise, the position remains at the end of the file. If you don't call Stop() first, Play() will result in nothing happening.

The following code is the class for SoundManager. This class can be expanded upon as needed for your game purposes.

```
public class SoundManager
{
    private Grid _parentElement;
    Dictionary<int, MediaElement>
          _activeMediaElements = new Dictionary<int, MediaElement>();
    int _nextID = 0;

    public SoundManager(Grid parentElement)
    {
        _parentElement = parentElement;
    }

    public int Play(string fileName, bool repeat)
    {
        int mediaID = GetNextID();
        MediaElement me = new MediaElement();
        me.Tag = repeat;
        me.Source = new Uri(fileName, UriKind.Relative);
        _parentElement.Children.Add(me);

        _activeMediaElements.Add(mediaID, me);

        me.MediaOpened += new RoutedEventHandler(me_MediaOpened);
        me.MediaEnded += new RoutedEventHandler(me_MediaEnded);
        me.MediaFailed += new EventHandler<ExceptionRoutedEventArgs>
                        (me_MediaFailed);

        return mediaID;
    }
```

```
private int GetNextID()
{
    _nextID++;
    if (_nextID == Int32.MaxValue)
        _nextID = 0;

    return _nextID;
}

public void Stop(int mediaID)
{
    if (true == _activeMediaElements.ContainsKey(mediaID))
    {
        MediaElement me = _activeMediaElements[mediaID];
        me.Stop();
    }
}
// Media elements are automatically removed when they are done playing
public void Clear (int mediaID)
{
    if (true == _activeMediaElements.ContainsKey(mediaID))
    {
        MediaElement me = _activeMediaElements[mediaID];
        me.Stop();
        _activeMediaElements.Remove(mediaID);
        if(true == _parentElement.Children.Contains(me))
            _parentElement.Children.Remove(me);
    }
}

public void ClearAll()
{
    foreach (MediaElement me in _activeMediaElements.Values)
    {
        me.Stop();
        if (true == _parentElement.Children.Contains(me))
            _parentElement.Children.Remove(me);
    }
    _activeMediaElements.Clear();
}

public void Mute(int mediaID)
{
```

```
        if (true == _activeMediaElements.ContainsKey(mediaID))
        {
            MediaElement me = _activeMediaElements[mediaID];
            me.IsMuted = true;
        }
    }

    public void Pause(int mediaID)
    {
        if (true == _activeMediaElements.ContainsKey(mediaID))
        {
            MediaElement me = _activeMediaElements[mediaID];
            me.Pause();
        }
    }

    public void Resume(int mediaID)
    {
        if (true == _activeMediaElements.ContainsKey(mediaID))
        {
            MediaElement me = _activeMediaElements[mediaID];
            me.Play();
        }
    }

    void me_MediaFailed(object sender, ExceptionRoutedEventArgs e)
    {
        // Log error
    }

    void me_MediaEnded(object sender, RoutedEventArgs e)
    {
        MediaElement element = (MediaElement) sender;

        foreach (int key in _activeMediaElements.Keys)
        {
            MediaElement me = _activeMediaElements[key];
            if(me == element)
            {
                bool repeat = (bool)me.Tag;
                if (repeat == false)
                {
```

```
                    _parentElement.Children.Remove(element);
                    _activeMediaElements.Remove(key);
                }
                else
                {
                    me.Stop();
                    me.Play();
                }
                return;
            }
        }
    }

    void me_MediaOpened(object sender, RoutedEventArgs e)
    {
        MediaElement me = (MediaElement) sender;
        me.Play();
    }
}
```

Using Timeline Markers

Timeline markers are preset points in the media file that are used to mark specific intervals that you can check against. These markers can be added using tools such as Windows Media File Editor and Microsoft Expression Encoder. You can also dynamically add them by creating new `TimelineMarker` objects and adding them through the `MediaElement.Markers` property. During playback of a media file, the event `MarkerReached` is fired whenever a marker is reached. This is useful if you want your application to perform certain actions when the markers are hit.

The following code shows how to dynamically add markers and how to listen for them. This method is called when the `MediaElement` has successfully loaded. Any markers added before this event is called are automatically cleared and overwritten.

```
void MyMedia_MediaOpened(object sender, RoutedEventArgs e)
{
    MediaElement me = (MediaElement) sender;

    TimelineMarker tm = new TimelineMarker();
    tm.Text = "First Marker";
```

```
    tm.Time = new TimeSpan(0, 0, 5);
    me.Markers.Add(tm);

    tm = new TimelineMarker();
    tm.Text = "Second Marker";
    tm.Time = new TimeSpan(0, 0, 10);
    me.Markers.Add(tm);

    me.MarkerReached += new TimelineMarkerRoutedEventHandler(me_MarkerReached);

    me.Play();
}

void me_MarkerReached(object sender, TimelineMarkerRoutedEventArgs e)
{
    string secondCount = e.Marker.Time.Seconds.ToString();
    string markerText = e.Marker.Text;
}
```

Summary

This chapter is a brief introduction into how sound and video work with Silverlight through the use of the `MediaElement` object. The `SoundManager` class is meant to help you get started adding sound in your game. This class can be expanded upon and further customized to meet your individual game's needs. The next chapter concludes this book with some additional game-related techniques you can apply to your Silverlight game.

CHAPTER 11

EXTRAS

So far, the book has given broad-level coverage of Silverlight 3 and Silverlight 3 tooling. It has discussed object management, animation techniques, and building custom, styled user interface controls for your game, including draggable/droppable buttons and dialog boxes. In addition, the book discussed how to write server and client applications in order to make your game multi-player. Finally, I demonstrated how easy it is to add full sound and media support to your Silverlight application.

This chapter concludes the book by showing you a few extra techniques you can use in your game. These techniques include map scrolling, player movement, a chat-box implementation, and finally, creating reflections and shadows for your game and UI objects.

Scrolling a Map Smoothly

In any given game, a player is represented by a character who is typically centered in the game's viewport. This section shows you a technique you can use to scroll your world maps while keeping the player centered in the viewport. Map scrolling is necessary in games when the viewport is not large enough to see the entire world map. As the player's character moves around the map, the map is scrolled within the viewport so players can see the entire world map.

In order for maps to scroll smoothly, you need to update their positions based on timers, where each new scroll position occurs over a predetermined set of intervals. The interval created for this example, called `ScrollDelayInMS`, is set to 50 milliseconds.

The map in this case is centered on the player's character. The player's character has a current X and current Y as well as a destination X and destination Y. These coordinates are relative to the map position. Depending upon the speed of the character, the player will move from the current position to the destination position over a given amount of time. This speed of movement is indicated by the player's `MoveSpeed` property.

The three methods `ScrollMap()`, `UpdatePosition`, and `CenterMap()` are used to scroll the map and update the player's position.

In the method `ScrollMap()`, the program first checks to see if a valid player object for this player has been created. If so, it checks to make certain whether enough time has elapsed to update the scroll. If enough time has passed, the player's position is updated and the map is re-centered to the player's new position. Once a player has reached her destination, the animation switches from walking/running to idling in the given direction.

```
public int ScrollSpeed = 5;
public int ScrollDelayInMS = 50;
private ObjectCreature _thisPlayer = null;
private DateTime _lastUpdate = DateTime.Now;
private Enums.Direction _currentDirection = Enums.Direction.South;
private object _scrollObject = new object();

public void ScrollMap(double windowWidth, double windowHeight)
{
    if (null == _thisPlayer)
        return;

    double elapsedMS = (DateTime.Now - _lastUpdate).TotalMilliseconds;
    if (elapsedMS < ScrollDelayInMS)
        return;

    _lastUpdate = DateTime.Now;

    lock (_scrollObject)
    {
        if (_thisPlayer.CurrentX != _thisPlayer.DestX
            || _thisPlayer.CurrentY != _thisPlayer.DestY)
```

```
            UpdatePosition();
        CenterMap(windowWidth, windowHeight);
    }
}

private void UpdatePosition()
{
    if (_thisPlayer.CurrentX < _thisPlayer.DestX)
        _thisPlayer.CurrentX += _thisPlayer.MovementSpeed;
    else if (_thisPlayer.CurrentX > _thisPlayer.DestX)
        _thisPlayer.CurrentX -= _thisPlayer.MovementSpeed;
    if (_thisPlayer.CurrentY < _thisPlayer.DestY)
        _thisPlayer.CurrentY += _thisPlayer.MovementSpeed;
    else if (_thisPlayer.CurrentY > _thisPlayer.DestY)
        _thisPlayer.CurrentY -= _thisPlayer.MovementSpeed;

    if (true == _thisPlayer.IsAtDest())
        _thisPlayer.Animate(_currentDirection, Enums.AnimationType.Idle, true);
}

private void CenterMap(double windowWidth, double windowHeight)
{
    if (null != _parentCanvas && null != _thisPlayer)
    {
        int leftPos = (int) ((windowWidth / 2) - _thisPlayer.CurrentX);
        int topPos = (int) ((windowHeight / 2) - _thisPlayer.CurrentY);

        _parentCanvas.SetValue(Canvas.LeftProperty, (double) leftPos);
        _parentCanvas.SetValue(Canvas.TopProperty, (double)topPos);
    }
}
```

Fine-Tuning Player Movement

A player can move in any one of the eight directions, including north, northeast, east, southeast, south, southwest, west, and northwest (see Figure 11.1). When the game receives keyboard input from the player, a call to `ScrollDirection()` is made to move the player. Alternatively, you can also listen for mouse clicks and calculate the direction based on the location of the mouse click relative to the player's position on the screen.

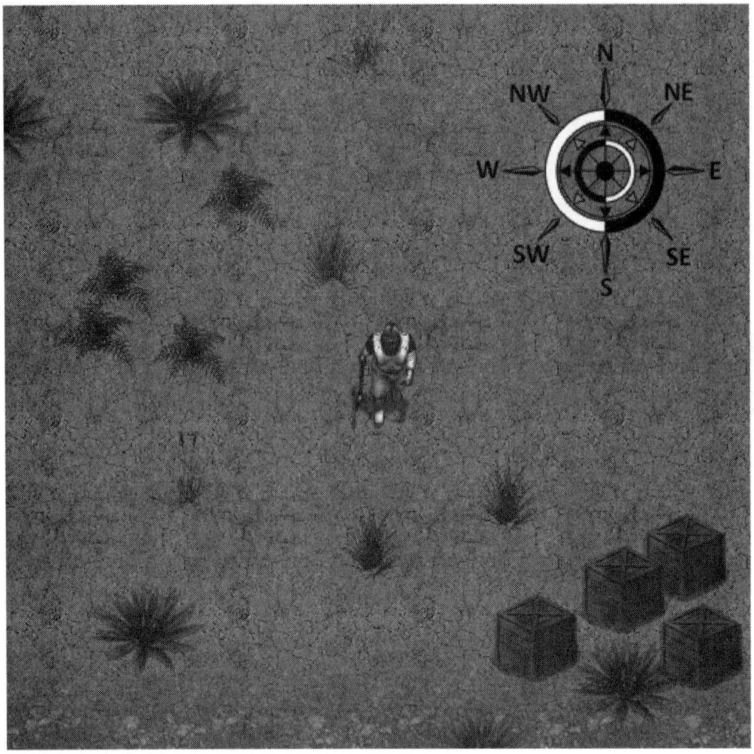

Figure 11.1
Player Movement

The following code for `ScrollDirection()` first checks to see if the player is already moving in the given direction. If so, it ignores the request. Otherwise, the new destination is calculated. Before you actually set the new destination, you must first check to see if the destination is walkable. That is, any position on the map that should block a player moving over it should be set to non-walkable. For example, you do not want a player walking over a tree, a river, the ocean, a large rock, and so on. Any movements to non-walkable positions should be rejected. Also, if the game is multi-player, the player needs to report the movement to the server. The server is the master of the world and will tell the player if a move is valid or not. This needs to be done in case the player decides to hack the local map files. If the player attempts to move somewhere he is not allowed, the server will report the actual true position and the player will find himself or herself jumping back to the last valid position.

You don't necessarily want to first ask the server for permission to move. It's better if the players have a predictable idea of where they can and cannot go;

otherwise, movement will be very choppy. Keep in mind that the server will always correct the players if they are wrong. The side effect of this is when the connection to the server itself is slow. For example, your players may honestly think it is okay to move somewhere but suddenly they will jump back because they weren't aware of an obstacle that suddenly appeared in the way due to the server not reporting it to you in time.

Finally, a call to `_thisPlayer.Animate()` changes the image so it's facing the right direction. You should also check to see if the character is walking or running to make sure the call to `_thisPlayer.Animate()` updates the player to the appropriate running or walking image frames.

```
public bool ScrollDirection(Enums.Direction direction)
{
    bool moveSucceeded = false;

    lock (_scrollObject)
    {
        if (direction == _currentDirection && false == _thisPlayer.IsAtDest())
            return false;

        // Stop the players from moving toward their old destination.
        _thisPlayer.DestX = _thisPlayer.CurrentX;
        _thisPlayer.DestY = _thisPlayer.CurrentY;

        // Calculate the distance the players will move based upon their speed.
        int distanceMoved = _thisPlayer.MovementSpeed * ScrollFrameCount;

        double newDestX = _thisPlayer.CurrentX;
        double newDestY = _thisPlayer.CurrentY;

        Enums.Direction newDirection = _currentDirection;

        // Are we walking or running?
        Enums.AnimationType animationType = Enums.AnimationType.Walk;
        if (true == _thisPlayer.IsRunning)
            animationType = Enums.AnimationType.Run;

        switch (direction)
        {
            case Enums.Direction.East:
                newDestX = _thisPlayer.CurrentX + distanceMoved;
```

```
            newDirection = Enums.Direction.East;
            break;
        case Enums.Direction.North:
            newDestY = _thisPlayer.CurrentY - distanceMoved;
            newDirection = Enums.Direction.North;
            break;
        case Enums.Direction.West:
            newDestX = _thisPlayer.CurrentX - distanceMoved;
            newDirection = Enums.Direction.West;
            break;
        case Enums.Direction.South:
            newDestY = _thisPlayer.CurrentY + distanceMoved;
            newDirection = Enums.Direction.South;
            break;
        case Enums.Direction.SE:
            newDestX = _thisPlayer.CurrentX + distanceMoved;
            newDestY = _thisPlayer.CurrentY + distanceMoved;
            newDirection = Enums.Direction.SE;
            break;
        case Enums.Direction.NE:
            newDestX = _thisPlayer.CurrentX + distanceMoved;
            newDestY = _thisPlayer.CurrentY - distanceMoved;
            newDirection = Enums.Direction.NE;
            break;
        case Enums.Direction.SW:
            newDestX = _thisPlayer.CurrentX - distanceMoved;
            newDestY = _thisPlayer.CurrentY + distanceMoved;
            newDirection = Enums.Direction.SW;
            break;
        case Enums.Direction.NW:
            newDestX = _thisPlayer.CurrentX - distanceMoved;
            newDestY = _thisPlayer.CurrentY - distanceMoved;
            newDirection = Enums.Direction.NW;
            break;
    }
    if (true == IsWalkable(newDestX, newDestY))
    {
        _thisPlayer.DestX = newDestX;
        _thisPlayer.DestY = newDestY;
        _thisPlayer.Animate(newDirection, animationType, false);
        _currentDirection = newDirection;
        moveSucceeded = true;
    }
```

```
    }
    return moveSucceeded;
}
```

Creating a Chat Box

For multi-player games, people often need a way to communicate with each other. A chat box, as seen in Figure 11.2, allows a player to type input that is then sent to the server. The server processes this input by sending it to everyone who is within visible range of the player.

The background of the chat box is a gradient `Border` control. It is made visible only when the mouse hovers over the chat-box region. This background border fades in when moused over and fades out when the mouse leaves the region. This is done through a `Storyboard` timer that is linked to the `Border` control's `Opacity` property.

The chat box is created as a custom Silverlight control with one list box that is used to show the chat messages and one text box that is used to receive input from the players. The following XAML represents the `ChatBox` control:

```
<UserControl x:Class="Client.ChatBox"
  xmlns="http://schemas.microsoft.com/winfx/2006/
                xaml/presentation"
```

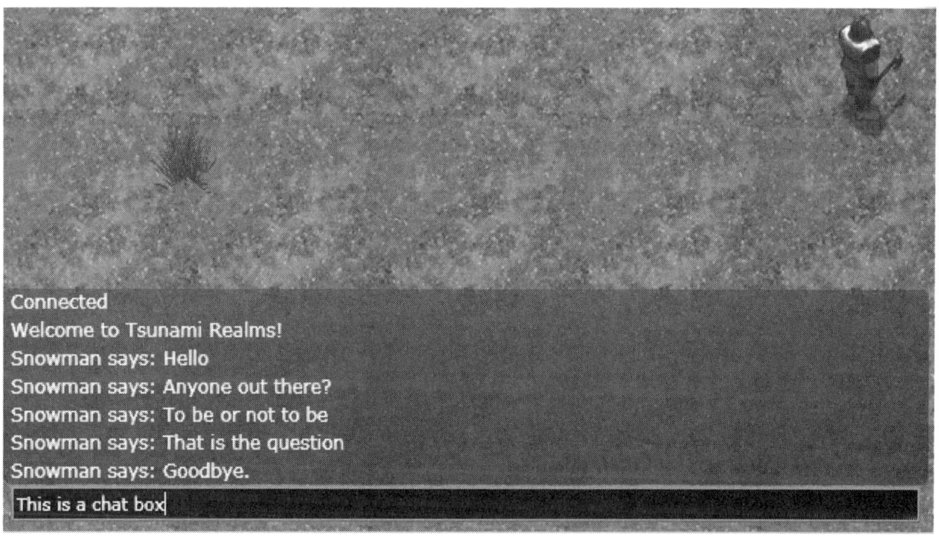

Figure 11.2
Chat Box

```
  xmlns:x="http://schemas.microsoft.com/winfx/
               2006/xaml">
  <Canvas Height="155" Width="600" Canvas.ZIndex="100000">
    <Canvas.Resources>
        <Storyboard x:Name="FadeIn" Storyboard.
                       TargetName="ChatBoxBG"
                       Storyboard.TargetProperty="Opacity">
        <DoubleAnimation From="0" To="0.6"
                          BeginTime="0:0:0.5"
                          Duration="0:0:0.9"/>
        </Storyboard>
        <Storyboard x:Name="FadeOut" Storyboard.TargetName="ChatBoxBG"
                        Storyboard.TargetProperty="Opacity">
           <DoubleAnimation From="0.6" To="0.0" BeginTime="0:0:1.5"
                    Duration="0:0:0.9"/>
        </Storyboard>
    </Canvas.Resources>

    <Border Canvas.Left="5" x:Name="ChatBoxBG" Style="{StaticResource
                            DlgBackgroundStyle}" Width="600"
                            Height="120" Opacity="0.6"/>

    <StackPanel Canvas.Left="5">
        <ListBox Visibility="Visible" Foreground="White"
                 Background="Transparent"
                 x:Name="MyMessageBox" Width="600" Height="120"/>
        <TextBox x:Name="ChatInput" Visibility="Collapsed"
                         Foreground="White"
                 Width="600" Height="23" Background="Black"
                 CaretBrush="White"/>
    </StackPanel>
  </Canvas>
</UserControl>
```

The chat box has a public member called `AddMessage()` that takes as a parameter the message to append to the `ListBox` control. Since you don't want players to have to scroll the list box vertically to see long messages that extend beyond the borders, you should automatically parse the text and create multiple lines of text from it if necessary (as is done here). Finally, this method ensures the last line of text is visible by calling the `ListBox` method `ScrollIntoView()` passing as a parameter the last message in the control.

In this game, the text box used to receive input from players is automatically hidden by default. To activate the TextBox control to type input, the players simply have to press the Enter key from anywhere in the application. This will cause the EnterChat() method to be called, which simply makes the text box visible and gives it the focus. Once players press Enter a second time, the game calls LeaveChat(), which resets the text-box content.

The final public method ShowBackground() is used to hide and show the background of the chat box. It kicks off the FadeIn or FadeOut Storyboard animation, which causes the background to gradually fade in or fade out.

The following shows the code-behind for this control:

```
public partial class ChatBox : UserControl
{
    public ChatBox()
    {
        InitializeComponent();
    }

    private void AddToChat(string msg)
    {
        ListBoxItem lbi = new ListBoxItem();
        lbi.Content = msg;
        MyMessageBox.Items.Add(lbi);
    }

    public void AddMessage(string msg)
    {
        TextBlock tester = new TextBlock();
        TextBlock actual = new TextBlock();
        string[] words = msg.Split(new Char[] { ' ' });

        for (int i = 0; i < words.Length; i++)
        {
            tester.Text += words[i];

            if (tester.ActualWidth < 500.00)
                actual.Text += words[i]+ " ";
            else
            {
                AddToChat(actual.Text);
                actual.Text = words[i] + " ";
```

```
                tester.Text = words[i] + " ";
            }
        }

        if (actual.Text.Length > 0)
            AddToChat(actual.Text);

        MyMessageBox.UpdateLayout();
        int count = MyMessageBox.Items.Count;
        ListBoxItem lbi =
              (ListBoxItem)MyMessageBox.Items[count - 1];
        MyMessageBox.ScrollIntoView(lbi);
    }

    public void EnterChat()
    {
        ChatInput.Visibility = Visibility.Visible;
        ChatInput.Focus();
    }

    public string LeaveChat()
    {
        string text = ChatInput.Text;
        ChatInput.Text = String.Empty;
        ChatInput.Visibility = Visibility.Collapsed;

        return text;
    }

    public void ShowBackground(bool show)
    {
        if (true == show)
        {
            ChatBoxBG.Opacity = 0.0;
            FadeIn.Begin();
        }
        else
        {
            FadeOut.Begin();
        }
    }
}
```

As mentioned earlier, on the client side of things, you should check to see if the Enter key is pressed; if so, call `EnterChat()` to start receiving input from the players. Once Enter has been pressed a second time, the program grabs the text from the `TextBox` control. If the length of the text is greater than one, the program creates a packet of type `PacketMessages.ChatMessage` and sends the text to the server for processing.

The following code from the class `PacketMessages` and the file PacketMessages.cs shows you how I create this type of packet:

```
public const string CHAT_MESSAGE = "CM";
public static byte[] ChatMessage(string message)
{
   return Encoding.UTF8.GetBytes(CHAT_MESSAGE + "," + message);
}
```

The code to handle the keyboard event checks can be found in MainPage.cs. The following snippet of code from this event handler shows you how to process the Enter key.

```
private bool _isInChat = false;

void MainPage_KeyDown(object sender, KeyEventArgs e)
{
  if (e.Key == Key.Enter)
  {
     if (false == _isInChat)
         MainChatBox.EnterChat();
     else
     {
       string chatInput = MainChatBox.LeaveChat();
       if(chatInput.Length > 0)
          _network.SendPacket(PacketMessages.ChatMessage(chatInput));
     }
       _isInChat = !_isInChat;
  }
}
```

Reflections and Shadows

Reflections can be used for a wide variety of effects, both in the game and in the UI for the game. For UI, you will commonly see reflections used on text as well as controls such as buttons. Figure 11.3 shows examples of both.

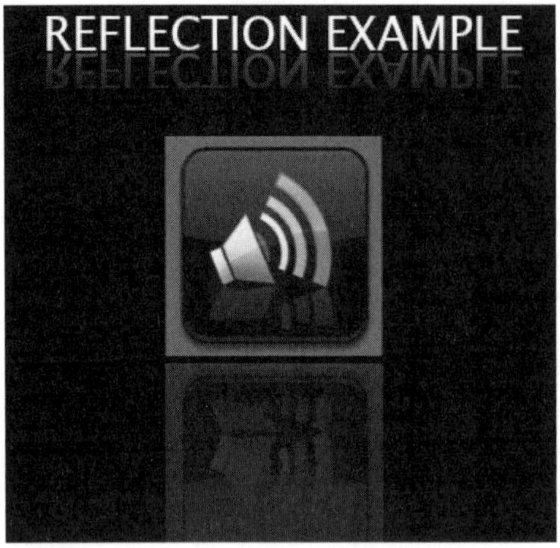

Figure 11.3
Reflections

The XAML used to create the reflection for the text shown in Figure 11.3 is as follows:

```
<TextBlock Text="REFLECTION EXAMPLE" Foreground="White"
                 FontSize="30"/>
<TextBlock Text="REFLECTION EXAMPLE" Canvas.Top="68"
                 FontSize="30" RenderTransformOrigin=
                 "0.5,0.5" Opacity="0.6">
<TextBlock.RenderTransform>
    <ScaleTransform ScaleY="-1"/>
</TextBlock.RenderTransform>
<TextBlock.Foreground>
    <LinearGradientBrush StartPoint="0.5,0" EndPoint="0.5,1" >
        <GradientStop Color="#FF000000" Offset="0.0"/>
        <GradientStop Color="#FFFFFFFF" Offset="1.0"/>
    </LinearGradientBrush>
</TextBlock.Foreground>
</TextBlock>
```

This XAML has two `TextBlock` controls. The first one is rendered as normal. The second one has a `RenderTransform` applied to it with the `ScaleY` set to −1. This causes the text to invert itself along the horizontal axis. To make the reflected text fade out, the program uses a `LinearGradientBrush` on the `Foreground` property, which makes the text fade from white to black, causing it to blend into the black background.

The reflected image is accomplished in the same way as the text. The only difference is that the `LinearGradientBrush` targets the `Opacity` property of the image rather than the foreground color of the `TextBlock` controls.

The following is the XAML for the reflected image:

```
<Image Source="Reflect.png" Canvas.Top="100" ></Image>
<Image Source="Reflect.png" Canvas.Top="370" RenderTransformOrigin =
"0.0,0.0">
    <Image.RenderTransform>
        <ScaleTransform ScaleY="-1"></ScaleTransform>
    </Image.RenderTransform>
    <Image.OpacityMask>
        <LinearGradientBrush StartPoint="0.5,0" EndPoint="0.5,1">
            <GradientStop Color="#00000000" Offset="0.0"/>
            <GradientStop Color="#FFFFFFFF" Offset="1.0"/>
        </LinearGradientBrush>
    </Image.OpacityMask>
</Image>
```

The same code can be used in your game to apply shadows to objects such as trees, creatures, and so on. Figure 11.4 shows an example of a tree with a reflected shadow.

Notice that the reflected shadow on the ground is a black-and-white mask of the original image. Figure 11.5 shows the original image and the black-and-white mask used in the reflection.

To take this one step further, you can have the shadow skew in the direction of the sun by applying a `SkewTransform` to your object. For example, if the sun is to

Figure 11.4
Shadows

Figure 11.5
Black-and-White Mask

Figure 11.6
Shadow Skew

the northwest of a given object, you will want the shadow to skew to the southeast. Figure 11.6 demonstrates this concept.

In order to apply a second transform to a `RenderTransform`, you will need to place them in a `TransformGroup`, as can be seen in the following XAML.

```
<Image.RenderTransform>
  <TransformGroup>
    <SkewTransform AngleX="-30"></SkewTransform>
    <ScaleTransform ScaleY="-1"></ScaleTransform>
  </TransformGroup>
</Image.RenderTransform>
```

You could then use a `Storyboard` timer that will move the sun across the sky, simultaneously updating the shadow skew of all your game objects as it moves. This is just one example of how you can make the game world seem more dynamic and real to your users.

Summary

Silverlight adoption is growing at an increasingly rapid rate. Each release brings more flexibility and power to help you quickly build high-quality games and other types of applications in Silverlight. To get an idea of what developers and designers are creating today, be sure to visit the Silverlight showcase at http://silverlight.net/Showcase/. To date, there are over 600 submitted applications from 62 countries around the world.

I have covered a lot of topics in this book and undoubtedly there are many more to explore. For updates, additions, and changes, please go to http://code.msdn.microsoft.com/Silverlight. As a reminder, the full source code for the following applications is available for you to download at that location:

- Map Editor—Create, load, and save maps.
- Client—A sample client application that allows you to connect to the server, walk around a map, and do actions such as combat, chat, and more with other players.
- Server—A sample server implementation that works with the clients.

Thank you for reading this book. I hope that by reading it, you were able to learn a lot about Silverlight. If you have any questions, feedback, or ideas, feel free to contact me at SilverlightGaming@live.com.

INDEX

H

I

J

K

L

M

N

O

P–Q